Chief Teale's

The Tools of Learning

Chief Teale's

The Tools of Learning

From GED
to
Master's Degree and Beyond

by
Charles A. Teale, Sr.

Teale Ink Inc.
Hartford, Connecticut

A Teale Ink Inc. production
Contact information:
Chief Charles Teale, Sr., Ret.
Tealeink@gmail.com
https://www.facebook.com/TealeInk.Inc

Book design by Charles A. Teale, Jr.

Edited by Lois F. Lewis

Except where noted, all photos courtesy the personal collection of
Chief Charles A. Teale, Sr., Ret.

ISBN 978-1511417297

Printed in the United States of America by AlphaGraphics, 915 Main Street,
1st Floor, Hartford, Connecticut 06103, www.alphagraphics.com.

In loving memory of my cousin
Hartford firefighter Kevin Lamont Bell.
He was killed in the line of duty on October 7, 2014.

This book may be used to instruct students in the Tools of Learning by certified instructors or teachers only.
The Tools of Learning Student Workbook must be given to every student learning this method.

Health, Strategy and Desire. These are "The Tools of Learning." As an organization, Teale Ink, Inc. attempts to address the most common of all emotional health challenges like discouragement, depression and despair. It also provides a strategy through the various "Tools" of the Tools of Learning found in this book, and it addresses the matter of desire through history tours, public speaking engagements and the publication of books that are inspiring.

It can all be described through one equation:
$$A = (H+S)\,D$$

It stands for "Attainment equals the sum of Health plus Strategy times Desire." In essence, this means if you want to <u>A</u>ttain any major goal, you must have a certain amount of physical, mental and emotional <u>H</u>ealth, you must have a <u>S</u>trategy, and you must have the <u>D</u>esire.

Each value is written as follows:
Attain 100% = (Health 5% + Strategy 5%) Desire 10%

Both sides of this equation are equal or proportional, meaning that the greater your total on the right side of the equation, the greater your ability to reach your major goals. Sadly, most of us attempt to Attain with no Strategy of any kind. This book was designed to address that problem.

It is my hope that this book will provide the portion of the strategy that seems to be missing from our daily lives — a strategy for learning, understanding and remembering information so that we can have academic and professional success. Whatever you think of these lessons, just remember that they were learned the hard way from the following experiences.

This book is dedicated to my daughter Kathleen and my son Charlie. Although the Tools of Learning made success possible, watching you both come into the world made it necessary. Charlie age 2 and Kathleen age 4 (1982).

Love, Pa

Contents

Contents

Chapter 5

Chapter 6

Chapter 7

Chapter 8

Chapter 9

Chapter 10

Chapter 11

Contents

Part 2
Chapter 12

Chapter 13

Chapter 14

Chapter 15

Contents

Contents

The following table of contents lists the Tools in the order that they appear in the Tools of Learning Student Workbook. Each Tool is placed in one of the following categories: Learn, Understand, Remember and Conclusion. The last column indicates the page number where each Tool can be found in the workbook. Each Tool with an asterisk is one of the "Top Ten Tools of Learning".

Contents

Remember

Conclusion

Foreword

To begin with, it should be noted that this book is not so much a book as it is a passport, and its creator is not so interested in being perceived as an author, as he is a conductor. The book's central tenant is based on the precept that the reason why a person finds himself in need of this type of information is not as important as the result of his not acquiring it. That thought is the engine that drives this effort. What the writer has done in effect is to perform an in-depth analysis of the items that inhibit a student's ability to absorb critical academic information, which in turn initiates a chain reaction of failures. As the student continues to decline, he is besieged by a lack of confidence. The author has demonstrated in his treatise the actual things that prevent many intelligent people from ever "getting off the ground". Critical lapses in the early stages of the student's curriculum vitae, such as not having a "personal study guide" or a "solid math foundation", will eventually turn a would-be accountant into a janitor.

Anyone who is familiar with Charles A. Teale will tell you that the possibility of this sort of thing happening to an unfortunate soul has been the bane of his existence, a thing among others that he has railed against his entire professional career and beyond. It was his ability to understand early on, in the days before he could acquire a GED, that propelled him from high school dropout to Chief of The Hartford Fire Department, the serious long-term effects of an inadequate education. This book was created to be a road map for people who feel as he does, and want to do something about it.

I was asked to write this forward by the author because I know the words written by him to be both inspiring and empowering. I witnessed first-hand the effect of implementing what is written here.

I should have — I'm the author's brother.

Edgar W. Teale

"Bad times have a scientific value, they are occasions a good learner would not miss."
— Ralph Waldo Emerson

"You measure the size of the accomplishment by the obstacles you have to overcome to reach your goal."
— Booker T. Washington

Preface

I'm from Hartford, Connecticut, born and raised. I still live here and have no plans to move. Most people in this city of my birth call me "Chief" because I was Chief of the Hartford Fire Department for 10 years, and I was the Deputy Chief of the Training Division for four years prior to that. Even though I have retired, I still conduct myself like I used to when I worked at the fire department, partly because it's the kind of career you can never totally retire from. When you least expect it, someone will call upon you to be the chief again. Also, the way I act now is a habit -- a habit that I choose not to break.

I am now a public speaker. Since I was 7 or 8 years old, I have felt more comfortable in front of a large audience than I do having a conversation with three or four people. I am frequently asked to be the keynote speaker for graduation exercises, especially graduations for people receiving their General Equivalency Diplomas (GEDs). I believe that the primary reason I am asked to say a few words at those types of graduation programs is because that's the way I received my high school education. I dropped out of school at the age of 14.

That was 46 years ago, but it still saddens me when I think about it today. So much so, that one day I sat down and wrote all the possible reasons why I made such a bad decision. I came up with six. Now, each one seems like just an excuse to make a foolish choice.

It has taken me many years to get up the nerve to publish this book, and I can't put it off another day. I decided to write this book because I finally figured it out. I know how to succeed academically and professionally, even though I made some mistakes that should have prevented me from ever succeeding at anything at all. Also, I have a cousin named Fenitia Armstrong who currently lives in Atlanta, Georgia. She also grew up in the city where I was born and raised. One day, she and I were reflecting on a terrible fire that took place while I served as chief of the fire department. Sixteen people lost their lives. After my cousin saw me on the news, she told me, "Write it down." I asked her, "Write what down?" She said, "I remember how hard life was on you when you were young. For you to go from where you were, to where you are is amazing. Write down everything you had to endure so that no one else in our family ever, ever has to endure it again."

I decided to take her advice just one step further by making those experiences available to everyone interested in the Tools of Learning. In essence, this is a book about the experiences I had that eventually led to my academic and professional success, in spite of the fact that I had such a bad start. Don't be concerned when you read about negative experiences. I had to have those experiences because *only a person who has faced challenges to succeed academically and professionally could write this book.* People who have never had those challenges won't sense the need to create something that they did not need. In other words, "Necessity is the mother of invention." (Plato)

Besides, by the time I became a mature adult, I found a way to turn every single negative into a positive.

This is a how-to book for anyone growing up anywhere who has made all the mistakes to become a failure, but then suddenly realizes that he or she owes a debt of gratitude to those who made his or her opportunities possible. This is a debt that can only be repaid by doing our level best to become successful and then helping others to do the same.

It is for these reasons that I tell everyone who has a story to write a book. What's your story? I'd like to read it. This one is mine.

Introduction

"That's like putting the cart before the horse."

This is an expression that is quickly loosing its meaning because we aren't accustomed to seeing horses or carts any more. However, some of us remember seeing this combination very well. Why is it not practical to put the horse behind the cart? When you think of it, there are some benefits to this arrangement, one of them being that the person in the cart does not have to look at (or smell) the back end of the horse for the duration or their journey. However, the primary reason why "putting the cart before the horse" does not work is you could not steer the cart if the horse was behind the cart. The horse could still "push" the cart, but the people in the cart would not go where they wanted to go. So it is with our means of getting an education or training. From the very beginning, whenever students are assigned something to learn, we teach it to them in a classroom setting and then we expect them to learn it. Then if the students do not learn the information, they receive failing grades. That's "putting the cart before the horse." The efforts of administrators, teachers and tutors in many of our schools far too often fail to direct the students to the rewarding careers that the students would love to pursue. Although it is past the time to change, it is not too late do so. Yet!

The rest of the world is surpassing our nation academically. Although it is sometimes not popular or perceived as professional, we must go against the norm and proceed in the following fashion:

1. First, teach our students how to learn, understand and remember information.
2. Then teach them what we want them to learn, understand and remember.

This book is about academic and professional success, which leads to economic independence, and fulfilling careers.

I served 28 years as a member of the Hartford Fire Department, the last 10 years as Chief. In all those years, I never had a written contract with the city. Many people wondered how I lasted that long without one. Well, I will tell you. I always felt as though I had a moral contract with those who truly care about the city. I can honestly say that in all of the time that I worked in the fire department, I never once broke that agreement. Not even for one day. Therefore, I always felt like I had job security. Well, when I retired, I didn't break that contract then either. I expanded it to include the entire country and changed my area of focus from saving lives to changing lives for the better. I now accomplish the goal of being of service by teaching others how to succeed academically and professionally. This book is one method I have chosen to accomplish that task.

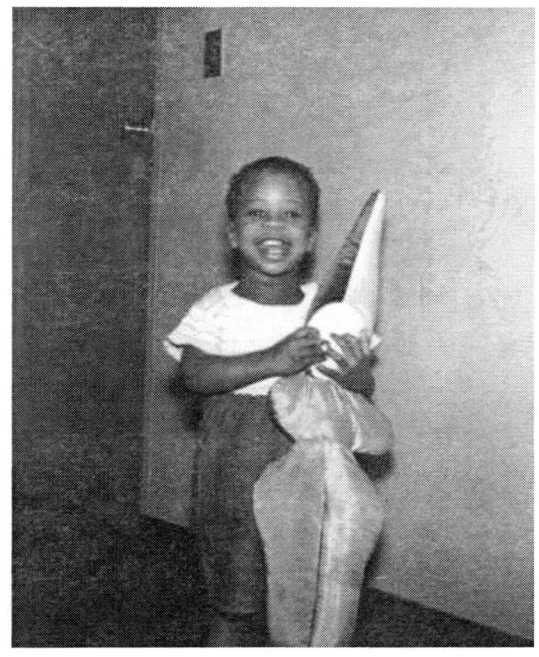

The future developer of the Tools of Learning.

There are three parts to this book. Part 1 consists of the 27 years of my life before joining the Hartford Fire Department. Part 2 consists of the 28 years that I served in that organization. Part 3 is post retirement.

"It's the story that makes the Tools of Learning program truly compelling."
— Jose Rodriguez, City of Hartford employee

Part 1
Chapter 1

The Square
1957

I was born and raised in the city that I currently reside in, Hartford, Connecticut. However, years ago, life in Hartford was very different than it is today. Back then, a man could find a job comparatively easily because there were so many factories in and around the city. Although most people will make this claim of their own town of residence, Hartford truly was different in this regard. So much so that three quarters of a century before I was born, when Mark Twain announced that he was moving to Hartford, he exclaimed, "I am moving to the wealthiest city in America." If he was right, it would not be for long. By the end of the 1950's, Hartford was transformed into a city on the decline. The exodus of the middle class to the suburbs started it; the civil disturbances of the late 1960's finished Hartford off.

During this time, I had my start. Until I was 2 years old, my family and I lived in a project called Charter Oak Terrace. I cannot remember a day of life there, but oddly enough I can remember moving into the next project we lived in called Bellevue Square, often referred to as "The Square". I remember sitting in the cab of the moving van, as my mother Francisca Teale held my infant sister Karen in her arms. When the van stopped, I jumped out of it and ran into the building we were moving into. I remember my mother saying, "Charlie come back here, you don't know where you are going." I replied, "I know where I'm going." She was right, but I kept running up the stairs anyway. Fortunately, we were moving to the top floor and I ran up until I couldn't go any further. I felt vindicated when I stopped at our new apartment. Sometimes I think that was the first experience that led to a series of errors. In time, I would make a lot of mistakes because I thought I knew where I was going, but I was just guessing and I was too proud to admit that I didn't know where my actions would take me at all. The big difference is that in the years to come, I guessed wrong!

Chapter 2

Junior Fireman
1958

My family consisted of my mother Francisca Teale, my father Charles Edward Smith, my brother Edgar Walker Teale (Rocky) and my sister Karen Ann Teale. We lived in one of the poorest neighborhoods in the nation, but I didn't know it because I had a father at home who was employed. What a difference that made. I cannot profess to remember everything that I experienced during those first few years. I probably don't want to. But one experience stands out among the rest. It was on a Christmas morning that I received some toys that were related to firefighting. I cannot recall my exact age. I do know it was before I entered the kindergarten. The toys consisted of a red fireman's helmet, a fire truck and two battery-powered telephones. The telephones were special to me because our family did not have a telephone in our apartment. So I had the only ones. During that time, most people who lived in the area did not have telephones. I remember playing with those gifts like no other toys I have ever received.

Little Arsenal
1960

Sometime later, I started kindergarten at Arsenal Annex School. One day in October, all of the kids in the class suddenly ran up to the window and started oohing and aahing. I wanted to see what all the commotion was about, so I ran to the window too. To my amazement, it was the Hartford Fire Department and they were coming into the school. I distinctly remember observing that the truck the firemen were on looked exactly like the truck I had at home. It was like seeing my toys come to life. Our teacher, Mrs. Anzoven, said to us, "Take your seats, the firemen will be here shortly." In a matter of minutes, there they were, standing at the doorway of our classroom with their arms full of red helmets for everyone. Their visit was simply unforgettable. So much so that when I became chief of the department, I never turned down the opportunity to visit a school and read to a group of kindergarten children a classic like, "Dot the Fire Dog". Our class even went up to Engine Company 7, the firehouse on the corner of Sanford and Main Street, which was only two blocks away, but it felt like an exciting field trip at the time. After seeing the shiny brass poles and fire truck, I wanted to be a fireman too.

I kept up the ritual of visiting the firehouse with my mother Francisca and my sister Karen, or with friends of mine. We were always treated like royalty by the firemen. They seemed to know that if you are to get respect in this world, you've got to give it. These guys were special, and for my entire career I remembered them and tried desperately to protect the legacy they helped to create.

At around this time, I was sitting on the porch of our building with friends of mine, when a police cruiser pulled up and an officer exited the vehicle. He had a purposeful step in his stride. Suddenly, one of my friends yelled, "Run!" During that time, there were many dogs without owners in our neighborhood, and I thought he saw one of them approaching. So, like everyone else, I took off as fast as I could. After a few steps I looked back and didn't see a dog so I asked, "Why are we running?" My friend said, "Do you see that man over there?" As he pointed toward the police officer, I said, "Yes." He then said, "I saw him hit a man over the head with that stick he's got in his hand." I looked at the officer and his nightstick and thought, *What a mean man.*

After that experience, I was afraid of police officers when one day, while I was walking with my father down Pavilion Street, just past Wooster Street in Hartford, we saw another police officer walking in the opposite direction on the opposite side of the street. Because I had developed a fear of police officers, I hid on the side of my father furthest away from the officer. He was artfully swinging a nightstick that looked just like the one the first police officer had. As the officer saw my father he said, "Hey, Charlie." Then my father replied, "Hey, Walt." I was surprised to see that my father knew the policeman, so I looked up at my father and said, "You know him?" He said surprisingly, "Yeah, that's your cousin. You don't know him?!" My father probably could see the look of fear and apprehension in my eyes. I still thought the purpose of the police officer was to harm people with their nightstick. So my father grabbed me by my hand and said, "Come on." As soon as he said that, he pulled me across the street toward the police officer. I went there obviously against my will. My father introduced me to the officer, and told me that he was my cousin Walt. With that, a friendship began that would last for the next four years. My cousin Walt could not walk his beat without me. On those rare occasions that I saw him from a distance, and I could not walk with him, I would shout out, "Hey, Cousin Walt." That way, everyone would know he was my cousin. I was obviously very proud of him, and getting to know him helped me interact with other police officers for the rest of my life.

During another day when my friends and I were sitting on our step, the police officer accused of hitting a man in the head with the night stick came to our building again. Once again, one of my friends yelled, "Run!" This time, I stayed where I was, and as the policeman passed by I said, "Good morning, Officer." He seemed pleasantly surprised by my greeting and replied, "Good morning" in a most friendly tone. Anyone growing up in Hartford at that time would recognize this man. His name was Matt Bolden and in years to come, he would become another relative. He was the cousin of a girl I met in the sixth grade named Helaine. More about her later. Interacting positively with these two police officers at such an early age would prove to be a very valuable lesson for me. A lesson that one night would come in very handy indeed.

A Visit from JFK
1960

You can never tell when you will have a brush with history. One October morning in 1960, my brother Rocky burst into our apartment and shouted to my mother, "The President is up the street." My mother exclaimed, "What?" Rocky said, "President Kennedy, he's up the street." My mother explained, "He's not the President yet, he's running for office." All of what she said seemed like unimportant details to him. He then said, "Well he's up the street." He grabbed my sister Karen by the hand, looked at me and said, "Come on, Charlie." Two blocks later, there sat Presidential candidate John F. Kennedy on the trunk of a convertible, speaking to the crowd. I saw him for just seconds because I was 5 at the time, and I could not see above the crowd that had gathered. But thanks to my 13-year-old big brother lifting me and asking me, "Do you see him," I was able to set eyes on the man and hear him in person. My sister Karen was 3 and remembers being there. She sat on Rocky's shoulders the entire time. Is that a special brother or what? The next month J.F.K. would be elected President of the United States of America.

Four years later, we moved out of Bellevue Square to 43 Greenfield Street in Hartford. From there, my brother and I would take the bus to Burr Mall. Burr Mall is the land that is in between Hartford's City Hall and the nation's oldest public art museum, the Wadsworth Athenaeum. It was at that location that several Presidents spoke, including Harry S. Truman, Dwight D. Eisenhower and John F. Kennedy (as a candidate). But on that day in 1964, Lyndon Baines Johnson spoke and I was in attendance. This time, I was not going to have anyone block my vision, so I stood on the windowsill of the Wadsworth Athenaeum's Morgan Building. When I got home, everyone saw me on television because I was on the news and above the crowd.

It was to be more than 40 years before I got to see another President in person. This time, I was Chief of the Hartford Fire Department, and I arranged to meet President George W. Bush after he spoke at the Boys and Girls Clubs of Hartford on Nahum Drive. There were many reasons why I decided to meet President Bush, and they had nothing to do with politics. It was during a difficult time for the President. As comparatively small as my duties were, I could empathize with the man. I reasoned that I could not always tell everyone why I made the decisions that I made, because it would create a sense of insecurity in the city. People would hear that we had challenges and would worry unnecessarily about them. Using that line of reasoning, I cannot imagine how much every President must withhold from the general public just to keep us from worrying about matters that they have under control. I also wanted to represent those members of my generation who were not able to meet the President. Those who, due to circumstances beyond their control, would never get to meet any President. Some of those people I wanted to represent were friends of mine who were dead and gone. I also wanted the President to hear a friendly greeting from someone who grew up in the neighborhood where he spoke. So when I got a chance to meet him I walked up to him and said, "Hello, Mr. President. Welcome to my club." I remember him saying, "Your club, Chief?" After that, I don't know what I said. Actually, prior to my meeting the President, I shared stories of my youth as a member of the Boys Club on Nahum Drive. So, when the President said, "Your club, Chief," one of the members of the Secret Service jumped in and told my story for me. I didn't mind. The Secret Service man seemed eager to distinguish himself by trying to hold a conversation with the President. I remember being that kind of eager to impress, and I got a kick out of watching this guy go! Besides, I couldn't think of much to say. No matter who you are, when you first hold a conversation with the President of the United States of America, your mind is kind of on automatic. Apparently, I was successful in making him feel welcome because he agreed to take a photo with me. (See photo below.)

To Charles Teale
With best wishes,

I had a lot of memorable experiences during my 28-year career in the Hartford Fire Department. This was one of them.

This experience taught me a lesson. Even though you may not agree completely with someone, you can still respect him or her, especially if that person is the President of the United States of America. As I write these words, Barack Obama is our nation's President. We accomplished a lot on his watch. However, if more people felt the way I do about respectfully disagreeing with one another, we could have made a lot more progress as a nation during his time in office.

Intro to the Great Hartford Fire Department
1961

It was during this time that my mother would sometimes work late into the evening. I had an aunt by the name of Margret Gomes, who I used to call Gida. One evening while I was sound asleep, I heard a great deal of yelling outside, and my bedroom window was orange, sort of like the way it looked when the sun was up. So, when I woke up, I looked at the window and said to myself, *Why is the sun up in the middle of the night?* Suddenly, my Aunt Gida burst into my room and said, "Charlie, get up! There's a fire!" I had no idea what she meant, but I could tell that it was something urgent, so my feet hit the floor, and I ran with her. We went down four flights of stairs and saw a neighborhood in complete chaos. There was a three-story brick apartment building with fire coming out of the windows. People were trapped inside. As one man kept pulling the firebox on the corner, other people shouted, "Somebody call the fire department!" I could not help but wonder, "Why call them? All they do is hand out red hats and keep the fire truck clean." Since very few people in my neighborhood had telephones at that time, the firefighters probably responded because of the pulled firebox. But within seconds, I could hear the sound of fire engines getting closer.

When the firefighters got there, they didn't look the same as when I saw them in school or at the firehouse. One of them had an axe in his hands and he approached the door to the building with aggression in his step. When he finished, the door he opened was just a pile of wood. The other firefighters followed him through, and none of them came out until they each had a man, woman or child in their arms. The sight was too much for me to see so I was whisked away from there as soon as possible. All survived. One of them was a classmate of mine. She was burned and had to stay out of school for quite some time, but eventually she was back. My teacher used to scold her because periodically she would display her wounds. Years later, I saw her as an adult and she had healed very well.

As I look back on that day, I believe that the Hartford Fire Department did more than save lives. They inspired a boy to become Chief of their department.

Life Changes
1961

It was during this time that things started to fall apart within my house and among my family. My father started to exhibit signs of alcoholism, and his presence in our home was on the decline. During this time period, whenever people asked me about my father, I always said that he was sick. That's because I view alcoholism as an illness. When he was present, I was constantly by his side. I loved my father and spent as much time as I could with him. When he was gone, it wasn't like a child missing a parent because of a divorce. In a case like that, you sometimes have the ability to see the missing parent on the weekends. This was different in the sense that I would sometimes see his car in the neighborhood, which meant that he was around, but I still could not see him. Sometimes I would not see him for months at a time.

Of even greater significance was the frequent loss of my brother Rocky in our home. We were living in a bad environment, which could have led to serious trouble with the law if he did not leave it. Rocky was recognized for his potential, so, he was sent away to a school in another town. I'm fortunate in the sense that I can still ask my mother how she broke the news to me that he would not be around for a while. My memories of the specifics are vague. I just remember the pain of his absence. To make matters even worse, even though we are eight years apart, we were emotionally close. One of my fondest memories of being with my brother was a few years earlier in downtown Hartford. During those days (the late 50's), you could go downtown on any given Saturday and get lost in the crowd. Nowadays, you can't find a crowd on a Saturday in downtown Hartford, but back then, my brother would grab his shoeshine box, and we would hit the streets with his friends. Whenever a well-dressed man would appear my brother would say, "Shine, sir?" I'll never forget trying to shine shoes with him. One day he placed the brush in my hand, and I did my best. All of his friends seemed to shout in unison, "He doesn't know what he's doing!" One of them grabbed the brush from my hand and finished the job for me. I decided then and there, that someday I was going to make money some other way. I obviously wasn't very good at shoe shining.

The visits were few, but from time to time my family and I did get to see Rocky while he was away at school. Initially, it was in Deep River, Connecticut at a place called Saint John's. To make matters worse, my cousin Bobby (pronounced BAW-by) was there too. The memory is faint, but I can remember saying goodbye to both of them as they stood on the steps of the school. They couldn't have been much older than thirteen.

These were the two main males in my life and I was about to lose them both at about the same time. As time passed by, these losses more than any other would have the most detrimental effect on my development into manhood.

First History Professors
1962

From the age of about 6, I remember visiting with my paternal grandparents, Pearl Woods-Smith and Benjamin Smith. I knew very little about their lives when they were children. They didn't seem to want to talk about it. I only know that they both came up from Americus and Plains Georgia around 1913, when they were in their early 20's. This was during a period commonly known as the "Cotton Migration." By 1960, they had a grandson who could not get enough of stories about how life was when they first moved to Hartford. Me. Whenever I could, I would say to my grandmother, "Grandma, tell me about the olden days." She would think back as far as she could recall and tell me about things like horse drawn fire trucks, which I found impossible to believe. Typically, after I asked my grandmother to tell me about Hartford's history, my grandfather would come out of his room, take a seat in my grandmother's kitchen, and start talking about how things were in Georgia when he was a young man. He would suddenly interrupt with a horror story of the Jim Crow South. I distinctly remember my grandmother shouting, "You can't tell children stories like that." My grandfather would reply, "Well how else are they going to learn then!?" For a couple of years, this was a regular event.

One day, my sister Karen, several of my cousins and I were sitting in my grandparent's living room. There were around ten of us. The area where they lived (Garden Street in Hartford) still had a large Jewish population in it. One of my cousins said, "There sure are a lot of white people living around here." Another cousin said, "They are not white, they are Jewish." I was 7 at the time, with the mind of a child, and someone who just did not know what the conversation was about. So I asked, "What's the difference?" Another cousin, Reggie, said in a whispering tone, "Be careful what you say about Jewish people. If granddaddy hears anyone say something bad about Jewish people, he'll have a fit!" As soon as Reggie said that my grandfather came storming out of his room. He had a huge chest and a baritone voice that made the whole house shake if he spoke loudly. With that voice, he said, "Who's in here talking bad about Jewish people? I won't have it, you hear? I won't have anyone talking bad about Jewish people in my house!" We were all so frightened that we could not explain that we were not trying to do anything of the sort. Reggie, the oldest of my cousins tried to explain, but my grandfather just roared, "**I don't want to hear it, I said!**" After that, no one uttered a word as he walked by.

Later that day, I just could not stand it any longer. I didn't like the thought of my grandfather thinking that I did something wrong when I didn't. So, I got up the nerve and walked into my grandmother's kitchen. My grandfather was sitting there in a location that I still get to see from time to time. I looked at my grandfather, and said to him, "I wasn't talking bad about Jewish people, I was just . . ." and then I started to cry. My grandfather looked at me and said, "I know, Charlie. It's o.k." Then he gave me a hug. It is the only time I ever remember him hugging me. That experience stayed with me for over 40 years when one day while helping my Uncle William "Rab" Smith write his autobiography entitled "I Remember Hartford", I asked my Uncle Rab why my grandfather would not tolerate anyone speaking negatively about Jewish people. My Uncle Rab said, "When he and your grandmother first started out in Hartford, the Jews were the only people who would hire them or rent them apartments. He's loved them ever since." Now I know why he was so livid!

Of all the experiences that took place around that time, the one in which I almost lost my life as a child stands out the most. It was at a school called Arsenal, which stood on Main Street at the time. A lot of things were called "Arsenal" in my neighborhood. That's because during the war of 1812, the State of Connecticut decided to build an arsenal on the corner of Pavilion and Main Street. I lived on the corner of Pavilion and Bellevue Streets. The Arsenal stood at that location until the State Armory was built in 1909. Anyhow, in this school called Arsenal was a swimming pool. The school is no longer there but if you ask any of the thousands of people who remember that pool, they will tell you that there used to be a lion's head in the shallow end, and every time filtered water entered the pool, it came out of the lions mouth (which was kind of gross to see). What was most memorable was the temperature of the water that came out. It was always ice cold so when it came out, everyone got away from that water. I could not swim, so I stayed in the shallow end.

One night I was playing there, and the ice-cold water came flowing out of the lion's mouth. As usual, I ran away from the water, but so did all of the other kids. In the rush, I got pushed toward the deep end. As hard as I tried to prevent this from happening, I was trapped. I then found myself in the silence that only comes with being completely under water. As I started to slide, I could clearly see the point where the pool quickly slopes. My feet were on the bottom and I could see the deepest end of the pool approaching. Suddenly, I could feel someone pushing me in my back so hard that it felt like a punch. That someone was pushing me back towards the shallow end. As I got closer to the shallow end of the pool, I distinctly remember seeing bubbles expelled from my mouth drift up towards the surface. Within a few seconds, I was in a safe area. I immediately turned around to see who had helped me and it was my friend O.C. Tolliver. He and his family lived on the same floor as my family did in Bellevue Square. I immediately looked around to see where the lifeguard was. He was in the deep end talking with the older kids that were around his age. He didn't even notice my close encounter with death at all. I came to realize that O.C. had saved my life and I thanked him as much as an 8 year old could thank one of his peers. Several decades later we lost O.C. He was a young, popular and incredibly talented athlete who was known for his basketball expertise like his big brother Dwight. One day, I saw Dwight who was working as the basketball coach for Weaver High School in Hartford. It was soon after we lost O.C., and I felt the need to share my experience with him just to let him know how important his brother was, and still is to me. I'll never forget that experience, nor will I forget, O.C. Tolliver.

My old friends and I still talk about O.C. He was truly unforgettable.

The Ranger Station
1962

One of the experiences that I had as a child will initially sound totally irrelevant to my academic and professional progress, but in time, it truly mattered. It was while I was 7 years old. For as long as I could remember, prior to that age a television show called *The Ranger Andy Show* was televised by a CBS affiliate known as WTIC, Channel 3. The show made it possible for children age 5 to around 10 to be seen on television throughout the region. For those of us who were fans of the show, it may as well have been televised worldwide because everyone we knew watched Ranger Andy. In essence, it consisted of a man named Orville Andrews who played the role of a park ranger. He would greet a group of children as guests every weekday at around 3:30 by going to the door of his station and saying, "Hi, kids!" The children waiting outside would reply, "Hi, Ranger Andy" as loud as they could. He would then say, "Come on in." As the children walked into the ranger station to have a seat on the benches, a song would play called "My name is Ranger Andy." Orville Andrews wrote the words to that and most of the other songs played on the show, which he sang while playing the banjo. Cartoons were shown as well. But the highlight of the show was actually the very beginning. After the children were seated, a microphone placed on a boom would go from child to child as they said their name. It was an enormous shock to see someone you knew on the show and everyone talked about it when they went to school the next day.

One day, my mother came up to my sister and I, and said, "I got tickets for you both to go on *The Ranger Andy Show*." I don't have the words to express how surprised I was to hear this. Our lives weren't extravagant by any stretch of the imagination, and this sounded like something only rich kids did. But she reassured us that we would be going, and that it would be on a day soon after my sister Karen became 5 years old, the age when a child was allowed to go on. As the day came close, I got more excited than I did for any occasion. Of course, I kept asking my mother if it was really going to happen, and she assured me that it would. On Saturday, October 15, 1962, my sister Karen turned 5. On the first business day following my sister Karen's birthday, my mother sent me to school with a note which said, "Please let Charles out of school early today because he is scheduled to be on *The Ranger Andy Show*." At the end of the day, my teacher, Mrs. Euglo (that's right, I remember her name), announced to the class, "Charles has to go home early because he's going to be on *The Ranger Andy Show*." The whole place went nuts. No one we knew personally was ever on that show up until that time. As I left the classroom, I distinctly remember saying to myself, *I sure hope my mother wasn't kidding when she said that I was going to be on that show, because if she was kidding, everybody will be laughing at me tomorrow.* It's no wonder that Mrs. Euglo wrote on my report card "Charles is a worry wart." (More about that later).

Well, eventually all the preparation had ended, and we found ourselves entering Broadcast House on Constitution Plaza, the newest addition to the city of Hartford's urban renewal program. It was new and exciting. Everything seemed to happen so fast. Before I knew it, I was lined up with my sister Karen and a friend of ours named Barbara Duncan, who we used to call "Barbie." Her brother Ralph was in the television audience because he was too young to be on the show. Both of our mothers were in the audience too. Soon after we lined up, Ranger Andy appeared. You would have thought we were looking at the President of the United States. We had seen him in parades, and even at Camp Courant, but not this close. He came up to me with the mail, which was kept in a large brown leather bag. He always had one of the kids bring it in. He said to me, "Would you like to bring in the bag?" I shook my head no and stepped back. It was my first time on television and I was full of nerves. Besides, it was too much responsibility for me and the bag was bigger than I was. He told me it was okay, gently placed his hand on my shoulder, and turned to one of the many kids who eagerly put their hands in the air as if to say, "Please pick me." One of the bigger kids was given the honor.

A couple of minutes later, it was show time. We had spent the last 30 minutes preparing, and now we were all ready to make our television debuts. Suddenly, Ranger Andy came to his door and said, "Hi, kids!" We knew what to do. We replied, "Hi, Ranger Andy" at the top of our lungs and we walked in. Because my sister had just turned 5 and she was the smallest of the children, she was placed on a tiny stool in the very front of the group of about 25 children, while the rest of us sat next to each other on benches. I still cannot imagine how nervous she must have been, being all alone and so close to the cameras and Ranger Andy. It was customary for every child to say their name as a boom microphone traveled over our heads. Because the microphone started in the front, Karen was first. She refused to say anything at all. It was close enough to her birthday to receive special recognition but she wouldn't even tell Ranger Andy her name let alone the fact that it was her birthday. My mother got as close to the group of children as she could without being on television and whispered to me, "Charlie, say her name." My memory of this day is so clear, that as I visualize it, my mother was so young that she looked like a kid. Now that I think about it, she was 33 years old. That's younger than my daughter Kathleen is today. But anyhow, I did as my mother told me, and I stood up and said, "Her name is Karen." With that, the show went on. After I said my name, I remember distinctly feeling very at ease speaking while on camera.

Thirty-three years later, I was asked to be on the 40th anniversary special of Channel 3. During my interview, I spoke as highly about Ranger Andy as I could. I even sang his theme song for the occasion. Several years after that, while serving as Chief of the Hartford Fire Department, I was invited to appear on "Face the State" with Al Terzi. As I entered the television studio, I remembered it all. Only the set had changed, and I believe that childhood memory made me feel comfortable in an otherwise uncomfortable situation. From that day forward, whenever I was interviewed as Chief, I have always harkened back on that time when I was first on television at the age of 7. I believe the experience expanded my comfort zone while in front of a group of people. After all, if you can speak when you think the whole world's watching, why should you be nervous when speaking before an audience of 10,000?

Camp Courant
1963

During my father's absence, things changed drastically for me. We never went a day without food, but sometimes the food was late. My mother would rely on my Aunt Gida to provide us with meals from time to time. In the midst of all of this were many families of like circumstance. I distinctly recall the first summer that my sister Karen and I spent living under these conditions. We were playing outside one morning when the children of the Jones family passed us by. Two of them were twins, Debra and Dianne, and one of them said, "Hey, Charlie, do you want to go to Camp Courant?" I said, "Camp Courant, what's that?" Upon hearing my question she stepped back and looked at me like I had two heads. She then replied, "You don't know what Camp Courant is?" Now one thing that all of the Jones kids could do was run, and Debra and Diane could outrun just about everyone. So, one of the twins ran up the four flights of stairs to my mother, and the next thing I knew I was standing in front of the Keney Clock Tower on Main Street in Hartford, waiting for the bus to go to Camp Courant. Immediately upon entering the bus, the children began singing songs that everyone seemed to know but me. I don't think I said a word until we reached the entrance of Camp Courant, which meant that we had to climb a huge hill. At that time, I joined in the chant, "We've got to make it up the hill," which we repeated until there was no more hill to climb. When we got off the bus, it was like stepping off of a plane and walking into Disney World. Because the project that I lived in was almost all asphalt and there was no level grassy area to be found, we used to go to the front lawn of Union Baptist Church on Main Street in Hartford to play football. From time to time, someone would kick the ball inaccurately and it would end up in Old North Cemetery. (You could prove how brave you were by just climbing over the fence, going into the cemetery and retrieving the ball). The basketball court was crowded with teenagers and a kid of age 7 wasn't welcome there. When we tried to play basketball, the teenagers would empty out a trash can, place it in a corner and say, "Play here." The trash can was our basketball hoop. But at Camp Courant, I simply followed my friends from one activity to another for hours until I heard someone yell the words "lunch time." As anyone will tell you who went to Camp Courant in the early 1960's, lunch was time for a milk, two cookies and a peanut butter and jelly sandwich. As we stood in line, I started worrying because I didn't have any money to pay for lunch. When I expressed my concern, I was told, "Lunch was free." After lunch, we had to wait an hour and then we could go swimming in the pool that still stands in the same location today.

As if days like these weren't exciting enough, there were special days for dignitaries and stars like Bill Savitt Day and Sheriff Pat Hogan Day. Bill Savitt was a jeweler in Hartford, and he had a store at 35 Asylum Street "just 35 seconds from Main." Although Bill Savitt Day meant free ice cream, my favorite day was Pat Hogan Day. Pat Hogan was the High Sheriff at the time, and he would have people hand out straw cowboy hats with his name embroidered on them. Walking home from the bus was always interesting on Pat Hogan Day, because if you were not careful, someone would snatch the hat off of your head and the next thing you knew your hat would be on someone else's head.

I was 9 years old when we moved from the neighborhood where I used to take the bus to Camp Courant, and it would be another 30 years exactly before I would return to celebrate the 100th anniversary of this institution. With the exception of the maypole (which was gone), everything was exactly the same as I remembered. When it was time for us to eat at this celebration, there was food for adults who wanted a good meal, but I was surprised to see that peanut butter and jelly sandwiches were also on the dining table. I could not resist the temptation to reminisce about my childhood, and made the obvious choice.

In the year 2000, I became Chief of the Hartford Fire Department, and Camp Courant was going through major renovations. My wife Helaine and I had the opportunity to participate in this capital improvement project, which transformed the site for the first time in 40 years. Now the camp has the same purpose, but the programs offered far exceed those that people of my generation enjoyed.

As I look back on those days before Camp Courant, I remember as a child wondering if anyone cared about me and other children in my neighborhood who faced the same challenges. I believe this question was answered in the affirmative by the actions of those who made Camp Courant possible, and their contribution helped to instill in me the desire to be of service to others.

I will always owe Camp Courant a great debt of gratitude, and nowadays I give history tours of the city of Hartford. My fee is a donation to one of three worthy causes: the Boys and Girls Clubs of Greater Hartford, the Connecticut Historical Society, and Camp Courant.

In 2009, I became the first lifetime achievement award recipient in the 115-year history of that institution.

First Loss
1963

I lost my grandfather that year. I was 8 years old. During the late 1960's, about five years after my grandfather died, Hartford suffered several riots that took the businesses of many Jewish people. I don't have the ability to write how sad I was to see people who helped African Americans during their most trying time since slavery, burned out of their businesses. I was just a boy of 13 or 14 at the time, but one day I was approached by a classmate who asked me, "Are you going to the riots tonight?" I said emphatically, "No!" He replied, "I am." I didn't go to the riots that night or any other, I am proud to say.

Then one night, while I was outside of the Boys Club on Nahum Drive, an official looking car pulled up in front of the building. From the passenger's side of the car stepped one of the most beautiful women I have ever seen. At first, I thought she was a movie star like Sophia Loren, but it was Hartford's first female mayor, Ann Uccello. She was outraged because of the rioting and the fact that many of the people participating were boys. One of the things that disturbed her most was the fact that one of the structures set on fire was the Ropkins Branch of the Hartford Public Library. This was my first library. It was the place where I distinctly remember my sister Karen and I getting our first library cards. We lost our library to the riots. Mayor Uccello put it best when she said, "What kind of people burn down a library?" More than 40 years later, I had the privilege of interviewing retired Mayor Uccello for the Hartford Public Library's history center. I am proud to say that I looked her in the eye and said, "I was not one of those who chose to destroy our city. I helped build it up." You can never tell when good behavior will pay high dividends. Mayor Uccello and I had a great relationship when I became Chief. That would not have happened if I had been a violence prone teenager.

I thought long and hard about including the following experience in this book. I was concerned that someone closely related to what happened would be offended by what is written. By the time I wrote this publication, my thoughts and feelings regarding this matter had been observed nationwide. Since I have received no complaints about the things that I have said, I must assume that my thoughts and feelings are not offensive. I have decided to include this information because it was one of the great learning experiences of my life. I learned how to empathize in a way that no other experience has taught me.

There Was a Circus Fire?
1964

During the aftermath of my grandfather's death, I thought that I would go by my grandmother's and help out around the house on Saturdays. I did this whenever my mother would let me, and my grandmother said it was okay. There wasn't much for me to do because it was a three-family house and I had cousins who lived on one of the other floors. However, I would do what I could which included working in the garden where my grandfather used to grow vegetables and fruit. I had no idea what I was doing, but I would try, and my grandmother showed her appreciation by fixing me the largest breakfasts that I have ever eaten. There would be pancakes and biscuits, bacon and pork chops, eggs with cheese and home fries. One day, after working in the garden for a while, my cousin Juanita (who was visiting too) called me and told me to come and eat. I sat down in front of the television set, and watched cartoons for a few minutes. Suddenly, Juanita said to my grandmother, "Hey, Gramps, we started a new school this week, and all of the kids had to carry their own desks and chairs from our old school to the new one." I must pause and ask the reader the following question: The walk was just a few blocks, but can you imagine the response if we tried to get children to do that today? Well, upon hearing this statement my grandmother said, "Where is this new school?" Juanita said, "On Barbour Street. It's called the Freddy Wish School." With that my grandmother said, "On Barbour Street? They shouldn't have built a school there. That's where the circus fire was." Upon hearing the words "circus fire," I envisioned the Shrine Circus that I used to go to as a child, and I pictured the fires that I used to see in my neighborhood, including the one that I saw that almost killed an entire family. I then tried to picture a circus on fire and I simply could not. So I stood up, walked into my grandmother's kitchen and I said what every child says when they first hear of this tragic event. I said, "There was a circus fire?" With that my grandmother shared the details of what she remembered.

The date was July 6, 1944, and the Ringling Brothers and Barnum and Bailey Circus tent caught fire on Barbour Street. More than 167 people died because of it and hundreds were very badly injured. It had been 20 years since it happened, but the way my grandmother described it, it may as well have happened the day before. Juanita and I were stunned. Perhaps we were too young to hear what Grandma had to say, but I distinctly remember returning to my place in front of the television with the newfound realization that children don't always grow up and then grow old. Sometimes they die while still children, at the circus.

Crown Gardens
1964

After living in Bellevue Square for seven years, my mother decided to move. It was during the summer of 1964. I was going from the third to the fourth grade and kind of looked forwarded to moving. I must admit that I didn't know what to expect, but I didn't make much of the matter because we were moving literally just three blocks away. What I didn't realize was that I was going to change schools. At the new school that I would be attending, named the Vine Street School, I would have to make an entirely new set of friends.

During my years living on Greenfield Street, there were people who made learning something valuable, unavoidable. One such person was a boy in my class named Michael M. We were in the fourth grade, age 9, and he was the richest kid I ever met. I can't remember why, but he had everything you could imagine. If there was a new toy on the market, he had it. There were times when he would come to class late with a box of donuts tucked under his arm. Of course, all of the kids would see him and ask him if they could have some. The children of this neighborhood weren't as bad off financially as the kids in my old neighborhood, Bellevue Square. I think the difference between what I was accustomed to and what I was now seeing had a profound effect on me. To me, everyone in the new neighborhood was rich by comparison. Michael M. was super rich. However, he wasn't a kindhearted person. If he had something that you wanted (like donuts), he would share them with people he liked, but if you didn't do everything he wanted you to do, he didn't like you. This made me unwilling to ask him for anything. He was even worse when it came to his toys. Usually, he was the only kid who had a football when we all wanted to play. One day the game wasn't going his way, and he literally did as the old saying goes "took his ball and went home." We were left without a ball and disgusted with Michael. Somehow we managed to make good use of the time we had together anyhow, and weeks passed by before we saw Michael on the block again. When he appeared, we saw him from a distance. He had his football under his arm and when he got within earshot, he shouted, "Go long." With that, he threw the football with all his might in our direction. The ball hit the ground and bounced into the street. No one picked it up until Michael picked it up himself. He then said to us, "Let's start a game." Two guys picked sides and Michael was not chosen. He then said, "If I can't play, you can't use my ball." With that, someone produced another football. It wasn't as nice as Michael's, but it felt great playing a game without being held hostage by a spoiled brat.

Michael went home, and my friends and I had won a moral victory. I don't know who won the game.

The Greatest Wealth (Round 1)
1964

At around the age of 9, I began having problems with my health. Sometimes it kept me out of school for extended periods of time. There were occasions, when I was absent from school for a couple of weeks at a time. Eventually, my mother received a diagnosis. It was rheumatic fever, a diagnosis that had even greater concern than it would normally have to a parent. The reason being is because one of my mother's brothers, Albert Pina, died from the aftereffects of rheumatic fever, which had damaged his heart when he was 14. Albert died at 21, so the concerns over my activities began. During that time, I started to think that I would live to about the age of 20 and that would be it, like Albert. Initially, the limitations placed upon me were related to the weather. I could not go outside and play in the rain. However, as time passed by, the concerns became even greater. So much so that by the time I was in the sixth grade, I was not allowed to take gym. As you can imagine, I looked real bad in the eyes of all of the boys who could. To make up for it, I used to go to the local Boys Club and try to prove that I was as athletic as the others. It was a foolish way to act, after all, I wasn't supposed to be physically active at all. However, I disobeyed the doctor's orders until one day, I was told that I could take gym again. By this time, I was in the eighth grade and I was way behind the other boys when it came to team sports. I never did catch up.

The strangest thing about the rheumatic fever diagnosis is that decades later, upon being evaluated as an adult, I was told by a cardiologist that there was no way that I could have ever had rheumatic fever. I could not help but wonder, well if it wasn't rheumatic fever then what was it? Only time would tell.

Don't Try This at Home or Anywhere Else
1965

From the summer of 1964 until the winter of 1966, our family lived at the Crown Garden Apartments at 43 Greenfield Street. Somehow, I managed to pack a lot of experiences into that short time frame. I knew absolutely no one in my new neighborhood. This was strange because if it were not for a hill that separated us, I could have seen my old place of residence, and the friends I left behind. My mother wanted me to be active during the summers, so she sent my sister Karen and me to Camp Hihoti. Camp Hihoti was similar to Camp Courant except that from time to time you got to spend the night at Camp Hihoti. This situation was to create a learning experience that could have easily cost me my life.

At my new camp, I made friends rather quickly with several of the boys who attended. On our way to camp, I was informed that we would be evaluated by a swimming instructor to determine if we could swim or not. Those who could not swim at all were called "minnows" those who could swim a little were called "pollywogs" and those who could swim well were called "fish." As we rode on the bus, somehow I told everyone that I could swim, and that I would be a "fish" for sure. The truth of the matter was that I was never in water over my chest in my life with the exception of the time that I literally almost drowned in the Arsenal School pool. However, the day of evaluation came. As all of us waited anxiously to show what we could do, I was probably the only one terrified about going in water that was at least two feet over my head. Before long, I found myself at the end of a pier ready to risk my life in order to save face. I jumped in. How I made it to shore I'll never know, but somehow I thrashed about long enough to get there. When I got there everyone was in hysterics, except for the swimming instructor who promptly yelled, "Pollywog." I left the deep end of the pool in disgrace. Everyone laughed at me for so long that I felt totally humiliated. So, I concocted a plan. That night, while everyone was asleep, I was going to go down to the pool and teach myself how to swim. As I carried out this plan, I determined that if I jumped in the area that was just over my head, I could jump up and down and get air so that I wouldn't drown. I tried my plan and it worked. I executed this plan around six times, each time I jumped into water just a little bit deeper. Before long, I was able to jump into the deepest section of the pool and then swim to the edge. By around midnight, I had taught myself how to swim. I was 10 years old. This experience could have easily killed me, but it didn't. The next day when everyone was at the pool, I asked the instructor if I could retest for the designation of "fish" again. Eventually he replied, "Yes, but if you can't swim, I'll never let you back in the deep section again." This time I dove in and did a sloppy version of the side kick, back stroke and the American crawl to the edge. Everyone was stunned. I made up some excuse like, "I had a cramp yesterday," but the truth of the matter was that at 10 years of age, while no one was around, I taught myself how to swim "round midnight." I learned more than how to swim that summer; I learned that some people would rather die than be laughed at by their friends. Now that's the power of peer pressure.

Chapter 3

The Tools of Learning became necessary for me as early as the fourth grade. Unfortunately, it wasn't invented yet. The following is the preparation for Tool #13.

Foundational
1965

Up until the age of 9, I was considered a good to excellent student. I don't remember studying much, but I do remember a lot of A's and B's on my report card. I now know that many students are good when the information is very elementary, but when it starts to get more advanced, the student may start to have difficulty. That's what happened to me. It was during my time as a student at the Vine Street School, in the fourth grade, that I missed the greatest number of days of school due to illness.

I was able to trace my first challenges with math to a specific time and place. When I was nine years old, my health challenges prevented me from going to school for weeks at a time. After being out for two weeks, I returned to a test on division. Next to the problems were the words "Check each answer." When someone tells you to check a division problem, they mean take the divisor and multiply it times the quotient. If the product you get in your multiplication is identical to the dividend you have in your division problem, then you have the correct answer. However, because I was out sick when this method was taught, I didn't know how to check my answers, so I just put a check mark next to each division problem, indicating that I had "checked my answer." When I got my paper back, I had all of the answers wrong. In addition to that, my teacher wrote in red ink the following words: "See me after school. Ms. Mills." I thought I was in big trouble, but when I spoke with my teacher she recalled that I was out sick when the "how to check division problems method" was taught. So, I sat there with her after school and learned it. Thanks again, Ms. Mills.

The problems that I experienced memorizing the multiplication tables also kept me from succeeding in math. My mother, who became a published poet in later years, helped me to clear that hurdle by making it fun. She would say "6 times 9 is 54, shut your mouth and say no more." Poems like this made it impossible to forget some of my multiplication table. Unfortunately, I failed to review the multiplication tables, which meant that eventually, I was no longer good at multiplying. Since multiplying is part of the foundation of math, it is like the ABC's of reading. I don't doubt that a person can read without knowing all of their ABC's, it's just that doing so makes learning how to read much more difficult, and certainly less enjoyable.

As I look back on these experiences, I also think of the many students in the cities of our nation who have similar experiences because they move from one apartment to another frequently. I once heard a man say that his family moved more than 30 times when he was a child. It stands to reason that children who move this frequently miss out on a lot of the prerequisite information that is necessary for building a solid math foundation.

Another problem that I had with math happened when I attended Hartford State Technical College (now known as Capital Community College). My first mistake was not reviewing what I had learned while getting my GED. That included the order of operations. Not knowing this basic mathematical concept would cause me great difficulty, until I relearned it from Assistant Chief Jack Kehoe of the Hartford Fire Department. One day, Chief Kehoe asked me how school was going when I was working on my Master's Degree in Public Administration. At that time, I was taking a course called "Quantitative Analysis", and I was not doing well in it at all. I had tried two times to pass this course and simply could not. When Chief Kehoe asked me how school was going, I replied honestly, "Not well." He then asked me what the problem was, and when I replied, he said, "It sounds like math, and you don't know your order of operations. How did you get this far in school without it?" As I look back on this question, I could have answered, "I got by with average grades," which is what I got for each math course I took. If information like the order of operations is not retained from high school, it will be lost because it is not taught in college. Colleges don't teach this information because the college instructor will assume that their students have learned it already. Also, I would take a math course, and then would not take another math course for several years, because I was going to school part time. This meant, that by the time I took the next math course, I had forgotten a lot about how to do math. I had allowed my foundation to erode away by not reviewing what I learned.

While taking my Technical Math Course at Hartford State Technical College, I received a C in trigonometry. I was so happy to just get that course over with that it didn't dawn on me that if I got a C, which is average, it could mean that I missed out on as much as 30 percent of the information taught in the classes given. The absence of that 30 percent caused me to have major problems in chemistry and statistics.

When I first learned algebra, it was while I was studying to become a firefighter. We all had to solve two basic hydraulic equations:

Gallons per minute (GPM)=29.7 times the Diameter Squared, Times the Square Root of the Nozzle Pressure

And

Friction Loss (FL)=2Q Squared Plus Q (Q, stands for quantity in gallons per minute divided by 100)

<u>I learned how to solve these equations, but I did not understand what I was doing.</u>

My way of solving them was to watch someone else do them, write their method down, and memorize how that person did it. Unfortunately, that did not prepare me for the future. In one college course that I took, there were 27 of these types of equations. Now, you may be able to memorize how to solve two such equations, but I could not memorize 27 of them. So, I had to learn the "order of operations" for solving algebraic equations.

Initially, I learned from Chief Kehoe, the PPRMDAS (Pretty Please Read My Dear Aunt Sally) method. In time, I converted to PEMDAS (Parenthesis, Exponents, Multiplication, Division, Addition, Subtraction). Whatever method you use, be sure to have a mastery of the order of operations, before you begin an advanced math course.

When I teach people how to read, I tell them that there are seven essential areas that we will cover:
1. The ABC's
2. Knowing the sounds that each letter makes
3. Combining letters to make sounds
4. Sounding out words one syllable at a time
5. Reading words by recognition or sounding them out
6. Combining words to make sentences
7. Comprehending what you read

It may be necessary to have a similar strategy when it comes to mastering math. The following, Tool #13, was designed to provide that strategy.

TOOL #13
(1964, 1974, 1982, 1983, 1990, 1998)

Dedicated to my first challenges with math, my mother Francisca and my former superior and mentor, Assistant Chief Jack Kehoe

Not knowing your multiplication tables multiplies your math problems.

Get a Math Foundation

One of the most common mistakes made by math students is trying to learn advanced mathematics without knowing the basics. When I say basics, I'm referring to addition, subtraction, multiplication and division. If you have learned that X times X = X squared, but you cannot tell me how much 9 X 7 equals, then when someone asks you how much is 9X times 7X you will get the "more advanced" portion of the answer right but you will get the elementary portion wrong just because you don't know your multiplication tables. Because no one will give you partial credit for a partially right answer, you will get the entire answer wrong. Learning advanced math without knowing elementary math is "like building a castle in the sky" (William "Rab" Smith). Also, if you don't know your multiplication tables, I can tell you that you are going to have problems with at least the following kinds of mathematics: multiplication, division, adding and subtracting fractions, algebra, geometry and trigonometry. And, if you don't know these subjects well, you will have problems with chemistry and physics.

Obviously, learning math is not good enough; you must understand it and then remember it. For some of us, the only way to remember math is to review it, and to review math means to do math, not just read about it, or hear about it. Reviewing math by reading about it only shows that you understand what is written. It does not prove that you remember how to solve problems. This means that reviewing math is a psychomotor function, which means you are physically solving problems while you are learning, like Tool # 11, which involves taking notes in class. So, there are three Tools of Learning that use the psychomotor learning domain, 11, 13 and 17.

For me, Tuesdays is times days. I do my times tables from 1-12 every Tuesday or I will forget them when I least expect it.

When a person has missed many math classes because of illness or frequently moving, or that person has not had a math course for a long time, it is as if someone has erased one or more of the steps necessary for a person to read. It is possible to learn how to read without knowing all of these seven steps, but it is so difficult to do that you learn to dislike reading. So you don't read frequently enough to become excellent, or even good at it.

If you are having difficulty with a particular math problem, try these six steps:

1. Relate what you are assigned to learn to something you already know. Money is one way to relate math to what you already know. Most people know how to work with numbers when you talk about dollars and cents. When I was learning right angle trigonometry, I would liken one leg of the triangle to a building. Next, I would liken the horizontal leg to the ground. Then I would liken the diagonal side to a ladder. This side is known as the "hypotenuse."

2. Try to liken the abstract to something concrete. I compare the words "abstract" and "concrete" in the following way: Abstract is something you cannot detect with any of the five senses, and concrete is something that you can detect with any of the five senses. Likening the abstract to the concrete is how we learned math. Initially, we were asked questions like, "If you had three apples and someone gave you two apples, how many apples would you have?" Number lines are often helpful too.

3. Make sure you have mastered the foundational knowledge of your math problem. In other words, make sure you know enough to get an "A" in addition, subtraction, multiplication and division before you tackle algebra. If you get "B's" it may sound good, but it means that you may not understand as much as 20 percent of the information needed to solve problems at the next level. Those 20 percents can add up to spell disaster in college.

4. Learn, understand and remember the rules and definitions that apply to solving a math problem. PEMDAS is a rule worth remembering. But what about the meaning of math words and terms. What is the difference between a digit, a number and a coefficient? The best way to insure that you know these rules and definitions is to practice:

    a. Reciting them
    b. Creating a personal study guide (PSG)
    c. Solving problems to practice what you know

(More about these three later.)

Developing a dependable review system means identifying a problem that tests your ability to remember the rules and definitions necessary to solve that type of problem. The Tools of Learning calls this type of problem "an ideal problem." You must then solve that problem as frequently as necessary to review those rules and definitions through the use of a personal study guide. A personal study guide is a notebook that has at least one example of each specific type of problem that is difficult for you to solve. It will help you to remember the general rules necessary to solve that type of problem. The numbers and variables may change, but the general rules will remain the same. If you can't remember the rules of the game, you cannot win the game. Once you know the rules, it is easier to apply them to problems with different numbers, coefficients, and variables. A personal study guide will also test your ability to remember essential definitions.

It is extremely important to remember that, "to review math means to do math." Just because you think that you are capable of understanding what is written in a book or what your teacher is saying about how to do a problem by just looking at it, does not mean that you remember how to solve the problem yourself. There's a big difference between "doing what you are told to do" and "knowing what to do on your own." Also, never look at a problem and say, "That one is too difficult. I could never find the right answer to that one." You may be surprised to see that you do know how to solve the problem once you try to solve it.

5. Be as specific as possible and write down each step necessary to solve a problem. The best example of how specific you must be is if someone told you to write down all of the steps necessary to come to class today, you could start with:

A. Get out of bed
B. Wash up
C. Get dressed

Or, you could start with:

A. Wake up
B. Open my eyes
C. Place my feet on the floor
D. Stand up
E. Walk to my shower, etc.

How specific you are depends on your specific needs.

6. Utilize free websites that provide tutorials on math. Sometimes watching a video several times without the pressure of a classroom can be most beneficial. However, make sure that it is a site that your teacher recommends. Sometimes it is not good enough to know how to solve a problem; you must also be able to solve it in the way that your teacher approves. "There are many roads leading to New York." (Mr. Howard)

If none of these six steps work, see Tool # 6.

This is Assistant Chief Jack Kehoe, the man who taught me the order of operations, pinning my Lieutenant of the Training Division badge on me in 1990. That's Fire Chief John B. Stewart, Jr. in the background.

Pleased to Meet You, Doc
Back to 1965

When I finished the fourth grade, I had completed the highest grade at Vine Street School. All of us who graduated from there had to attend Northwest Jones School on Woodland Street in Hartford. This was a particularly exciting time because Northwest Jones went up to the eighth grade. It had teenagers in it. To me, they were grown-ups. This would be the first time that I was to attend school with kids that close to adulthood, and I was truly excited by the thought of it all. My mind was filled with anticipation, and I thought that I would be able to distinguish myself even among the big boys. My plan was to be the best at something but I didn't exactly know what.

On the first day of school, while everyone was gathered outside the school waiting for the bell to ring, two of the boys walked around asking if anyone wanted to play football. It was a show of respect if you were just asked. When I was asked, I said, "Sure!" As we were choosing sides, I remember saying to myself, *This is my chance. I'll be the best football player at Northwest Jones School.* The game was just a couple of plays long when suddenly a fight broke out between two of the big boys. While they were throwing punches, they looked to me like grown men. All of the kids were shouting, and teachers came to the windows of the school shouting, "Mr. Hurley, Mr. Hurley!" Suddenly, the doors of the school burst open and there stood the biggest man I had ever seen in my life. My father was 6'3", but this guy was bigger than my father, and he was built like a professional athlete. I turned to another student who was standing next to me away from the action, and I said, "Who the heck is that?" He replied, "That's Mr. Hurley, the gym teacher." I then asked, "Are all of the teachers in this school that big?" He replied, "Nope, just him."

Well, Mr. Hurley got in between the fighters and shouted, "Stop that fighting, stop that fighting!" The two boys kept swinging at each other, but I noticed neither one wanted to come close to hitting Mr. Hurley. At that point, Mr. Hurley said, "Oh, you still want to fight, huh?" He then shouted to the boy I was standing next to "Bobby, go get the gloves." He then said to me, "You go help him." As I turned to assist Bobby in getting the gloves I thought to myself, *This is my chance.* I'm going to be the best glove getter in the history of Northwest Jones." Suddenly, two questions came to my mind: "Why is he sending two boys just to get some gloves? Also, what kind of gloves are these?" At the top of the stairs we were climbing were the biggest boxing gloves I had ever seen. Bobby and I grabbed them and ran down the stairs. For a moment, I thought that Bobby and I would be directed to put the gloves on so that we could fight with the teenagers. My fears were quieted when Mr. Hurley took the gloves from our hands and placed them on the fighters. With that he said, "Now, go to a neutral corner. When I blow my whistle, come out swinging."

A split second later, and the fight became a boxing match. Well, sort of. The two boys looked like Sonny Liston and Cassius Clay (now Muhammad Ali). They were dancing, bobbing weaving, hooking and jabbing. However, there was one thing they weren't doing, and that was hitting each other. With all of the showmanship there wasn't a ghost of a chance that anyone was going to get hurt because neither one could actually hit their opponent. After around one minute, those gloves started to look like cement blocks at the end of their arms. They could not even lift their hands. Upon realizing that, Mr. Hurley stopped the two boys and asked, "Do you still want to fight?" They looked at him and shook their heads as if to say "no." They were too tired to even say the word. So Mr. Hurley said, "Good. Take off the gloves." I never saw those two boys fight again. I came to find out many years later that Mr. Hurley knew what was going to happen. I know this because 49 years later, I wrote the life story of Mr. Hurley. It's entitled *The Making of a Legend: The Life and Times of Walter J. "Doc" Hurley*. If you want to know how to become as great as a man can become in this world, you've got to read that book.

There's Nothing on TV
1965

That was the start of the fifth grade. During that year, my challenges with the learning process seemed to intensify. However, I still found time to watch television. Television in the mid 1960's consisted of two or three television stations and a very limited variety of shows. The only exception was Saturday, which had lots of cartoons for kids to watch. Therefore, because there was nothing else for a kid to watch during the week, I would watch shows designed for adults like *Biography* starring Mike Wallace. It was a show about the men and women throughout the world who distinguished themselves in one form or another. Watching this show and the following experience led to the development of Tool #5.

I frequently give history tours of the city of Hartford, and I once gave a tour to a group of young executives. The reason why they took my tour was to familiarize themselves with the city they would be working in. Before I started my tour, I wanted to encourage them to ask questions, so I recited a portion of Rudyard Kipling's poem "I Keep Six Honest Serving-Men", which includes the following lines:

I Keep six honest serving-men

(They taught me all I knew);

Their names are What and Where and When

And Why and How and Who.

When I got finished, I asked the group, "Do any of you like Kipling?" (Referring to Rudyard Kipling.) That expression "do you like Kipling" is the opening line to a joke. I expected to hear the old punch line which is, "I don't know, I've never Kippled," but what I heard from them instead was, "Who is Rudyard Kipling?" I wanted to tell all of them to go back to the college where they got their degrees and demand their money back, but I didn't. I just reflected on why I knew who he was and why they did not. It didn't take me long to figure it out. It was because of that show *Biography*. One of the men whose life was presented was Rudyard Kipling. I remember talking about Kipling after the show with my mother. It was then that she taught me the poem "If".

That show is no longer on, but there are comparable ways to familiarize yourself with people whose names are mentioned in a classroom by your teacher. You can usually find a video of the person on the Internet. However, just telling someone "go online" and look up the name of someone may not be good enough. They might look at the wrong video. From time to time, I will email a link or write out the URL to a specific video to a student. I call this process "Writing a YouTube Prescription."

By the way, in 1999, when I graduated from the University of Hartford with my master's degree, Mike Wallace, the host of the show *Biography*, was our keynote speaker. I shook his hand, said who I was, and welcomed him to Hartford, but I was too impressed to say much more.

TOOL #5
(1961-1964)
Dedicated to Mike Wallace and *Biography*

Unknown contributors must be researched.

Know Their Contributions

You must also know why a person's name is mentioned during a lesson. If your teacher uses the name of someone you don't know, write it down phonetically if you must, and look it up later. Because, according to recent statistics, six billion hours of YouTube are watched every month, YouTube is often an excellent source for looking up names like "Dr. Jonas Salk". It must be remembered however, that no one source of information should be the only one you use. When firefighters respond to a hazardous materials spill, they use at least three sources of information before they decide how to handle the emergency. Before you are certain that you know what kind of contribution a person has made, use several sources of information.

On the Road Again
1966

My mother had a severe distrust of one of the friends I made while living on Greenfield Street. His name was Owen. This wasn't his real name, but I choose not to use his real name for reasons I will elaborate on later. I met Owen the month before fifth grade was to start. All of the kids I was talking with were excited about going to Northwest Jones. One of my friends Allen May said, "No more baby Vine Street," referring to the Vine Street School we had left behind. As I discussed the teacher I was going to have, Mrs. Vasquez, I heard Owen say, "I'm going to be in Mrs. Vasquez's class too." I was shocked to hear this from this kid because he was so much bigger than the rest of us. We introduced ourselves to each other and I soon came to realize that the reason why he was going to be in my class even though he was so big was because he had stayed back three times. While the rest of the students in Mrs. Vasquez class were 10, he was 13 years old. What made matters worse is that he fit right in with the rest of us. He was just as immature. As time passed by, I got to know Owen, and several of my classmates very well. Unlike the neighborhood where I came from, there was no community center where kids could to hang out. In my old neighborhood, we had the Good Will Boys Club, the Parker Memorial Center and the Arsenal School. The center and the school had swimming pools in them. However, there was nothing of the sort in my new neighborhood so we passed the time working and spending the money we earned. We would work at anything that paid any wage. Because I used to make money in the Bellevue Square project emptying garbage, I introduced my new friends to the concept. In Bellevue Square, the garbage from each household had to be carried to either one of two structures known as the incinerator building. This building always had a fire in it, and when you threw your garbage into a chute, the garbage would be disposed of. Unfortunately, the incinerator buildings were down four flights of stairs and a block away from some of the apartments, and some people were reluctant to make the trip. So, when kids needed money, they would knock on residents' doors and say, "Would you like your garbage emptied out in exchange for some bottles?" The bottles were redeemable at almost any store in the area. Some of the bottles were worth five cents. This was during a time when a candy bar cost a nickel. In the new neighborhood were the kind of kids that loved to go downtown and have a good time. If you saved up your money for about a month, you could go to the go-carts or horseback riding at Laredo Ranch in Keney Park. That's the way I made and spent money when I was a kid, but as I transitioned into my new school, Northwest Jones, I started trying to impress the older students. It was during this time that my brother Rocky returned home from school. He was eight years older and wore a shirt, tie and blazer to high school every day. Watching him created a change in my mind set that decreased my desire to ride go-carts and increased my desire to impress older boys, and of course the girls. I was growing up... sort of.

Suddenly, my appearance became important. I wanted to look as prosperous as possible like some of the other students in my school. By that I mean if they could afford to be in fine looking clothes, that's what they wore. At the age of 10, I started wearing P.F. Flyer sneakers. These weren't just any old sneakers. They were brand name. In fact, you could catch a television commercial about them from time to time. It went something like this: "Run your fastest and jump your highest with P.F. Flyers." Normally, a pair of sneakers cost $1.25 but P.F. Flyers cost $2.50. Since I was at that age when a boy starts to think that real men are athletes, I wanted a pair of P.F. Flyers. One day, my mother actually bought me a pair. This was astonishing because you could buy two pairs of Blue Tips for the price of a pair of P.F. Flyers. I wore them proudly and when I had them on, I felt like I could outrun anyone. However, as soon as my first pair wore out, all of the boys I knew were talking about sneakers called Converse All-Stars. Only the older teenage boys in my school were wearing them. After seeing some of the older boys with some on and the response they got from all the other kids, I started to want some too. I knew that my mother would not buy me a pair, but I laughingly walked up to her and said, "Ma, can you get me some All-Stars?" My mother asked, "What are All-Stars?" I replied, "Sneakers." She asked, "How much do they cost?" I said, "Eight dollars and 95 cents." She was stunned. She could hardly speak she was so shocked. When she could speak, the only words that would come out of her mouth were "Absolutely not!!!" I understood completely. After all, that was seven times the amount of a pair of Blue Tips. So, I concocted a plan. I knew my mother liked the thought of me earning the things that I got so I approached her again and I said, "If I pay for half of the sneakers, will you pay for the other half?" She said, "Yes." For the next couple of months I emptied the garbage of anyone who would hire me. I even got a job working at a local grocery store. Instead of watching cartoons on Saturdays, I was bagging groceries at the age of 10, and I got paid a dollar a day. I counted the money I saved so frequently that you would have thought it could accrue interest sitting in my dresser drawer. One day my mother and I proudly walked into Herbs Sports Shop on Asylum Street in Hartford, Connecticut. I told Herb that I wanted a pair of All Stars. Herb got my size and started lacing them up. While doing so, I noticed that he was using a different method of lacing sneakers than the one that I used. As I tried to correct him, he stopped abruptly and said, "I've been lacing up sneakers before you were born. Don't you think I know what I'm doing?" I knew to keep my mouth shut after that. The next day I walked to Northwest Jones. I was intentionally late because I didn't want anyone to step on my new sneakers. As I walked into Mrs. Vasquez's classroom, everyone noticed my feet. My friend Owen asked, "Are those All-Stars?" I said "Yup" and for the first time in my life, I was the coolest kid in my class. It was to be my grand finale, but I learned a very valuable lesson. If you want to be proud of yourself, earn the things you are proud of.

These were great times but they lasted for a short time because my friend Owen started getting money by stealing. I watched the beginning of his demise. Initially, when we went into someone's apartment to empty their garbage for them, he would take things that he thought they would not miss. I remember him reaching into a man's refrigerator and taking an egg. I was no older than 11, but I remember looking at him and telling him to put it back. He took it anyway. As we went about our garbage emptying duties, the egg broke in his pocket. I remember telling him laughingly, "It serves you right." Apparently, one day he was found in someone's basement. To get in, he had to force entry. Once my mother heard this story, she literally said, "We're moving because I don't want you around that boy anymore." I didn't believe she would move our entire family just to get me away from one friend but the next thing I knew, we were on our way to a new home in a project called Bowles Park.

This is a photo of my mother and me in 1965. I was 10 years old. She was 5'3", which gives you an idea of how short I was at that age.

Here we are when I was 50. I grew a little and put on a whole lot of weight. The building behind us is the former Everett School in Wareham, Massachusetts. It is where my mother went to grammar school during the Great Depression.

This is jumping ahead a few years but one day while I was at the Boys Club building on Nahum Drive in Hartford, one of my new friends came up to me and said, "Did you hear about Owen," referring to my friend in my previous neighborhood. I said, "No, what happened?" He said, "Owen and some of his friends broke into the Cadillac dealership. They hot-wired a car, and drove it through the showroom window. Then they went joy riding until the cops caught them." When I heard this, it dawned on me that if I had been foolish enough to remain close friends with Owen, I would have probably been with them when they were arrested. The next time I saw Owen after his joy ride was around ten years later. I was working part-time as an administrative assistant at a shelter for wayward girls. Sadly, Owen, who was at least 25 at this time, was visiting one of the teenage girls. I didn't dislike the man but after seeing him trying to date a teenage girl, I had nothing to say to him. We had grown completely apart. A few years later Owen was dead. My recollection of this man and the time we spent as kids reminded me of the words in the Bible spoken by the Apostle Paul: "Do not be mislead, bad association spoils useful habits." Fortunately for me, my mother knew those words and took them literally.

Since each move to a new neighborhood felt like a life changing experience, I was in the fourth chapter of my life. It would be the last one of my childhood.

Chapter 4

The Beginning of the End
1966

"Sometimes a person will not fit in with most of their peers because they were not destined to be part of the crowd; they were destined to be leaders."
— C.A. Teale, Sr.

I never adjusted. These are the first words that come to mind when I think of my life as a youth living in our new home. Moving is nothing new to the average child of Hartford. By the age of 11, I had lived in four different housing projects. Every change in schools disrupted my ability to get an education. I don't know how someone who moves more times than I did can get an education at all. We arrived in Bowles Park in November of 1966. This wasn't like when I was 9 and we moved from Bellevue Square to Greenfield Street. Bellevue Square was just three blocks away from Greenfield Street. Bowles Park seemed like a foreign country because it was miles away, and the kids there were very different from the ones in the previous neighborhoods. In the new neighborhood, there was a commitment to sports that I found impossible to adjust to because of my health challenges. I couldn't take gym in school so each week I fell further and further behind the culture of my new neighborhood. I desperately wanted to be an athlete but I was literally forbidden to engage in organized sports. I truly felt like an outsider my entire time there.

Some of the most talented athletes in the history of Hartford came from that area. One of them was a high school student by the name of Wayne Jones. Wayne wasn't just respected as an athlete; he was loved. I came to know hundreds of people by the time I met Wayne, and no one had a bad word to say about him. After seeing the affect he had on people, I decided that I wanted to become a basketball star like Wayne. That way, I could be respected and loved too. I got off to a bad start because if I tried and was accepted on a team, it meant having to get a permission slip from my mother. She of course knew of my diagnosis and would not allow it. I tried sneaking in some athletic activities by visiting the local Boys Club where you could just appear on the basketball court without anyone inquiring about your physical health. By the time I concocted this plan, I was way behind the kids of my age. Some of them had been playing organized sports for years and I had never been involved in a sports program at all.

From 1966 to 1969, I attended a school named after the author Mark Twain. The kids and the teachers at Mark Twain probably had the wrong impression of me because of my appearance. I say this because of the following incident. One day, while living on Greenfield Street, my brother Rocky came home and looked at my hairstyle. I use to wear a "pump" like the boxer Floyd Patterson used to wear. To wear a pump you had to let your hair grow, and the front of your head had to have more hair than the back. Sort of like a little ski slope, for those of you who can't remember Floyd. Well, my brother Rocky looked at me and said something to this effect: "Why don't you cut that sorry looking pump off your head and grow an Afro?" I asked him, "What's an Afro?" He told me by trying to mold my hairstyle with his hands. The next thing I knew, I was in a barber's chair trying to look like Huey P. Newton. Even the barber, Charles Robinson, was confused. I bring this experience to mind because it had an unexpected effect on the students in my new school. They thought I was some kind of militant even though I didn't even know what militant meant.

Since my activities in sports were nil at my old school, Northwest Jones, I took an interest in music. I wanted to play the saxophone at the time but there were none left in the board of education's inventory, so I started playing the clarinet, which had several similarities to the saxophone. I was told that I could get a saxophone the next year.

When I moved to Bowles Park, I still had the clarinet that I obtained at Northwest Jones, but I did not resume my lessons at the new school. I was too busy trying to learn the game of basketball at the Boys Club to be concerned about a clarinet. One day I got hate mail from the Board of Education. I can't remember exactly what it said, but in essence they wanted to know if I wanted to play the clarinet or not. If I was not interested in playing anymore I should turn the instrument in at once or pay for it. The next day I brought my clarinet in to school so that I could return it. It had to have been at least three weeks since I even saw the instrument, but I visited the band room to do as directed. I wanted nothing to do with this instrument and I was relieved to be getting rid of it.

As I entered the band room, I immediately noticed the prettiest girl you could imagine. She would have been "fine" if she wasn't so skinny. But I was impressed anyway. The teacher asked me, "Do you still want to play the clarinet?" I took one look at this girl, and shook my head to indicate "Yes." He then said to me, "Wonderful. Assemble it and we will see where you are."

I did as I was told and tried to play the notes in the book he placed in front of me. The screeching and squawking that came from that clarinet was so bad that the pretty girl and a girl she was sitting next to, named Dorothy, started laughing at me. The teacher scolded them immediately, telling them how rude it was for them to treat me in that fashion. I felt vindicated by what he said, and somehow, I decided to stick with the instrument. I'm sure the girl I've been referring to had a lot to do with my decision.

We each had "too young" marriages before long, but a few decades later, I asked her to marry me. She's my wife Helaine, and I've never met a better person. She has been with me during the most challenging times of my entire life. In spite of a lot of bad decisions that I made when I was very young, I've been able to accomplish more than I once dreamed possible. The main reason why this is true is because of Helaine. The year this book was released, we celebrated 20 years of marriage.

Here's Helaine from Mark Twain, 1968 to 1969.

The challenges my teachers had to face with me as their student were so great during this time that I decided to write about some of them. I'm not the kind of person who blames teachers when a student's grades are bad. I know from personal experience that the teacher can teach, encourage and even discipline a child but if the student is not interested in learning, the teacher cannot succeed, no matter how good the teacher is. I'm proof of that. The first of them at the Mark Twain School was my sixth grade teacher named Mr. Lapenta. He was to become very important to me in the months and years to come. He was known to give you pages of dictionary to write if you didn't do your homework (which was common for me in those days). Mr. Lapenta seemed to understand the children in his classroom in a way that I cannot express. He communicated, entertained and engaged all of us as he tried to teach us how to become better citizens. My grades by this time had gone into free fall. I could get an A, but only if I had a special interest in the subject I was being tested in. After I had been there around a month we received our report cards. Because I had just changed schools, my report card came from my old school, Northwest Jones. I had A's and B's. I had more A's than any other grade and was very proud to show them to my classmates. One of my fellow students turned to Mr. Lapenta and said, "The reason he got A's in his old school is because our school is harder than his old one." In his wisdom, Mr. Lapenta replied, "I believe a lot more is going on with Charles than just school work." He said a lot of things like that that I will never forget. If only I had the ability to positively interpret what he said when I was a child, I could have saved myself a lot of grief, but such was not to be the case. Many years later, after I had gone through my many academic and professional failures, I then succeeded in acquiring three college degrees. Less than a year after graduating, I was appointed Chief of the Hartford Fire Department. One day, while sitting in my office, reflecting on how I got there, I received a postcard from Mr. Lapenta congratulating me on my accomplishment. On the card he wrote:

"Dear Acting Chief Charles Teale, Congratulations on being appointed Acting Chief of the Hartford Fire Department. Best of Luck------Sincerely, Hugo R. Lapenta. It couldn't happen to a better kid."

When people you respect say good things about you, it does not matter what other people think. This lesson would come in handy real, real soon. I decided to give Mr. Lapenta a call so that we could have lunch and get caught up. We arranged to meet in my office and have lunch at one to the finest restaurants in Hartford at the time, The Goodwin. When Mr. Lapenta came into my office, I was so glad to see him that I was almost moved to tears. This was a man who taught school every day wearing a blazer and a tie. On this day, he showed up in Dock Siders, blue jeans and a sailor's cap. I was the one in the tie this time. We had reversed roles, and it was great to see him enjoying what every good teacher deserves, a long retirement. After sitting and talking about everyone who we both remembered from decades ago, we went out to lunch. At one point, I looked at him and told him that the reason I wanted to have lunch with him was to thank him, and to tell him that I believed that I owed part of my success to his instruction. Although I told him these things more than 14 years ago, I distinctly remember telling him this: "You taught us much more than reading, writing and arithmetic; you taught us how to become ladies and gentlemen." With that he said, "Well thank you Charles. You remind me of an old saying I once learned that goes: A teacher teaches not for the present but for all eternity; he never knows when his influence will end."

How our time together came to an end I don't recall. I only know that I did correspond with him through letters or the telephone after that. My life had changed. Sadly, there were days when I wouldn't have time to visit my own mother, who lives in the city where I was Chief, for two weeks at a time. One day, I read it in the obituary section of the newspaper that Mr. Lapenta had died. Although I felt the loss deeply, I was relieved that I at least got the chance to tell him how much he meant to me and all of us who he helped become contributing members of society. At his funeral his daughter gave his eulogy. During the service, she said, "My father was especially proud of the many students he helped into adulthood, among them was Doctor" (whose name I cannot recall) "and Charles Teale who became Chief of the Hartford Fire Department."

There are times when it all comes together, times when you ask yourself, "Why did I go through so much to accomplish the things that I did?" On that day, I got my answer.

You might have guessed it by now. Of all the teachers that I ever had, Mr. Lapenta was my favorite.

From GED to Master's Degree and Beyond

Here's Mr. Hugo Lapenta, sixth grade teacher from Mark Twain, during the 1966 to 1967 school year. That was when I joined his classroom.

These are the boys of Mr. Hugo Lapenta's class, 1966 to 1967. They are:
Standing (left to right) Danny Christoforo, Tommy Perkins, Kirky Means, Robert Zaccanino. Seated (left to right) Joey Quinn, me, Sam Harrison, John Dunn.

Ms. Lacker
1968

Over the course of the next two years, seventh and eighth grade, my academics worsened, but somehow, I stayed with my music. By the seventh grade, I made the transition from clarinet to the saxophone. It was the only thing that I seemed to stay with even though I cannot profess to have ever been very good at it. I took lessons during the school day, and that created a huge problem for one of my teachers by the name of Ms. Lacker. Ms. Lacker was the math teacher at Mark Twain, and she took her job very seriously. My music lessons were given during the school day when I was supposed to be in other classes. Whenever I would get up from Ms. Lacker's classroom to go to music lessons, she would comment on how difficult it was for her to teach me math if I wasn't there to learn it. One day she said that she was going to complain to the principal about the situation. I felt perfectly justified in doing what I did, and besides, I wasn't fond of math anyway. I really enjoyed walking out of her classroom. It wasn't until I tried to get through math in the ninth grade that I came to realize that Ms. Lacker was right. I had a very poor foundation upon which to learn even basic algebra.

Ms. Pustello
1969

My inability in math seemed to fuel resentment for the overall learning process. My attitude toward all subjects was starting to suffer. Also, because I was bigger than most kids of my age, I thought that I was becoming a man. However, I was just an oversized kid. One day it all came to a head during one of my social studies classes. Exactly what foolish thing I did I cannot recall, but my social studies teacher, Ms. Pustello, called me into the hallway, which had never happened to me before in all of my years of going to school. This much I remember clearly. She said, "Charles, you have a real chance of making something good of yourself in life, but if you aren't careful, you're going to throw it all away." When she could see that I wasn't listening, she then said, "You don't want to grow up to become like some of those other guys in the classroom, do you?" She was obviously referring to some of the members of my class who had already had run-ins with the law. I took offense to what she was saying, and with her words I just rolled my eyes and looked away from her. She then said, "All right." She then opened the door and I reentered the classroom. I felt cool, brave and even a little tough, but what I didn't realize is what many children don't know as they try hard to impress their peers. I had just thrown away an opportunity to get on the right track. Our conversation that day must have reached the other teachers in the school because no other teacher ever tried to steer me straight again. It would be another four years before someone, other than family, would try. This is one of the reasons why I say the public school system didn't fail me; I failed it by trying to gain acceptance from my fellow students instead of listening to my teachers.

Mrs. Dickerson
1969

At Mark Twain, we were accustomed to seeing an African American teacher. Mrs. Gwendolyn Hurley taught fifth grade there, and she taught my sister Karen. However, with the exception of Mrs. Hurley's husband, who was my gym teacher at the last school I attended, I personally never had an African American teacher. That was about to change.

With the assassination of Dr. Martin Luther King, Jr. came an increase in African American teachers throughout the Hartford public school system. One of those teachers was Mrs. Thelma Dickerson and she taught English. To make things even more interesting, Mrs. Dickerson wore an Afro, so some students thought she was a militant type teacher. I remember being misclassified like that for the same reason, so I made no such assumption. Upon realizing that we had an African American English teacher, Barbara, one of my fellow students exclaimed, "We can do what ever we want to now." Nothing could have been further from the truth. Mrs. Dickerson was nothing less than strict and she wasn't taking any crap! If you were inclined to act out in school, you didn't let Mrs. Dickerson see you. This was during the days when if a teacher wanted to, she could hit you with a paddle. I never knew Mrs. Dickerson to do so, but everyone thought that she had the potential to paddle. She did everything in her power to prepare us to succeed in what she knew would be a difficult world. Decades later, while serving as Chief of the Hartford Fire Department, I would receive the privilege of speaking at an event where a school she had started was being named in her honor.

I strongly suspect that there are people in every city who strive to distinguish themselves by being of service to children throughout their lives. Mrs. Dickerson was one of them, and that's putting it very mildly.

Goodbye Mark Twain
1969

The other times spent as a student at Mark Twain were tumultuous at best. Oddly enough, some of the people who I felt like I hated became people who I would someday love dearly. However, during this time I simply could not get along with my teachers, fellow students or family. I was coming apart at the seams. A once good kid, suddenly angry with the world. By the age of 14, my fate was sealed. Prior to this time, my brother Rocky tried to intervene by introducing me to people who were successful. One of them was my brother's boss. His name was Curtis Robinson and he was the head of the Small Business Development Corporation in Hartford. While every pimp and hustler in Hartford was driving a Cadillac, Curtis Robinson was driving a Bentley, and it had a telephone in it. I knew of no one else who had a car like that. In a sense, I wanted to be like Curtis. Curtis Robinson was the reason why I wrote in my Mark Twain school year book that I was going to be a "Black Business V.I.P." when I grew up. Unfortunately, I didn't have the discipline necessary to succeed in business or anything else for that matter. I was on my way to high school with a bad attitude about learning. I actually thought that I knew how to succeed, and everyone else didn't know as much as I did. I had stumbled upon the perfect formula for failure because I became a "know-it-all."

This is my mother Francisca and me on the day of my graduation from Mark Twain in 1969. It would be another 22 years before I got to graduate from another school. The suit is Bill Blass, but it wasn't mine. It belonged to my brother Rocky. During that time, we were about the same size so I wore his clothes a lot. When people saw me they would say, "That kid sure is clean!"

Chapter 5

Just Passing Through
1969

During the mid-1960's, my brother Rocky attended Weaver High School in Hartford. I was around 10 years old. He was on the photography team, so he got to go to all of the major events like football games and watched from wherever he wanted. Sometimes he brought me with him. I loved the place. Weaver High was truly more like a prep school than a high school in those days. I knew my father had attended there, so I envisioned myself going there when I turned 14. That day came sooner than I thought it would, and I was not prepared for the changes that took place after the assassination of Dr. Martin Luther King, Jr. By the time I got there, it was an act of courage to just go to the restroom. Gangs roamed the halls, and the smallest, most defenseless person in the school could become a bully if he was in a gang. I hated the place, and I wanted out the first day I walked through the doors. A student should not have to choose between studying and safety, but I did. For a little while.

One day after school, while playing a game of softball with some white friends of mine, two guys walked up to the field. As they were coming, one of my friends said, "Here comes trouble." Just as soon as he said that, one of the guys said, "We want to play." They were told that the teams were chosen and there was no more room for other players. (In other words, "Get lost.") One of the guys decided to grab a bat and approached home plate. Since they were of my race, and all of the other players were not, I was starting to feel embarrassed. I often felt that way when people of my race acted poorly around white people. My friends seemed scared of these two so I stepped in, and told them to get out of the way so that we could finish the game. As I did that one of them pulled out a switchblade. I suppose nowadays he would have pulled out a gun. He still had the bat in his hand so I told him, "You must be mighty scared of me if you need a knife and a bat to fight me." He tossed the bat aside, so I picked it up and approached him saying, "Drop the knife or I'll knock your head off." Neither one of us was thinking. He dropped the knife and I grabbed him by the throat telling him what I would do to him if he ever pulled a knife on me again. When I let him go, he and his friend walked away from all of us shouting, "We'll be back." I wasn't concerned at all until one of my friends turned to me and said, "He's the brother of a gang member. They always come back with at least six guys.

You'd better go home." I did exactly as he said as quickly as my legs would carry me. Although I stood my ground, I lived from that moment onward in constant fear. I never knew if or when that gang would exact their revenge, but it made an already uncomfortable learning environment worse.

I found high school humiliating because of my bad grades and terrifying because of the possibility for violence. One day, just a few months after I started my freshman year, I left school and vowed never to come back. I came very close to keeping that promise.

Sorry Charlie

1970

What I did with my time during those days saddens me now. I used to go to the YMCA building when it was on Jewel Street in Hartford and watch TV in the lounge. Because my mother worked, I would just stay at home if I wasn't at the Y. In time, it became apparent that I wasn't going to school. A lack of report cards was all it took to make that obvious. My household was in turmoil over the matter. No one knew what to do with me. Not even me. I started drifting. However, I discovered that I could still enjoy life if I had a little money in my pockets. In my neighborhood, you could make money if you walked over to the local golf course and caddied. Although this was an opportunity for some, it proved to be a serious problem for others. I say this because, if you lived in Bowles Park and you wanted to go caddying, you had a college campus as an obstacle. The guards on the campus did not allow those of us who were obviously not students to cross through school property. Trying to do so would lead to apprehension by the security guards and possible arrest by the local police. Therefore, you had three ways to get there: get a ride with someone who had a car, walk around the entire campus, or try your luck with the guards. As anyone who has ever caddied will tell you, you usually have to get to the golf course by 6:30 am or all of the good paying golfers would be gone. That meant that it would be very difficult to get a ride because no one with a car would be up that early on a Saturday or a Sunday. As for walking around the campus, when you caddied you walked for four hours with two bags on your shoulders. The thought of walking another hour to get there and another hour to get home was not a viable option. The only other choice was cutting through the campus. In those days, there was only one barbed wire fence between Bowles Park and that university. Now there are two fences. A hole in that fence made accessing the campus possible but getting across the campus was the tough part. Although most of my friends and classmates tried ducking behind cars and other objects to avoid detection, I decided to try another method. I surmised that the guards were less likely to impede my progress if they could see me. Because I was a big kid, I tried to act and look like a student. I flashed the peace sign to those I passed because that's what many of the college students did in those days. I hoped that the guards would not think that I was an outsider. In five years I was never stopped by any of the guards, but I never felt safe until I reached an anchor on the other side of the campus. When you reached that anchor, you were no longer on the campus. I remember tapping it triumphantly as I passed it.

I learned much later in life that that anchor once was attached to the USS Hartford. It was on that ship that the first admiral of the United States Navy, David Farragut, who was of Hispanic descent, uttered the words "Damn the torpedoes, full speed ahead" during the battle of Mobile Bay. That anchor came to mean so much to me that several years later, I took a picture of it with me standing next to it.

Here I am standing next to the anchor that I touched on my way to work when I was a kid. This time, touching it meant that I had made it through my third collegiate degree program. Thanks to the Tools of Learning, I had gone from GED to Master's Degree.

As you can imagine, the weather sometimes got in the way of my caddying. So, after a year of doing this, I decided to get a more permanent job. Initially, I tried to apply for jobs and simply telling people that I was 16 instead of 15. The first job offer I received doing this was from G. Fox and Company in downtown Hartford. To longtime Hartfordites, G. Fox wasn't just a store; it was an institution. In my immature mind, I thought that if I could work there, it would be proof that I didn't need a high school diploma to be successful. Their department of personnel informed me that all I had to do was get my working papers, and I would be hired. I was so new at everything that I had to ask, "Where do I have to go to get working papers?" They informed me, "At the Board of Education building on High Street." So, off I went. When I got to the board of education, I was still 15, but I had told the people at G. Fox that I was 16. To prevent myself from being caught in a lie, I tried to be consistent. So, I told the person at the Board of Education that I was 16. She looked for about 10 minutes and informed me that she could not find anyone of my age in their records. I then said, "That's because I'm 15." She looked at me in mild disgust and said, "You can't get working papers at 15; you will have to wait a year." So I left, totally embarrassed. It took me a couple of days but it dawned on me. Working papers are for people who are less than 18 years old. Therefore, if I tell people that I'm 18 they won't ask me for working papers. So, I got a false birth certificate and told people that I was 18 instead of 15. Within months, I was hired by E. J. Korvettes, a store that was right across the street from G. Fox. It was my first real job, and I was only 15. What a shame that I could not use my ability to strategize for more productive things like getting a high school diploma.

My job at E.J. Korvettes did not last very long. This was during the time period when people and businesses were leaving Hartford and flocking to the suburbs. E.J. Korvettes was closing, so, in less than a few months, I was laid off and looking for work. Fortunately, I was nearing 16 and getting a job would be much easier.

The Truth Unveiled
1971

I had been drifting for a while when school authorities finally contacted my mother. They tried reaching her earlier, but I used to intercept the mail they sent her before she got to see it. They tried calling a few times but I would answer the phone pretending to be my father, and I would promise to address the problem ASAP. I don't recall how the school administration figured me out, but by the time that they did, I had been out of school for almost two years. By this time, my brother Rocky was a man, living in his own apartment. My mother spoke with him about this matter, and he said to me, "We just got word from Weaver you haven't been in school for almost two years. What are you going to do?" I should have said, "I'm quitting school so that I can get a full-time job." If I had said that, I would have been telling him what I really wanted to do with my life. If I had said that, he would have hit the ceiling and started lecturing me on the importance of an education, which I was in no mood to hear. By this time, my brother had tried to inspire me to pursue academic and professional excellence by introducing me to successful people. They would inspire me but for only a short amount of time. When my brother asked me, "What are you going to do," I didn't have an answer that was acceptable to him. So, I said, "I'm going back to school" to get him off my case. I cannot tell the reader how much I wish that I felt some sense of determination about succeeding when I said those words. But the truth of the matter was I was just saying what I thought other people wanted to hear me say.

However, before long, I was walking through the front door of Weaver High School for an appointment with my guidance counselor. Entering the school was one of the strangest experiences of my life. I didn't fit in at all. People who did know me thought it laughable that I was even there. When my guidance counselor saw me, he exclaimed, "Well, look who's here!" I never forgot that greeting. Because there were several students in the area when he said it, I felt humiliated when I heard it. Up until that point, I believed that all of the teachers and administrators wanted what was best for me. He became the exception. As I waited to talk with my guidance counselor, I had a conversation with a student who said, "Why don't you go to Hotchkiss for the summer? You can get two credits." Hotchkiss is a school in Lakeville, Connecticut. The name of the school is actually "The Hotchkiss School" and it was part of the G.O. program. G.O. stood for "Greater Opportunity" and it meant summer school for students from Hartford and Harlem since 1965. I figured it out. Since I had actually passed a band and a typing class in my first semester at Weaver, I had more than two credits. With the two credits that I would receive at Hotchkiss I could become a sophomore. That sounded a lot better than being a 16-year-old freshman. I looked into the matter through my guidance counselor and the head of the program, Father David Kern. I was told that I could attend Hotchkiss, but I would have to go to school the rest of the year to qualify. In those days if you were 16 and you had less than three credits, you sat in a freshman homeroom. I had to endure all of the jeering and the ranks. Some students called me "the world's biggest freshman", and they even stood at the doorway of my homeroom just to laugh at me, but somehow, I endured it all until summer. The next thing I knew, I was on my way to Lakeville, Connecticut.

Chapter 6

My Walden Pond
1971

I'm sure that to many of the 100-plus students who attended the program at Hotchkiss that summer, it wasn't a big deal. For me, it was to be the first time I had been in a classroom consistently in close to two years. The bus took off from where I used to leave for Camp Courant, right in front of the Keney Clock Tower on Main Street in Hartford. The ride from Hartford to Lakeville took about an hour and a half. Oddly enough, I got along well with everyone, the way I did before I moved to Bowles Park. These were no ordinary students. They were great guys, people who you want to be friends with for life. I was surprised because I expected to receive taunts about my not showing up for school during the year but showing up for summer school. Not everyone was attending because they needed the credits. Some had been there during previous summers and simply enjoyed the experience. I didn't know what to expect. Fortunately, I had the experience of working while I was not at school. Otherwise, I would not know how to talk to other people. I believe the reason I remember my experiences at the Hotchkiss School so vividly is because it was my only successful high school experience. I remember being in my dorm room and placing my personal belongings in my dresser and photos on my walls.

Believe it or not, I had a girlfriend at that time. Her name was Darlene Hayes. I haven't mentioned her in this book so far. My reasons for that are twofold: First, I want to focus solely on those experiences and people who had an effect on my academic and professional development. Second, I'd like to protect the innocent as much as possible. I can't imagine any girl wanting to admit that she was my girlfriend at that age, but I could not conceal her identity any further.

I made friends quickly with the guys on my floor. Some of them were from Harlem. What a combination we made. Somehow however, I could tell that we all cared for one another, and that this would not be an atmosphere filled with negative competition. We would compete athletically but that was all. I felt right at home from the start. This environment was so productive that it resulted in the creation of the very first Tool presented in the Tools of Learning program. It's about using a study schedule.

A study schedule keeps you from doing anything but studying, when you should be studying. It is number one in my program because if you aren't willing to set time aside for studying, then you don't have the desire necessary to succeed academically or professionally.

While I attended classes at The Hotchkiss School, every student was directed to study at a certain time of the evening. To insure that students abided by this rule, we were given a study schedule and told to place it on the desk in our room. The room was so small that all it could hold was a bed and a desk, so no matter where you went in your room, you could see your schedule. We were also directed to be in our rooms, at our desks, with our books open, during the time specified on the schedule that they gave us. There were no locks on our doors, so we knew that any time the school wanted to determine if we were studying, all they had to do was open our door. I distinctly remember them doing so. Fortunately for me, I was at my desk with my books open. If we were not at our desks with our books open, it would spell trouble. Eventually, you would be sent back home.

Although this method may seem extreme to most students and adults, it was most effective when I took classes there.

I didn't start using this method away from The Hotchkiss School until 11 years after I left there. It was one of those Tools that I had to remember from my past positive learning experiences, so that I could get through firefighter training. I was learning how to become a firefighter when I first started using this system at home, and the place I put my schedule was on my television set. The reason why I did this was because I knew that after having a hard day of learning how to fight fires, the most relaxing thing that I could do was watch television. But as I sat down to watch TV, that schedule would be there, reminding me of what I should be doing.

Remembering this method 11 years later led to this requirement becoming Tool #1 of the Tools of Learning program. Every student studying the Tools of Learning method receives a workbook, and on the copyright page of that workbook are the words "Portions of Tool Number 1 'Use a Study Schedule' were reprinted with permission from The Hotchkiss School in Lakeville, CT." It has been over 43 years since that experience, but thanks to the incredibly positive learning environment I found at the Hotchkiss School in Lakeville, Connecticut, I still consider that place to be my Walden Pond.

TOOL #1
Use a Study Schedule, 1971
Dedicated to The Hotchkiss School in Lakeville, Connecticut

A study schedule will keep you from scheduling other things when you should be studying.

A study schedule is more important today than it was in 1971. Back then, we had one black and white television in our homes, and we were content to have that. Since that time, the following things have competed with the time we used to invest studying:

1. More televisions in the house
2. Color television
3. Cable television
4. Personal computers
5. Video games
6. Smart phones
7. Computers with internet connection
8. Social media

With each new development, we have had less time for studying. These changes have contributed to our nation going from being number one in the world in some subjects in 1945 to being number 26 in 2014. A study schedule can help reverse this trend, especially if you tell your friends and family about your study schedule.

Your study schedule should be placed in a location you walk by frequently in your home or on any device that you have with an alarm on it.

Television was once known as "the great thief of time." Well, if television was the thief of time, then the smart phone is time's assassin. Unless you are using your smart phone to accomplish or learn something, you are not investing your time wisely. If you find yourself using a lot of social media, place your study schedule on your favorite device (like your smart phone), put an alarm on it telling you that it is time to study, and use that phone only after you have accomplished and learned what you should have for that day.

My Walden Pond (Continued)
1971

The week's activities consisted primarily of schoolwork and athletics. Since there were no girls around, the guys didn't seem to compete against each other the way we did at home. Competition at home was personal. If you defeated someone in a game of basketball, you felt like more of a man in front of the girls. At Hotchkiss, we were competitive, but it was all just sports, and there were no hard feelings between rivals. The one time I remember experiencing an exception to this was when there was a wager for money. It was after that that I learned never to gamble again. I came close to loosing a friend just because of a stupid race.

However, during athletic events I was a fish out of water. School obviously provided the other students with gym classes, something I hadn't been in consistently since I was 10 years old. For some reason, I could jump well at that age, which meant dunking a basketball in the fanciest way I could think of, but I had no athletic ability other than that. One day, we were broken up into teams to play baseball. This wasn't by choice; we were directed by the administration to play. I hadn't played baseball since I was 8 and living in Bellevue Square. Since I have no depth perception, I struck out every time I was at bat through at least four tries. I later came to realize I had a serious eye impairment that was caused by an illness that would later create some of the most challenging days of my life. But before this game ended, the following event occurred.

It was the top of the ninth inning, the score was 9 to 8 in favor of the other team, the bases were loaded, there were two outs and I was up at bat. The other team all seemed to be laughing. I was so furious that I knew if I just made contact with the ball, it would be a home run. I can still see that pitch and the look on everyone's face as I made contact. I don't think they have found that ball to this day. I rounded the bases and swore out loud "I will never play this game again" as I crossed home plate. In over 43 years, I never have. The next day in school, some of the guys came up to me and said, "One of the teachers was talking about you in class. He said that you are an example of how a person can do great things if he doesn't quit." The reader might detect, that as bad as that experience started, it became a shining moment for me. Since I had very few victories in those days, it was a moment I have cherished since then.

The Ragamont Inn
1971

We received an allowance of seven dollars per week, which was pretty good money during a time when gas was 29 cents a gallon. How we spent that money was our choice. Usually, we spent it as a group. Each floor would have a supervisor who coordinated our activities. I remember going to a car race, the circus and other events. But, one day, someone said, "Let's save out money and go to the Ragamont." The Ragamont was a restaurant in Salisbury, Connecticut. It was the next town over but it may as well have been a world away. The Ragamont Inn (which was its formal name back then) had been in existence since the mid-1800s. Only the wealthiest people ate there, and when they did, they were dressed to the nines. However, we wanted the experience. So, for two weeks we stayed on campus. It was difficult seeing guys from other buildings and floors on their way to a good time, but we persevered.

The day finally came. Because my mother made arrangements for me to attend a religious convention while I was at Hotchkiss, I had a suit that I wore. The guys were surprised to see me in it. Everyone was nicely dressed, but I think I was the only one in a suit. I wish I had photos of that experience. All of us, so young, with our entire adult lives ahead of us, trying to act like men. That was a truly memorable experience.

Just before the conclusion of the program we had family day. My mother, brother, sister and my brother's girlfriend came up to see me. It was one of those experiences I'll never forget. I hadn't seen them in a while. Because I was able to send most of my personal belongings home with them, I just had a grocery bag of items to carry when the summer was over. On the bus, we discussed all the things we were going to do when we got home. The bus was going to the Keney Clock Tower, the place where we got on a couple of months prior. It passed by the corner of Albany Avenue and Garden Street in Hartford, which was close to where my girlfriend lived at the time. All the while that I was in Lakeville, she wrote to me. As we got within a block of her house, I asked the bus driver if he would let me off. There really wasn't much point in him doing this. My girlfriend's mother was very strict. In the almost two years that we saw each other, we never went on a single date. The only way I was able to see her was to go over to her house. Most of the time I wasn't allowed to even do that. I can still envision myself looking back at the guys on the bus as the door opened saying, "See you guys in school." It was to be the last time that I saw most of them again.

I decided to include a photo of the entire group. That's me standing in the top row, second person from the right, in a double-breasted pinstripe suit. It's amazing how well I could dress when you consider the fact that I seldom had any money. Fortunately, I knew the value of the word "layaway".

Here I am at The Hotchckiss School. Back then, I would run three miles before breakfast and three miles after dinner. I would return on many occasions throughout the years. Usually, I would take a photo at this same location. This one is from the summer of 1971.

With all the things that happened on that campus, the days I remember most were Sundays. I brought a stereo with me and I remember listening to the Delfonics, Carole King, the Stylistics and others. One day, I promised myself that I would ride my bicycle there from Hartford. It took me about 40 years but one Sunday, I struck out from my Hartford home, and five and a half hours later, I arrived on the campus. I didn't have the strength to ride back so I had my son Charlie come pick me up. While waiting for my son, I sat on a wall I used to sit on decades earlier and reminisced about those days when we would throw parties. Girls from other summer school programs would visit us. It was the days of Hot Pants, so it was definitely worth it to sit on that wall and wait for the bus to show up. As I was sitting on that wall I found myself thinking about Hotchkiss during the summer of '71.

Here I am in the same location 42 years after the 1971 photo. This time, I decided to drive there. Thanks primarily to a former student named Daryl Collins, we had a reunion at last. What a difference four decades and 80 pounds make. There are no words to describe what I had been through between then and now. This book is designed to share with the reader the most valuable lessons I learned in those four decades. In the first photo I was 16, and in this photo I am retired and 58. Oddly enough, in both photos I didn't have a care in the world. That year, a group of us decided that we would form a group called "G.O. 2". Our mission: to recreate this program for today's youth. After all, this was an experience worth sharing.

Chapter 7

Back Home
1971

I cannot remember if I saw my girlfriend that day or not. If I had, it would have included a hello along with sitting in her living room. Her mother would have looked in on us every five minutes, so I probably can't remember because it was an experience I choose to forget. Somehow I made it back to my place of residence, Bowles Park. I probably walked. I walked everywhere in those days. Living in Bowles Park was an experience that came very close to destroying me completely. My family and I moved there when I was 11 years old. I felt hated from the start. I never completely knew why I received the reaction I got, but it's important to reflect on those years at this time because it demonstrates one of the reasons why I had such a difficult time transitioning from my old school, Northwest Jones, to Mark Twain and from Hotchkiss back to Weaver High. Within a couple of weeks, I was scheduled to start school at Weaver High. I was excited about school again. Thanks to Hotchkiss, I felt like I was well known and well liked by at least some good students in the school.

Before I entered school, I was notified about my homeroom assignment. To my horror, it was the same one as my little sister Karen. What that meant was the credits that I should have gotten from going to school all summer had not been added to my record. Alarmed, I called the school and explained my situation. The best response I got was, "We have no record of you ever attending Hotchkiss." No matter how hard I tried, I could not convince them. Over the coming days, all I could do was envision how bad it was to be a freshman when I was supposed to be a sophomore. Surely, it was going to be much worse for me to be a freshman when I was supposed to be a junior. The representative from Weaver's office told me, "Just come to school; it won't kill you to be in your sister's homeroom for a little while." Such words sound sensible to an adult, but as we all know, a teenager is driven by peer pressure. The last thing I remember telling the office at Weaver was, "When you find the records of my attending Hotchkiss, call me. Then, I'll come to school."

That day never came. I cannot tell the reader how often I have felt that if I had gotten that call, I would have returned to school as a sophomore, gotten the grades to become a junior, went back to Hotchkiss for two additional credits and graduated with my class. This realization has driven my desire to intervene on behalf of any student who is trying to stay in school. Many of the challenges our students now face are resolvable, if everyone works together to help keep the student in school.

The following days and months had me back where I was before Hotchkiss. I'm sure that no one could understand it. How did I go from doing so well during the summer to not showing up at school again? Even I couldn't explain it. One day, about a month after the start of school, my sister came home and said, "They keep calling your name at school and asking where you are." That made me realize that the problem with my record had not been resolved — and that it never would be. I was certain that I was not going back.

I started working again, drifting from one job to another. Although I thought that I was being productive by working, most people didn't see it that way at all. That was especially true where I lived, in Bowles Park. I was looked upon as a "dropout" and "sorry" to some people. I even earned the nickname "Sorry Charlie". I never had the right to dislike them for the way they thought of me. After all, if I didn't start doing things differently in my life, eventually I would prove them right.

Chapter 8

Shanti
1972

As you might have guessed, word of my not returning to school after Hotchkiss got to the ears of my family. However, it didn't take long this time for my absence from school to reach my mother and brother. We were at an impasse. I was not going back to school to be a 16-year-old freshman!

About a year after Hotchkiss, my brother Rocky proposed a solution. He found out about a school called Shanti. It was called "a school without walls" because the homeroom was at the train station in Hartford (yes, I wrote "the train station"), and other classes were given all over the city of Hartford and beyond. It sounded like something that I was willing to try, so I signed up. I took gym at Trinity College, political science at Hartford City Hall with Mayor George Athanson, and astronomy at the Children's Museum in West Hartford. Some of the courses we could take even included skydiving. I signed up for that course but my mother refused to sign the permission slip (thank God). Getting a sense of rhythm was difficult because there was so much freedom. If you were missing from school, who would know? One day, I realized that there was a company called Kelly Labor that was attached to the building where my school was located. At Kelly Labor, you could work for a day and get paid the very next day. If you wanted to work, you could. If you didn't want to work, you didn't have to. You just wouldn't get paid. I applied for work there every day I had available. I told them I was 18, so I could work as late as the job required. Most of the men who worked there were alcoholics who needed money so that they could buy supplies the next day. Sometimes I would be working at 12 midnight even though I had school the next day. That wasn't so bad except that after work, I had to walk home, which was up to an hour away. Thanks in part to this schedule, one night, I had a late night meeting with a police officer.

As I said in an earlier chapter, I was particularly fond of firefighters and police officers when I was a boy. The firefighters in my neighborhood and my cousin, Officer Walter McBride, deserve the credit for that. By the age of 17, however, I wasn't thinking about the police or firefighters until the following incident occurred.

I was taking temporary work at Kelly Labor, working at demolishing buildings in Washington, Connecticut. Late one evening, I was coming back to Hartford from Washington. Temporary workers seldom had their own transportation, so the company we did work for gave us rides to and from the job site. On our way back from Washington, Connecticut, I asked to be dropped off as close to my home as possible by the driver. Although I was dropped off at least two miles from my house, in those days, to me that was just a stroll. I should have been home resting up for a day in school, but I found myself walking two miles to get home instead. I could not have been walking for more than 15 minutes when suddenly a police cruiser pulled up next to me with its lights flashing. The police officer got out of his car and said, "A woman has been assaulted and you fit the description of the person who did it. Put your hands on the hood of the car." I did as directed. He put the handcuffs on me behind my back and then placed me in the back seat of the cruiser. Then we drove to a project called Westbrook Village in Hartford. It was there that we stopped, and the officer got out of his car to approach a crowd. I could tell that one of the women in the crowd was very upset and the others were trying to comfort her. I saw the officer go up to the woman who was crying, and she and her friends approached the car. It's times like these that make you realize how unpredictable life is. I could sense that all she had to say was "yes, that's him," and my life would be over. As she took a close look at me, she turned to the officer and said just the opposite: "No, that's not him." Forty-three years later, I can still feel the sigh of relief I felt at that very moment.

The officer got back in his cruiser and said, "I'm sorry, but you did fit the description." I told him that I understood, and that he was just doing his job. Then he said, "Where were you walking to at this time of the night?" I told him, "Bowles Park." He couldn't believe his ears. He knew that I was about an hour away and that it was close to midnight, so he asked me, "Would you like a ride home?" I said "Sure!" He let me out of the car, took off the cuffs, and let me sit in the front seat. We had a good conversation, and he even encouraged me to stick with my schoolwork. He then brought me right to the front of my apartment building at 211 Nahum Drive. I thanked him emphatically for the ride but after he pulled off, I couldn't help but think how differently things could have gone. If I had been rude to that police officer, he would not have given me a ride home. In fact, it could have been a lot worse than that on that night.

Working late evenings and trying to go to school during the day lasted all of three months. Suddenly, everyone in the school started talking about the class of '73 graduating. Although I was old enough to be in that class, I didn't have nearly enough credits. All totaled, I believe I had around six months of high school, including The Hotchkiss School. I should have been preparing for graduation, but because I didn't have more than three credits, I was still a freshman. I tried desperately to conceal my true academic standing and was successful until one day, one of the students made an announcement to a group of students. He said that one of our teachers showed him my folder, and that I didn't have enough credits to graduate next year or the year after that. I couldn't believe that a teacher would do that, so I approached the teacher and asked him about the matter. I remember the teacher's name but I don't care to list it here because he is now deceased. I do remember him saying that at the rate that I was going, I would not be able to get a high school diploma until I was in my early 20's. In light of all the circumstances, I decided to withdraw from school. On my next birthday, I would be 18. I was closing in on becoming a man, and I sensed the need to get a real job to support myself. Accomplishing the task of getting a full time permanent job was to be more difficult than getting day work at Kelly Labor. After all, I had little more than an eighth grade education.

School's Out
1972

I never could determine one single reason why I gave up on my education. Although my academic challenges were the main reason, there always seemed to be several reasons why my grades were so bad. Although those reasons seemed valid at the time, they seem like poor excuses today. However, in 1982, when I began developing my system of learning methodology called the Tools of Learning, I decided to look back on the previous decade and write down why I arrived at such a self-destructive decision. My reasons were:

1. Poor grades
2. Bad student, good worker
3. Sleep disorder
4. Wanted money now!
5. Distracted by the possibility of violence
6. A total lack of confidence in my ability to live long enough to use the information taught to me

I now teach and tutor students taking GED (General Educational Development) and N.E.D.P. (National External Diploma Program) courses, high school students who appear to be on the verge of dropping out and college students who are having a difficult time transitioning from high school. In an attempt at empathizing with current-day students who may be thinking of quitting, I decided to analyze each of the six reasons I mentioned. Things may be somewhat different nowadays, but I have discovered that these reasons provide me with the experience needed to connect with a lot of students who are having a difficult time with school.

1. Poor Grades

How I wish that I could determine why my ability to learn diminished so greatly when I became a teenager. If I could, I would be able to solve a major challenge faced by so many children and their parents. Common concerns like the effect poverty has on the learning process, and the fact that courses become harder with each semester are possibilities, but most of the other students had the same challenges as I did. They didn't drop out. Why did I? I now believe it was because I had no strategy for succeeding academically. In some homes, there is an adult who graduated from high school. Other households have college graduates. But, if you live in a house where no one has a high school diploma, who will teach you how to succeed academically if you aren't learning that strategy in school?

In high school, the only exception to my academic failings was (of all things) my typing classes. I can still envision the room. It was large and filled with desks, chairs and typewriters. The primary reason why I liked going to this class was because some of my friends took the class too. One of them was a guy by the name of Terry. I remember his last name but I won't mention it here just in case he wouldn't want to be mentioned. The main reason why I remember Terry so well is because he had a severe stammering problem. It was so great that when he spoke, he created ridicule that led to the most memorable fights in school history. This was one of the nicest guys I had ever met but when he got mad, a whole gang of kids couldn't beat him. There was one story of a group of three brothers attacking him all at once. These brothers were great athletes so you would think they could defeat Terry easily. Guess again. At one point Terry got so angry during the fight that he pulled the piping from an underground oil tank out of the ground and chased these brothers all over the schoolyard. The brothers were so terrified that they ran and threw rocks back at Terry like he was an approaching monster. I know all of this sounds unbelievable and irrelevant but I had to mention Terry somewhere in this story. That's because he was one of very few friends I made in high school. One day, a group of us were walking from Weaver High School when one of my friends looked at Terry and asked, "Why do you stutter so much?" The rest of us were shocked to hear the question but didn't want to overreact (After all, if this guy got angry, he probably could have beaten us all like we were rented mules.) Terry just smiled and said as clearly as he could, "When I was 5 years old, I saw my mother frying some chicken. I wanted to help, so I went to the stove and grabbed the frying pan handle. Hot grease spilled all over my chest and back and legs. I have stuttered ever since." As he said this, he opened his shirt and showed us his scars. They must have been left by third-degree burns they were so pronounced. Since that day, Terry has come to symbolize for me every school child who can't seem to stop fighting in school.

When I think about attending Weaver High School, those are the only memories that I have. Fortunately, I had a positive experience in that typing class. If I didn't learn how to type, this book, all of the other books I have written, and the program I developed called the Tools of Learning, would never have been written.

Getting poor grades is a prelude to dropping out of school. Think about this: When was the last time you saw someone give up on something they were really good at? Just try to imagine someone who is great at baseball saying, "Yeah, I stopped playing that game. It got on my nerves because every game I hit a home run." It would never happen. We keep doing the things we are good at, and because we keep doing those things, we become better at them. I say all of this to say that the Tools of Learning are designed to make good students out of students who would otherwise not do well in school, because if this program can make them good in school, they will be more likely to keep going to classes and less likely to drop out.

2. Bad Student, Good Worker

Prior to leaving Shanti, things got slow at Kelly Labor, so I found a job washing dishes at a place called the Last National Bank Restaurant. It was in the Travelers Insurance building on Main Street in Hartford. I was working there so many hours that the management asked me if I wanted to work there full time. Under the circumstances, I should have said yes but I declined the offer because somehow, I still considered myself to be a student. I've always been sort of a neat freak, and where I worked was a total mess. One of the reasons why is because we worked so hard just trying to keep up with the dishes that had to be washed that we had no time to clean anything else. One day, I decided to punch out at 3:30 am and keep working. It was 6:30 am when I finished, and I still had to walk home to Bowles Park because it was on the weekend when the busses ran poorly.

Walking home always took at least an hour and five minutes. I know the time it took because I used to time it. The next day I came to work and the manager, a man named Dave, came up to me and said, "This is for you." It was a bottle of Blue Nun wine. I couldn't tell him that I could not take it because I was just 17. It would have been ungrateful of me, and he would have had to fire me because I lied about my age to get the job. He then said, "We came in and saw how beautiful everything looked, and we just stopped and stared. We are giving you this bottle of wine along with a fifty cents an hour raise. You now make more money per hour than anyone else in the restaurant except three people: the manager, the maitre'd and the owner." Somehow I managed to say thank you and relished the fact that I had become the highest paid employee in the Last National Bank Restaurant. Later on that evening, my brother Rocky came by to give me a ride home. I gave him the Blue Nun wine. I was more of a Boones Farm Strawberry Hill kind of guy anyway.

Although it didn't register as a life lesson at the time, I now believe that it was the first time that I saw the direct correlation between extra effort and success. That was a lesson that would come in real handy one day.

3. Sleep Disorder
As stated in the beginning of this book, the mission of the Teale Ink organization is to address a formula A=(H+S)D. The "H" stands for health. If a person suffers from a physical health challenge like a sleep disorder it can prevent that person from being able to concentrate while in school, and it can decrease a persons ability to study because they will fall asleep while studying. I have for as long as I can remember, had a tremendous sleep disorder. Three clinics that specialize in the matter have been unable to correct the problem. Decades ago, I decided to turn adversity into advantage and simply study when most people are sleeping. It isn't the way I would like to spend my nights, but it beats lying awake doing nothing, and I've learned a lot while others sleep.

4. Wanted Money Now!
When I was 16, I stood around 6'2" and was starting to think that I was a man. Exactly where I got my desire for nice clothes I'm not sure, but it could have started a couple of years earlier when I could wear my brother's clothes. I was accustomed to being seen periodically in Bill Blass and Pierre Cardin suits, but I had outgrown my brother, and by then he had moved out of our apartment. I also had friends who were much older than I was who worked full time. They had money when we hung out. I couldn't ask my

mother for the money I wanted, and the amount I desired far exceeded anything a part time after school job would have paid back then. These are some of the reasons why I believe I got accustomed to wanting and earning money. Please notice that I did not say "needing" money. Of course, I should have been investing my time in school and not spending it working as someone's dishwasher. I should have known that the job of a teenage boy is to prepare himself for manhood by getting an education.

5. Distracted by the Possibility of Violence

I write about this concern partly because I have heard it expressed by other students too. I'm thinking primarily about a GED graduation ceremony where I was asked to be the keynote speaker. The valedictorian was a young lady who was absolutely brilliant. Her name I do not recall but for the sake of this account, I'll call her "Anna." As Anna spoke, she talked about her days in high school before she dropped out. Essentially, she said that she loved high school and looked forward to going there every day. Then one day, one of the other girls started to pick on her. Each day the situation got worse until the two girls got into a fight. Anna then said that she defended herself very well, and this caused the girl, who was in a gang, to get her friends so that she could get even. The situation got so serious that Anna and her mother had a meeting with the principal. When the principal came to realize who Anna had problems with, he said, "We cannot guarantee your safety and you should leave school." As Anna relayed this account, she was so emotional that everyone in the audience gasped at this decision. Anna left high school but remained determined to get an education. Armed with her GED, she was on her way to college!

I relay this story to illustrate a point. Sometimes a child will take a disinterest in school because they perceive the place to be too dangerous to be there. Boys don't want to say "I'm afraid to go to school" because they don't want to be thought of as cowards, but when you take into consideration the potential for extreme violence in some schools, they sometimes have a right to fear their "learning environment." I remember having days like this before I dropped out.

I was pleasantly surprised to see that college is not like high school in the sense that your fellow students in college don't look down on you because you are smart. Those students who think poorly of smart students don't last long in college because they get thrown out due to bad grades.

6. Didn't Think I Was Going to Live Long Anyway

When I was diagnosed with rheumatic fever as a child, I didn't take the diagnosis seriously. I wanted to do all the things that I was accustomed to doing. However, to make me aware of the potential harm that I could do to myself if I wasn't more concerned about my health, I was reminded that I had an uncle who died at the age of 21 from heart disease. His early death caused me to believe that I too would live a very short life. The year that I published this book, I turned 60 years old. I bring this to the reader's attention to encourage you to make long-term plans even if you don't think that you will live a long time. You might fool yourself.

Out of Road
1973

I left the Last National Bank Restaurant on December 31, 1972. I just couldn't settle in one place for long. In time, I would come to realize that I quit at everything because I thought that I would get fired eventually anyway. I had lost all hope or confidence in winning at anything. My self-esteem had declined to a level so low that I had no confidence in my ability to maintain any positive relationship for long. That included friends and jobs. One day, there was a change in managers at the Last National Bank restaurant. The new manager didn't care for me, and I was no longer considered a valuable employee. This was typical of me during those days. I never made it any further than December 31st because I was told by the new manager that I would not be paid double time for working New Year's Eve. Dishwashers I knew who worked in other restaurants and hotels in Hartford were getting at least that amount, so I refused to show up for work that day. When I went in to pick up my last check, I was told that everyone was paid quintuple time or five times their hourly rate. The new manager was honest when he said, "We are not going to pay you double time." I didn't appreciate his tactic. They lost a hardworking employee, and I lost my job.

It was a sad way for me to separate from a place I had come to enjoy, but I was on to another job in a matter of weeks. Finding a job was easy in those days if you were willing to take minimum wage for doing meaningless work without benefits. Eventually, I found myself working at the 7-Eleven store in Bloomfield, Connecticut. I didn't last long there either, but the demise of that position led to a very important experience in my life. I had just quit the 7-Eleven job. I wasn't afraid of quitting jobs because I had a safety net that I could rely on. It was called "caddying." I was still 17 at this time, and I had been going to the local golf course off and on since I was 11 years old. As long as the weather was right and it was a Saturday, Sunday, holiday or a Wednesday, I could find work carrying a golf bag for four hours. By the time I was around 14, I could carry two bags (known as a double 18). This was like a promotion, and I was envied by those of my age who could not do it. But at the age of 17, caddying had become second nature to me and my friends from Bowles Park. However, to get to the golf course I had to cut through the university again.

Unfortunately, I was just passing through . . . for now.

No More Bridges
1973

In any event, during the aftermath of my quitting my job at 7-Eleven, I went caddying. The amount commonly made at that time was $12.00, which of course was a lot of money when the price of gas was 29 cents per gallon. I knew that because sometimes I got to drive my mother's car. On one particular day, we were having a golf tournament, so there was plenty of work for everyone. As usual, I got a double 18 and was preparing to start when suddenly, a couple of my friends, the Dunn Brothers (John and Billy), came up to me. The Dunn Brothers were true friends; they had been since I was 11 years old. We always made money together, shoveling snow or delivering newspapers or caddying. We were real working kids and proud of it. On this day however, one of them said, "Hey Charles, the guy you are caddying for is a racist." This was during the aftermath of the many civil disturbances of the late 60's and early 70's. I knew the attitude some people had against young African American men and boys but I wasn't about to let someone treat me like I was one of those who rioted and burned down stores in my own city to protest. I turned to my friend and said, "I'm not here for any of that, I just want to make some money and go home." My friend said, "I know that, I just wanted to tell you so that you will know to be careful." They were wise words that I believe kept me from doing something truly foolish in the coming minutes.

A short time later, our tournament began. There were many people waiting to tee off where we were, which is unusual. Most of the time there are just four golfers and two caddies together. On this day, however, some golfers had a gallery of a hundred people or more. If you were a golfer, it had to be a little intimidating because you were not used to performing in front of a crowd. One of my golfers, the alleged racist, approached me, and we had the usual conversation held between a golfer and a caddy. He seemed all right to me. Eventually, it was his time to tee off. This is a strange time period for an amateur caddy. Part of you is thinking, *What a great day it is to be standing in the sun on a golf course.* The other part of you is saying, *It's time to get to work. I can't wait to get the next four hours over with.* My golfer approached the ball, swung at it, and looked to see how well he had hit it. I distinctly remember hearing him strike the ball, but I could not see it take off, in flight or hit the ground. These were the three things every good caddy knows to look for so that the golfer does not lose his ball. If he loses a ball, it will probably come out of your tip. When he couldn't see the ball, he looked around at everyone and said, "Did anyone see that ball land?" Everyone kind of shrugged their shoulders as if to say, *Don't blame us for losing your ball. We were not your caddy.* Suddenly, he looked at me and said, "Well, caddy, where did it go?" I explained, "I didn't see it take off, in flight or land. I don't know where it is." To say that this man was angry is an understatement. He started cursing at the top of his lungs, and telling me how he had to keep his head down, and that it was my job to watch the ball. For the first time in six years, someone told me that I didn't know how to do my job. My mood was changing from embarrassed to extremely angry. With the exception of the other caddies, everyone around me all looked real old. I thought, *I could knock this guy out, and nobody here could catch me as I run home.* His words were so harsh that one of the men he was golfing with said, "Okay, Bob, you've made your point!" But that didn't stop him at all. Saying these things in front of the crowd that had gathered was bad enough but having my friends witness it was particularly humiliating. I was real ready to defend myself. What caused me to act in the following manner, I'll never know, but what I did next was to approach the golfer. He backed up with fear in his eyes. I could tell that he was expecting me to retaliate physically. What I did was grab one of his golf tees. I scraped the ground under where he had swung, and I found his ball buried in the ground. He had hit it so poorly that it didn't go anywhere but down. I placed the ball in my hand and I tossed it up in the air toward the golfer. As I did this I said to him, "Here's your f*****g ball," and I left. Because this was a tournament, all of the caddies were working, and there were no caddies left. I can distinctly remember him shouting at me, "If you leave, you'll never work here again!" He was right about one thing. I never worked there again because I never went back. Well, I never went back there to work. As I walked away from the crowd I heard the other man that I was caddying for say, "Who's going to carry my bag for me now Bob, you?" Everybody laughed.

As I look back on that experience, I wish I had stayed. I wish I had just found the ball and placed it in his hand. Caddying for him for the next four hours would have been just the humiliation he deserved. My leaving meant that I had just quit another job. Now, I had nowhere else to go.

Thirty-five years later, while serving as Chief of the Hartford Fire Department, someone I know who is a member at that very same golf club, invited me to have lunch there. Initially, I just couldn't bring myself to accept his offer because of the way I left so many years ago. However, after about a year of stalling, I found myself sitting down in the lunchroom of the golf club with him and an insurance executive who was raised in Bowles Park too. The insurance exec used to caddy there also, and both of us were considering becoming members of the golf club where we used to caddy. We had grown, and the golf club had grown too. When our luncheon was over, I bid both gentlemen a good day and thanked the person who invited me emphatically. He had helped me to proudly come back to a place that I left in a very negative way. I actually found myself thinking about being a member. I have not as of yet, but it has nothing to do with the confrontation I had with the irate, irrational golfer. I just don't have the time to enjoy the benefits of the club. I had years of part-time employment there when I was a child, and most of the time the members treated me with kindness. One person does not have the power or the right to diminish the image of an otherwise great organization. Periodically, I drive past that golf course and I find myself straining to see sections of the course that I once walked as a kid. I guess you could say that I remember the place fondly.

As strange as this may sound, during this and the most challenging experiences up until now, I always had this feeling that when I turned 35, something great was going to happen to me. The truth of the matter is that the greatest thing that happened to me at that age was that I finished the requirements of my first college degree. If the Tools of Learning turn out to have the impact on our nation that I know it can, then and only then will I have been right. If there is one central theme to my life it would be how the most trying circumstances happened so that I could benefit sometimes decades later. It leaves me thinking constantly, *Oh, now I understand why I had that experience!*

Chapter 9

The Return of Mr. Hurley
1973

The reader may recall that when I was ten years old, I met a giant of a man who was the gym teacher at Northwest Jones. Throughout the years he would play a major role in the lives of many people. I was one of them.

The following experience has been relayed to thousands of people through speeches and presentations of the Tools of Learning that I have given over the course of the last 20 plus years. However, it has always been a condensed version of what happened. Until now.

Although many people my age called him "Doc" I called him "Mr. Hurley." I did for 49 years. When I retired from the Hartford Fire Department, I had the honor of interviewing him for a history project I was working on through the Hartford Public Library. I saw it as an opportunity to sit down and talk at length with a man who literally changed my life when I was 17. He was raised in the city of Hartford from the age of 16 months. He got the name Doc because his father wanted him to grow up to become a doctor. I mean no offense to doctors, but he became much more than that to millions of people. All through his life he distinguished himself, and he lived to be 91 years old. Among the many successes he had as a youngster in Hartford is the fact that among the major sports, he is the only four letterman in the history of Weaver High School, a school that has been in existence since 1923. He went on to go to college, serve in the Marine Corp during World War II, and had a scholarship fund named in his honor that has helped more than 500 kids go to college.

I'd like to bring the reader back to the time and place where I was leaving the golf course after having an altercation with a golfer that I was caddying for.

Initially, I was concerned about getting off of the golf course. I was certain that the man who I was caddying for would tell the caddy master that I had assaulted him and that he wanted the police to intervene. As soon as I got off the course, I felt safer, but I immediately started to wonder, *Now what am I going to do for money?* In the following weeks, everything changed. It seemed like if I didn't need a job, I could be confident and friendly when interviewing for one, but as soon as I needed one, people could sense my desperation, and no one wants to hire a desperate person. I went about a month when it became evident that no one was going to hire me at all. I also started thinking about what should have been my high school class, getting ready to graduate the following year. For the first time in my life, I was in a total state of despair. I had lost all hope or confidence in winning. To top it all off, I got the distinct feeling that something sinister was gaining on me.

Eventually, I thought of a plan that would help me to get out of my bad situation. I thought that if I could get some good references, I could get a job at a factory near Hartford called Pratt and Whitney. Pratt and Whitney was hiring, and I knew that they paid big money. You also didn't need a high school diploma to work there. The most respected man that I knew of was Mr. Hurley. Surely, if he gave me a reference I could get a job. So I decided to consult with Mr. Hurley. I hadn't had a conversation with him in three years, since I was 14, but I was going to try. By this time in my life, I had burned so many bridges. There was nowhere else to turn.

It took me about a month after quitting as a caddy before I got up the nerve to go to Mr. Hurley's house at 289 Ridgefield Street in Hartford, and knock on the door. I remember going by it three times before I did. I finally got tired of stalling, knocked, and when the door opened, it was Mr. Hurley. I said to him, "My name is Charles Teale and I use to be one of your students. I've made a few mistakes since I last saw you and I think I'm in trouble. I need your help." To this day, I don't know why I said those words. I only wanted a job reference. Mr. Hurley looked at me, and said, "Come on inside! Have a seat!" As we sat, he told me to tell him about myself. Somewhere in my answer to him, I told him that I had dropped out of high school at the age of 14. When he heard this, I could tell that he couldn't believe what he was hearing. What I did not know was that Mr. Hurley had a master's degree before most people in Hartford had a college degree at all.

I continued to tell him about the experiences I had had since leaving school. Somehow, through the experience of talking with him, I thought Mr. Hurley would help me to get a good job when I turned 18. When I think back on this line of logic, the only excuse I have is that I was 17. When I stopped talking, he paced the floor and with the most distressed look on his face said words barely audible like, "I can't believe it," and "Oh my God." Eventually he turned to me and said, "How could you give up on your education?" I had no answer for the man and the words "I don't know" were not about to come out of my mouth. He told me many things about the importance of an education and how important it was to my future. At this point those words only made me feel worse because I thought an education was not in the cards for me. He then said, **"I'm not going to help you get a job because you're going back to school!"**

When he said that, I was too shocked to say anything for a couple of seconds and then I said, "I'm not going back to Weaver. I'll be an 18-year-old freshman." He then told me, "You don't have to go back to Weaver. You can get a GED, and with that, you can go on to college. I could help you to get a good job, but that would not make you happy because you are the kind of person that needs to be of service." When he said the word "service," I thought he meant the kind of service a waiter gives to a customer. I had been washing dishes and bussing tables for money, and I used to hear the waiters say, "My name is Dave and I'm here to <u>serve</u> you." So I asked Mr. Hurley, "You mean like a waiter?" He looked at me in astonishment and said, "No, I mean you are the kind of person who likes to help others. But look at you. You have no job, no education and no future. Who are you going to help? You can't even help yourself." With those words I began to place my chin in my hand like someone trying to think. However, I wasn't thinking anything good. I was thinking that I came all the way here to get some help, and Mr. Hurley was just coming down on me like all of the other adults that I had been talking to lately. Seeing that I was starting to feel badly, Mr. Hurley asked me, "How do you feel right now?" I said, "Huh?" That's what I always said when I was trying to buy some time to formulate an answer. It wasn't working with Mr. Hurley. He rephrased his question: "How do you feel now that you have let down your family, given up on your education, and you have no job or and no future?" I said, "Bad." he then said, "Naw, naw, that's not good enough. How do you feel?" I restated my answer, "<u>Awful. I should not have quit high school.</u>" Although this admission might seem minor to some, up until that time I had not admitted to making a mistake by dropping out. As long as I could not admit to making a mistake, I could not correct my mistake. Mr. Hurley then said, "Good. That's how you should feel, and that's how I want you to feel for the rest of your life because as long as you know how badly it feels to quit at something important, you will never quit at anything important again." He then said, "I know of a way you can get your high school diploma and even go on to college." When he said these words he may as well have told me to buy a Learjet. I had been out of school for so long I could not even imagine that I would be going back at all, especially to college, but Mr. Hurley assured me. He said, "You're the kind of person who needs to be of service to others, but to do this, you need a college degree. I'm going to send you to a school counselor at Greater Hartford Community College by the name of Bill Edmonds. He will be able to get you started on this process." Mr. Hurley then wrote Mr. Edmonds name and phone number down on a piece of paper and gave it to me.

As I left Mr. Hurley's house, I distinctly remember having for the first time since I was 11 years old <u>the desire to receive an education.</u> To me, it became obvious that if I was going to accomplish anything in life I would have to maintain that desire. Years later, I would express this belief in the form of an equation:

$$A=D$$
Which stands for Accomplishment equals Desire

When I got to my car, (actually my mother's car), I said to myself, "I should have taken notes while Mr. Hurley was talking." So, before I even left the front of his house, I tried to summarize the things I had learned during that meeting on the only piece of paper I could find. It was the flap of a common white envelope. I wrote "be of service, get an education," but by the time I got to the words "don't quit," I ran out of ink. I searched around the car, and I found another pen. It wrote in red ink so under the words "be of service, get an education." I wrote the words "Don't quit" in red ink. Persistence and my newfound desire for an education more than anything else have given me the things that I need and want out of life. I kept that piece of paper with me for more than a decade. By the end of that decade, generating desire and remaining persistence were habits I could not break even if I wanted to.

To conclude this section I would like to share the following words with the reader:

Never give up on young people in your family. Even if you can't reach them, have then talk with someone else. All it takes is the right person, with the right message, telling the right person at the right time, and someone's life will change.

Here's Mr. Hurley, (center), my wife Helaine (left), Mr. Hurley's daughter Muriel and me at my retirement celebration, April 9, 2010. Location: Hartford's Municipal Building, City Hall. Four years later, I wrote Mr. Hurley's autobiography. It is entitled *The Making of a Legend: The Life and Times of Walter J. "Doc" Hurley*. I would recommend that anyone who would like to make a real difference in this world read it. The net proceeds go to Mr. Hurley's scholarship fund.

Mr. Edmonds
1973

As soon as I could find a telephone, I contacted the person Mr. Hurley told me to call, Mr. Bill Edmonds. It took several weeks but eventually I got an appointment to see him. I arrived at his office on time. Since it was in Greater Hartford Community College, the place was busy with students running from one place to another. They all had books in their hands. I hadn't been in an environment like it in several years. Although I had left Shanti High just a few months earlier, Shanti was not like this. Because most of the courses provided by Shanti were away from the main building (the train station), you didn't see the level of intensity commonly found at a school. The home base or train station was simply more laid back than the rigid collegiate environment displayed at Greater Hartford Community College. I felt like a fish out of water and an imposter, but I was determined to follow through on the discussion I had with Mr. Hurley. Mr. Edmonds's administrative assistant told me to have a seat, and that he would be with me shortly. I did as directed. At exactly the time I was scheduled to see Mr. Edmonds, he bolted from his office! He looked at me and said, "I'll be with you in one minute." I waited for at least 15 before he came out again, and again he said, "I'll be with you in one minute." This actually happened a third time. Each time I could tell he was busy helping one of the students in the school. This was a very busy and committed man. I decided that I would give it five more minutes and if he did not have time for me, I would just leave.

Fortunately for me, he called me into his office before those five minutes had passed. We greeted one another in the usual way when suddenly he said to me, "Tell me something about you." As I told him about myself, I had to mention that I had dropped out of high school. When I said that, he slapped his desk, turned his head to the side, and looked away in disgust. When he looked back at me he said, "<u>Do you know how many people spent their lives, risked their lives and sometimes gave their lives so that you could have the opportunity to succeed?</u>" When he said this I suddenly felt very ashamed of myself. Although I was now 18, it was the first time I ever felt this way, and in retrospect, I can honestly say that I should have felt that way sooner. It would have probably saved me from making a lot of foolish mistakes. Feeling ashamed of yourself should be a result of allowing yourself to make huge mistakes. If you don't, then you become a person who "has no shame." I suddenly came to realize that that's not a good person to be.

As Mr. Edmonds spoke, I also found myself thinking back on conversations that I had with my grandparents Pearl Woods-Smith and Ben Smith. As I have already shared with the reader, when I was a child, they would constantly tell my cousins and me what life was like a century ago in this country, and more. Our Grandmother Pearl would tell about the wonderful things the State of Connecticut had to offer. Both of them moved to Hartford from Georgia, and they both worked throughout the Hartford region. The comparisons between living in Georgia and living in Connecticut were truly like living in another country. As Mr. Edmonds told me about the people who "spent their lives, risked their lives and sometimes gave their lives so that I could have the opportunity to succeed" I envisioned it all. The conversations I had with my grandparents and the people they told me about who made things better for all people. I even thought about the people my teachers used to tell me about when I attended elementary and middle school, when I attended Northwest Jones and Mark Twain School in the fifth through the eighth grades. In those years, I went on many history-based field trips. Places like Mystic Seaport, which taught us how some of the men who sailed on ships like the Charles W. Morgan were men from the Cape Verde Islands, where my maternal grandparents were raised. I also thought about the writer of the novel *Uncle Tom's Cabin*, Harriet Beecher Stowe. Her last place of residence is in Hartford just two blocks from where Mr. Edmonds office was. As I thought about these people, I listened carefully as Mr. Edmonds directed me on how to get my GED, and how to get started on attending college. I was years away from success, but from that day on, I knew which steps I had to take to get a college degree. Taking those steps successfully, however, was another thing entirely.

Reset
1974

My sights were now set on college. I also had to do something about finding a job since I could no longer rely on caddying for spending money. There were also great personal changes taking place in my life. I'm not inclined to discuss personal matters in this book because I don't sense they have relevance. This is a book primarily about how to recover from making bad decisions about your academic and professional life. My goal in this publication is to inform people about the challenges I faced getting an education, and a career and how I overcame those challenges. It is my hope that by reading about how those challenges turned into successes, the reader or their students will be able to do likewise. That way, no one has to reinvent the wheel. However, the greatest personal change to take place in my teenage years was about to take place. My mother and father, who had not been together since I was about 7 years old, had started seeing each other again just prior to my 18th birthday. I must remind the reader that I was now 18, and the thought of my father being around was a nice one, but I was on the way out of that household. I was thinking about finding my own place to live, and perhaps, starting my own family. If I had that time period to live over again, I would have done it differently. I would have stayed in my parent's household and obtained an education. During that time, I would have simultaneously gotten to know my father again. After all, I had seen him an average of just once each year for the past 11 years. I loved my father, but I didn't know him like I should have. However, I was on to other things. For the summer, I took the first job that I could get with a company called Burns International Security. When the summer ended, within months of my seeing Mr. Edmonds, I heard that Hartford Hospital was hiring. This was not just a job; it was potentially a career if I wanted it to be. What I found most attractive about this job was that Hartford Hospital had a GED program for its employees. The representative of Hartford Hospital's personnel department was a friend of my brother Rocky. His name was Michael Thomas. Mike Thomas did everything the way it was supposed to be done. As a student at Weaver High, he was highly regarded for being a studious, respectable person. On top of that, he was a very fine musician, playing the piano to a level that was the envy of the entire city. I liked him from the start, probably because he reminded me of my brother. My attitude toward him and his realization that I would be more than an employee, that I would be an aspiring student at Hartford Hospital, meant a lot. I was hired. Shortly after that, I started taking GED classes at Hartford Hospital. I had found a home. It seemed like everyone there liked and understood me. I would take classes there until the time came for me and the rest of my classmates to take the exam to get our high school diploma. With that, I planned on going to college. I was on the right track at last.

"You can be on the right track but if you aren't moving fast enough you'll get run over by a train." — Will Rogers

The day came; I took the test and waited for the results. The results of a GED exam were delivered by mail in 1974. If you got a large manila envelope in the mail it was your diploma. If you got a small white envelope you failed. One day, I looked in the mail and my heart sunk. It was from the State of Connecticut and it was a small white envelope. I had flunked the GED exam. When you have an experience like that, you think about several things like the people who will be disappointed in you because you didn't pass. However, the most dangerous thought that I had at this time was that I was just not cut out to succeed in school. I started to think that I was not smart enough to do anything of any great significance with my life. I had a good job. I thought about just doing my job and forgetting about this entire college thing. Then I heard in my mind the words of Mr. Hurley: "Don't quit."

I went back to my GED instructors and told them the news. They were disappointed, but they informed me, "You aren't the only one who didn't pass. We will keep trying." Their attitudes were perfect. They were reassuring, but they made it clear that this was going to require more effort. It wasn't going to happen on its own. I took more classes and then I retook the exam. One day, I went to my mailbox and there it was, a large manila envelope, for me. It had been many years since I could say these words but I told everyone that I could, "I passed the test!" It took around two years but persistence won out in the end.

Chapter 10

"The Greatest Wealth is Health"
— Horace

Shortly after I received my GED, I started feeling restless again. At this time I had moved with my mother, father and sister to East Hartford. I was 19, had a real good job at Hartford Hospital, and was starting to acquire material possessions that only people making a comfortable living could get. I had the clothes that I wanted and even bought a new car. Buying new things didn't really mean that I was making it because the only reason I could afford them was I still wasn't paying any bills. This whole matter got very old to my parents who were starting to complain about my coming in at all hours of the night. I knew that I was going to have to find another place to live but I didn't have any idea where. One day, I decided to move to Norwalk, Connecticut. My girlfriend, Sue, had moved there just months earlier, and we really enjoyed each other's company. I found work near the town that was very close to where she worked, so we rode into work together.

On our way to work one day, she looked at me and exclaimed, "What's the matter with your eye?" I didn't know what she meant, so I looked in my rear view mirror. There was a dark discoloration to my right eye and the lid was drooping. The sight was not alarming to me but everyone I met that day kept asking the same question regarding my appearance. After a couple of days of this, I made arrangements to see a doctor. His initial diagnosis was not complete, and he wanted me to be admitted to the hospital for testing. He obviously sensed something serious but didn't seem too alarmed. I didn't think it was serious because I felt fine. During this time, the situation worsened. Whatever the problem was, it was starting to affect both eyes. In addition to the drooping eyelids, I had double vision. For a while, I was in and out of the hospital. After a total of 28 days of tests, my doctor gave up and told me to see some doctors at the New England Deaconess Hospital in Boston, Massachusetts. Now, I was starting to get concerned. At the New England Deaconess Hospital, I underwent more tests. Prior to the most serious test, my doctor came in and told me that the only thing that was left to assume was that I had a brain tumor, and it was resting on an optic nerve. I found this particularly alarming because while I was at the Norwalk Hospital, there was a young man there who had had a brain tumor. There were four of us in that room, and one of the other patients remembered the young man with the brain tumor from high school. He told us that the young man with the brain tumor seemed to be fine when he was in school. However, this young man was not fine now. After his operation, the only thing he could say was the word "garbage," and he said it loud and clear when interacting with the doctors and nurses who took care of him. As I heard this diagnosis, I thought about that young man. I still do today 40 years later, and I hope things turned out better for him as time passed.

After hearing about the possibility of having a brain tumor, I started thinking about the challenges I had learning in school. Was this the reason why I had such a difficult time academically? The doctor assured me that there was technology available that could remove the tumor, but they would have to locate it first. So a test was conducted to locate it. As I lay in my hospital room after the test, my doctor came in and informed me that the test was negative; they could not find a brain tumor at all. However, he did say that it might be there, but it was too small to seen at that time. He seemed sure that I had nothing to worry about in that regard, but he still didn't know what was causing my health challenge. It was great news, but due to the test that I had taken, I was in too much pain to appreciate anything. The next day, I called my brother Rocky for a ride home. I was certain that these doctors weren't able to help me and I was tired of being tested on. It was May 29, 1975. I know that date precisely because it was my 20th birthday, and I was spending it in the hospital, not knowing what was wrong with me but determined to get on with my life.

I could not have been home in Norwalk for more than a week when one of my friends approached me and told me that he had been watching the Phil Donahue Show. For people of my generation, that was the talk show to watch. This friend informed me that he saw a doctor and several of his patients on the show. All of the patients exhibited the exact same signs that I did. All had an illness called "Myasthenia Gravis." To those with the illness at that time, it meant paralysis and even early death if not treated with an operation. Upon hearing this, I made arrangements to visit the doctor who was on the Phil Donahue Show. When I got there, there was another doctor in his office who was suffering from the disease. Both were certain that I had it, and both were disgusted to hear that I had had been diagnosed with a brain tumor when it was so obvious that I had had Myasthenia Gravis. At this point, I didn't know who to believe. I just wanted to be cured of this condition. For a while, I was placed on a medication that seemed to address one symptom and aggravate a group of others, but I felt certain that I knew what my problem was. Throughout all of this, I had a girlfriend who was starting to long for a married life. I wanted the same, but I was hesitant because of my health concerns. In a few months' time, we decided to move forward, and so, in November of 1975, we got married and settled in East Hartford, Connecticut, Myasthenia Gravis and all.

Sue was 19 and I was 20. Considering our ages, we did well. However, the cloud concerning my health affected us both. It was strange in the sense that I felt great and was as athletic as I ever was, but my eyes made me appear to be very sick. My contact with my doctor in New York continued until he informed me that it was time for me to have the operation needed to cure this illness. It didn't sound like a very big operation, but I had to go under anesthesia, which was something I had never experienced. I was informed that the operation would not take very long.

After living with a nerve and muscle disease for more than a year, I thought that I was about to be cured. I was rolled into the operating room and placed on the operating room table when suddenly the anesthesiologist and I had a very serious disagreement. To my astonishment, what seemed like a simple operation sounded dangerous and complicated. A discussion occurred between several people in the operating room and me. I was forced to make a decision about moving forward with the operation or not right then and there. I decided not to have it and was placed back on the stretcher and wheeled out of the operating room.

Later that afternoon, I got a call from my doctor. He first explained that the likelihood of me suffering from complications for this operation were about as great as me getting hit by a bus while standing in my hospital room. I then asked, "If it isn't risky, then why are they making an issue of this matter?" He had no answer, just this statement: "If you don't have this operation, you will be in a wheelchair by the time you are 25, and you will be dead at 35." I left there that day and never spoke with him again. I never had that operation.

This year I will turn 60 years old!

In the months that followed, several friends of mine were talking about fasting for health reasons. The more I thought about it, the more I became interested. One day, I decided to give it a try. As I recall (almost 40 years later), there were ways to determine when to break a fast. I was going to consume nothing but water until I saw those signs. I fasted for seven days and nights, drinking water at a rate recommended by a book that I had acquired on the subject. When I saw signs that it was time to break the fast,

I started eating. Almost immediately, I went into remission from the signs of Myasthenia Gravis. In about a year, all of the signs were gone. It had left as quickly as it came.

Chapter 11

New Careers
1976

As I said earlier, this is not a book about personal experiences that are not directly relevant to my eventual academic and professional success. This book is a road map for those of like experience, those who are going through or have gone through something similar to what I experienced and still want desperately to be successful in spite of their past academic and professional challenges.

Less than two years after moving to East Hartford, Sue and I moved to Hartford. I wanted a career that could only be obtained if I got a college degree. Time was going by, and I had no more time for plans. It was time for action that yielded positive results. I applied for and got accepted into a program called "New Careers." It was a program that allowed you to go to college part-time, to go work in your field of study part-time, and receive full-time pay. I started working at a home for wayward girls and attending college classes, at last, taking courses in accounting and business administration. My school of choice was Greater Hartford Community College, the school where I met Mr. Edmonds several years earlier. I felt so certain that this was going to be my road to success that Sue and I started planning a family. Before long we were expecting. I was working, taking classes and trying to prepare for the day when I would be a father. On July 21, 1977, Kathleen Rene Teale was born. She was, and still is, the most beautiful girl I have ever seen. When Kathleen was on the way, I knew I had to kick it into high gear.

Although I did well in some of my classes, I did very poorly in others. The challenges outweighed the accomplishments. I received warnings about poor grades but could find no way to improve them. I read everything I was assigned to read and did my homework to the best of my ability, but my test scores were awful. In time, I was dismissed from the program, and that meant unemployment with an infant child in the house. I responded by taking a job as a plumbing apprentice. It was the first job I could find, and I thought it could pay the bills, but even that didn't work out for long. The owner of the company I was working for paid us less than the mandated wage for some of the job sites that I worked for. When state labor representatives learned about this, he was forced to give us back pay. As you can probably imagine, the atmosphere at work was beyond tense. I was diagnosed by a doctor with stress, and I distinctly remember imagining that the depression I was experiencing being so thick that I could cut a hole in it and look through to the other side. That way, I could see life as it once was, worry and stress free.

Within a year, layoffs had hit the company and half the workforce was gone. I was one of the ones to be laid off. Laid off with a child, I had no other choice but to vacate my apartment and move in with my sister-in-law and her family. I found myself feeling depressed to the point of reaching for any means to console myself. Fortunately, I was able to find work at Hartford Hospital again. To me, it was like returning to the place where I was when I was doing well, when I had a new car, lots of friends and money to spend. The money got better, but the depression remained. To get me through this time, I developed what would become Tool #2 of the Tools of Learning.

This is how it was developed:

As stated earlier, I played the clarinet and the saxophone as a child. That was between the ages of 10 and 14. At 14, I just stopped because I was no longer in the school band because I had dropped out of school. However, when I turned 19, a group of my friends decided to form a band, so I took up the saxophone and the clarinet again, and since the fingering pattern was so similar, I added the flute to it. We weren't any good, but we had a lot of fun. To learn and practice, I used to study at a school called the Artists Collective on Clark Street in Hartford, which was founded by the legendary alto saxophonist, Jackie McLean and his wife Dolly. By the time I moved in with my in-laws, I had been playing off and on a total of seven years, and if I practiced, some true jazz fans said I sounded like the tenor saxophonist Sonny Rollins. This was high praise considering the source. My new little girl and my music were the only things keeping me from completely losing my love for life. While employed at Hartford Hospital, I still relied on my music as a means to console myself when I was feeling especially depressed. It actually worked quite well, so much so that I wrote a note and placed it in my soprano saxophone case. It read, "The next time you find yourself lazy as to practice, think about how it feels to have a lack of accomplishment."

Out of necessity, I had discovered on my own the secret to fighting depression. It's called "Aspiring and Accomplishing." I learned that if I had major goals that excited me (like performing in front of an audience), and I got something done every day to reach those goals (like mastering a new song), I would not be as depressed as I would be if I did not do something worthwhile daily. Years later, I would add a third "A" to the group called "Attain", which means to reach a major goal. And so was developed what I refer to as Tool # 2 of the Tools of Learning, the "Triple A's of Enthusiasm":

Aspire
Accomplish
Attain

My musical studies may have seemed like a waste of time to many, but it kept me aspiring to something and accomplishing something. This carried me through to the year 1982. It was in that year that I joined the Hartford Fire Department. The day I found out that I was hired, I sold my instruments. Somehow, I knew I had found a new way to fuel my enthusiasm. I aspired to become Chief of the Department and the things that I accomplished included learning, understanding and remembering new things related to my profession. I attained major goals by getting promoted and graduating from three college degree programs. I had found a new way to pursue the Triple A's through the Hartford Fire Department.

The following is the presentation on Tool #2.

TOOL #2
(1978)

Dedicated to my musical studies: "The next time you find yourself lazy as to practice, think about how it feels to have a lack of accomplishment."

We must keep goals in mind that fuel enthusiasm.

Enhance Enthusiasm

Although most of us know what depression is, most of us have a slightly different understanding of what despair is. Well, Webster's Dictionary defines it as "to lose all hope or confidence of winning." The problem with despair is that it can prevent you from even trying to succeed. You will assume that solutions to problems, like the Tools of Learning will work for some people but definitely won't work for you. Statistics show that in 2013, the city of Hartford, Connecticut had over 27,000 adults without high school diplomas. Why aren't they all working on their GED's, the classes are free? They could be suffering from despair. It may have been one incident or a combination of challenges that led up to their state of mind.

And now, back to depression. Some psychologists call depression "the common cold of psychology." The problem here is that depression can prevent us from studying effectively. Sometimes it can stop us from studying at all. To help prevent this from happening to us, the Tools of Learning recommends the Triple A's of Enthusiasm.
They are:

    a. Aspire   b. Accomplish   c. Attain

a. Aspire

Ralph Waldo Emerson once said, "Nothing great was ever accomplished without enthusiasm." Getting a "quality education" is a great thing because we can do great things once we have one. Well, we can enhance our level of enthusiasm by "aspiring" or thinking about the great things we are going to do with the information that we are about to learn. For some people, this means getting an education, a good job and then paying off all of their bills. Other people need something more, like thinking about all the people they will be able to help once they learn the information they are about to study. The importance of determining what your ultimate goal is cannot be overstated. If your goal is meaningful enough, you can overcome even the greatest tragedy. Having a goal well worth pursuing will get you out of bed when you otherwise won't have the ability to do so. Whatever it is that you want to do with the information you are about to learn, think about it. It will help fuel your enthusiasm.

b. Accomplish daily

To insure that we stay enthusiastic, we must write up a list of all the things we feel we should accomplish on a daily basis. That way, we can feel like we have done something positive. Getting the things on that list done builds enthusiasm.

c. Attain

Unless you know everything, one of the things that you should have on your list of things to accomplish is "study." That's because of the importance of "Attaining" an educational or professional milestone when it comes to building enthusiasm. Attaining means reaching a long-term goal via the short-term goal of studying. It's taking all the studying you have done and graduating or getting promoted or starting your own business! If you don't think this works, then think back. When was the last time you saw a depressed person at their graduation?

Remember that the ultimate goal here is to improve ourselves at least two percent per week. In that way, even if we take two weeks off a year, we will have improved ourselves 100 percent every year. That kind of improvement builds enthusiasm.

And remember to keep in mind your ultimate goal that keeps you enthusiastic.

Plenty of Jobs but No Career
1978

Before the start of my career with the Hartford Fire Department, I sill had some struggling to do. The job I got at Hartford Hospital was not like the one I had there the first time. I didn't fit in like I did before. For a time, however, it helped pay the bills. I will always owe that organization for providing me with a job in 1974, the courses I needed to pass my GED and for providing me with the second job in 1978. With it, I was able to move my family out of my in-laws' house and into our own apartment at 178-A Stonington Street, Hartford, CT.

It was during this time that my depression was starting to lift. After seeing the negative affect that depression and my double vision problem had on my ability to learn information, and to keep a job, I determined that it took more than desire to succeed. You had to have physical and mental "health."

Therefore, the formula that I had created for my ability to succeed changed from:

Accomplishment equals Desire
to
Accomplishment equals Health plus Desire:
$$A=H+D$$

My "Health" concern was more than just physical; it was mental and emotional too. I determined that it would be necessary for me to take care of both by exercising regularly and staying away from anything that could damage my mind. Especially illegal drugs!

Soon after finding the second job at Hartford Hospital, my second child was on the way. On February 4, 1979, Charles Alan Teale, Jr. was born. His birth and the raising of my two children caused me to try a variety of methods when it came to their well-being. Determined to succeed at getting a degree, I took classes at Manchester Community College. That didn't last long because my grades were just as bad as the ones that I got at Greater Hartford Community College. My brother Rocky had opened his own nightclub, the Club Charisma, and I worked there for a little more than a year. When that business closed, I went to work as a custodian at the Wadsworth Athenaeum. This is the oldest public art museum in the nation. The job was close to home, paid the bills and provided benefits. Cleaning floors didn't bother me in the least bit. I took pride in the appearance of my area, so much so that my supervisors would comment on how well I was doing. This display of pride in my work resulted in a major discovery. It dawned on me that I hated being told to "get to work." It actually caused me to dislike my supervisors, so I concocted a plan. If I did my work before they told me to do it, they wouldn't have any reason to tell me what to do. The plan actually worked. Within days, my supervisor stopped telling me what to do. Within months, my direct supervisor was quitting. His name was Joe, but I knew him as "Tiny Joe" the singer, and wow, could this guy sing! Upon leaving, he recommended me to take his place. Initially, I accepted the offer. Then I found out that his supervisor would be leaving a few months after him. Within six months, it appeared as though I would become the highest-ranking person in my area of approximately 12 men. At the same time, I landed a part-time job as the superintendent of my housing complex on Stonington Street. In total, the money was good and so were the benefits. It looked like I had found a home all because I took pride in my work. I was paying the bills and putting food on the table. I should have been satisfied, but none of the work felt fulfilling. I still longed to distinguish myself and be of service to others. I had to keep looking because I felt certain that I was destined to do something great with my life. I knew that once I found it, I would also be able to support my family the way they deserved. So, I left the Wadsworth to work for a man I came to respect in the greatest way possible. His name was Norris Graves, and he owned a real estate management agency. We did great together, but this still was not it. Finally, one day I decided to go for broke. I remember not having the confidence necessary to pursue a career because of my fear of failure, but something in me kept telling me to search for a job that paid well, had good benefits, and gave me a true sense of fulfillment. Then one day I got a reminder of what I wanted to become when I was just 6 years old.

That Burning Desire
1980

My family and I were crowded into the only car that I could afford at the time, a Volkswagen Beetle, as we traveled south on Main Street in Hartford. Every true Hartfordite knows where the Keney Clock Tower is. As a child, I used to stand in front of it to go to Camp Courant. As a teenager, I stood in front of it to take the bus to The Hotchkiss School. It is the location where Hartford's first residents lived, the Sequin Indians. Arriving at that location made me think back to when I was a child. I found myself looking at the place where we used to stand and I remembered old friends. Slowly my eyes drifted back to the center of the road when all of a sudden I noticed smoke coming from one of the buildings across from the Clock Tower. I said out loud, "Is that building on fire?" With that, I pulled over and went into one of the stores of the building. I said to the owner, "Call the fire department, this building is on fire." He said, "Are you serious?" I said, "Yes, if you don't believe me, give me the phone and I'll call for you." He took my word for it, and we stood outside as the fire grew. From that location, a person can literally see the firehouse on the corner of Main and Belden Streets in Hartford. The house is called Company 2's and in it are two fire trucks, Engine 2 and Ladder 3. A deputy chief and his aide are there also. I watched in amazement as both companies and the district deputy chief pulled out of the firehouse and took the steps necessary to extinguish the fire. Some men went to the roof, some forced open the door, and some laid a line up the stairs. It was totally impressive. Everyone seemed to know exactly what to do, and they did it like it was no big deal. When it was all over I finally knew what I wanted to do with my life. This time it was not a childhood dream. I wanted to become a member of the Hartford Fired Department. I knew then that nothing else in life would do.

In Earnest
1980

Becoming a firefighter in any city is a time consuming process. You don't just apply, and in a couple of weeks you get hired. However, I sensed that every job was easy to get but starting a career took time and persistent effort. I was right. The firefighter's exam consisted of six sections and was known to eliminate many inner city candidates, so I was concerned about my chances of succeeding from the beginning. There was the written exam, the oral interview, the strength and agility test, the background investigation, the physical, and the interview with the chief of the department. A person could do exceptionally well at one phase and be totally eliminated at another. Of all of the steps, the written exam concerned me the most. I had a history of doing poorly on tests, and you didn't get a second chance to pass the firefighter's exam like you did with the GED My brother Rocky came to the rescue again. Because he knew a man in the fire department named Mike Booker, he spoke with Mike and asked him how he got on the job. Mike told Rocky that there was an organization in Hartford called Plan B Incorporated. Their main purpose was to prepare people to take examinations for jobs in the Police Department, the Post Office, the Corrections Department and the Fire Department. Rocky then told me, "Mike said they can get you in!" As soon as I could, I signed up to take their classes on how to pass the fire department's exam. When I finished taking the first class, I asked the director, Cynthia Jennings, if I could take it again. She said, "You can take it as many times as you want." All totaled, I took that course on how to pass the firefighters exam four times. I knew I had problems with exams, and I wasn't taking any chances with this one. The day came when I was scheduled to take the written exam. There were 33 jobs available and more than 2,000 applicants. With my preparation, I felt I had a good chance anyway. I took the test and waited for the results.

During this time, I was periodically underemployed. Although I still drifted from full-time job to full-time job, I never let go of the part-time job I had as the superintendent of the apartment complex where I lived. At least that job provided me with a salary and a rent-free apartment. However, it did not pay all of the bills or provide benefits. I knew that I may not make it through the fire department's testing process successfully, so I applied to other organizations that offered careers, and jobs that I could see myself working at for several decades if necessary. One of those organizations was the Metropolitan District Commission (MDC). Coincidentally, the written test to get the Metropolitan District job was almost identical to the one that I had to take for the fire department. I did well enough to be offered a job there, and I took it. It was in the waste treatment plant. Although the job was not in a clean environment, it provided the best salary and benefits I had ever had up until then. As I was being hired, one of the men in their personnel department said, "You've got it made now. You'll be working for Tony Broncato. As long as you show up and do your job, he'll treat you right." Truer words were never spoken. As he said these words, I saw others nod their heads in agreement. It was obvious, I was about to work for a highly and widely respected man. You don't want to disappoint a man like that. I prepared myself to work hard.

The best part about the job was the fact that if you knew what you were doing, there were promotional opportunities. One of my supervisors informed me that if I was serious about my position, I should pursue a degree in Civil Engineering. It all sounded very promising, and I looked into the matter. The fire department examination process was taking a while. All totaled, it took about a year and a half to complete, but I had stopped drifting when it came to my full-time work. With a family to support and a good job to support them with, I was completely content working at the MDC.

Rita
1982

Working at the MDC was hard, dirty work, but the guys were great. I found myself actually telling people that even if the fire department comes through, I'm not leaving the MDC. Not only was I paying the bills, but for the first time in my life, I was saving money. Time went by quickly however. I spent the following months enjoying friendships that I had formed throughout my life. I couldn't do this before. Financial challenges prevented me from doing so.

My best friend, Marcus, and I would hang out playing basketball or riding our bikes. One day, we rode from Hartford to Agawam Massachusetts and back together. When people ask me who was the best friend I had when I was young, I always think of Marcus. His children, three girls, and my two children were close friends. My wife, Sue, and his, Rita, were best friends too. We were truly like brothers and sisters together. We even lived in the same apartment complex, and saw each other frequently. Although I could tell that although Rita loved her three girls totally, she wanted a son, and so, she became pregnant again. Her pregnancy was a difficult one this time, so before she was due to deliver, she was put in the hospital. She had to be in there for several weeks. We kind of got used to her being there, safe and sound under the care of physicians, when one day I got a call from Sue. She was at work and crying hysterically. I couldn't even understand what she said, but eventually I heard her say, "Rita just died." Everyone I knew was just destroyed by grief. Rita was a marathoner, winning some races in her category. I can honestly say that I have never cried so hard in all of my life. She delivered the son she wanted while in childbirth. I include this recollection because even though I promised the reader not to discuss matters of a personal nature, I did say that I would discuss matters that resulted in my academic and professional success.

When I became Chief of the Hartford Fire Department, I actually was sworn in twice. (Please excuse my lack of explanation here; I never understood why myself.) During my second speech, I informed the crowd present that my career in the Fire Department was a tribute to all of my friends who I have lost throughout the years. When I said those words, I thought of several people, including Rita. I have done so every day since she died. Almost 20 years after she died, I decided to do something special in remembrance of her. The Hartford Fire Department was attempting to take over as the primary first responders to first-aid calls in the city. This was major, and it meant the saving of many lives. I faced stiff opposition from some very prominent people. However, as I did my part to make this a reality, I knew I would succeed because I did it in memory of Rita. I wasn't going to quit, and absolutely nothing beats persistence. Especially when that persistence is fueled by the memory of a lost loved one.

That loss was in early May of 1982. I was still working at the MDC and really settling in. I had forgotten about the fire department. With Rita's death came a shift in priorities. I just wanted to raise my family; I wasn't in the right frame of mind for any kind of change. One day, while in the locker room and preparing to go home, a coworker came in with what appeared to be a pair of firefighter boots. I looked at him and asked if that was what they were, and he said, "Yes." He said that he worked as a volunteer firefighter for one of the surrounding towns, and that he liked to wear the boots around the plant. I could see his point immediately. I informed him that I had taken the test to become a firefighter in Hartford but that I was no longer interested in taking the job. He looked at me and said, "Are you nuts? Have you ever seen the chief of the fire department, Chief Stewart?" I said, "No." Well, he said, "Before you make a final decision regarding that, take a look at him. After you see how respected he is, you'll change your mind." I did exactly as he said. Chief Stewart, John B. Stewart, Jr., was Hartford's first African American fire chief. He truly was a respected man in the community. People knew who he was across the nation. When I finished looking into his career and community service, I no longer wanted to become a firefighter. I wanted to become Chief!

Captain Epps
1980

During the application process, I interacted with a fire captain named Richard Epps. He was the man in charge of Special Services, which was the public education division of the department. At one point he told me, "You'll have no problem getting on the job, and when you do, apply yourself. Turn off the television and pick up the books!" This statement hit me like a ton of bricks. I was reminded of my days at the Hotchkiss School. I did very well there, even though I had not been in school during most of the school year, or the year before that. The fact that we were mandated to use a study schedule at the Hotchkiss School helped, but after hearing these words from Captain Epps, it became very apparent that there was another reason why I was successful in that environment in spite of the fact that I lacked so much prerequisite knowledge. Televisions were not allowed in the rooms. So, I didn't have the temptation many teenagers give in to. They keep the television on with the volume down. Somehow they think that if the volume is down, they can study in front of it. This is not true at all. If we aren't watching the television, then why have it on? Therefore, with Captain Epp's words, "Turn off the television and pick up the books," Tool # 3, "Avoid Distractions" to enhance my ability to learn, understand and remember information, was born.

During my first three years as a firefighter, there would be other reminders of the importance of this Tool of learning. One of the reminders was the sight of a member of my company who was studying for the Lieutenant's test while he was holding the watch. You had to have five years on the job to take the test, so I was not eligible. From a distance, I observed him. While he was studying, he had the television on with the volume all the way down. Periodically, he would lift his head up from the book he was "studying" to look at the television. When I saw this I walked in on him and asked, "What are you doing?" He looked at me and said, "Studying for the Lieutenant's exam." I then said, "With the television on?" He said, "I'm not watching it." I then said, "If you are not watching it, then why do you have it on?" He just looked at me in disgust, and kept doing what he was doing. Sadly, he never did make Lieutenant.

To illustrate the importance of "avoiding distractions," I often tell a classroom of students to picture doing the thing they like to do most during the summertime. For me, it's riding my bike. Next, I tell them to picture the thing they don't like to do during the wintertime. For me, that's waiting for the bus. Next, I tell them to picture doing both things at once. They can't picture both things at once, and no one can think of two things at the same time either. Our minds can bounce from one thing to the other, but we cannot think of two things at one time. That's why we should not try to study with anything that can distract us around us. Including but not limited to, the television.

TOOL #3
(1980)

Dedicated to Captain Richard Epps, those firefighters who wanted to make lieutenant, but never made it because they studied in front of a television, and to Dale Carnegie

Success is all about focus.

Avoid Distractions

Four out of 5 college students text while driving. *(The Hartford Courant,* October 2013.)

Texting while driving kills nine people per day in the U.S.A. (Brian Williams, *NBC Nightly News,* 2013.)

That's a lot of pain and suffering caused by the fact that many of us refuse to believe that we cannot think of two things at one time.

Let's all try something. Think of what you like to do most when you are on summer vacation from school. Now, think about what you don't like to do in the wintertime. Can you think of both of them at the same time? No you can't. No one can think of two things at the same time. Either we are thinking about one thing or we are thinking about another. We may quickly bounce from one thought to the other (which is what multitasking truly is), but while we are thinking about one thought, we are missing something important about the other one.

All of us want to make the learning environment as comfortable as possible, but some of us take this desire to the extreme by playing music or having the television on while we study.

Whenever I see someone studying with the television on, I can't help but ask, "How can you study with such a distraction?" The usual reply is, "I'm not watching it." Well, my next question is, "If you are not watching it, then why do you have it on?" The same is true of the radio. Watch a teenager studying with the radio on. Their head will bob to the beat; they may even tap their feet. Sometimes a song will come on, and they will stop what they are "studying" and they will say, "Ooh, that's my song." They will then turn up the volume until their song has ended. Well, if they weren't listening to it, how did they know it is their song that was playing?

The reason we enjoy having the television on or music playing while we study, is because our minds are capable of hearing thousands of words per minute, and we are only capable of studying (with some possible exceptions) hundreds of words per minute. So subconsciously, we are actually listening to the radio or watching the television and not giving our undivided attention to the material we are reading. So, in effect, we are just reading and not studying. Don't be fooled into thinking that you can avoid being distracted by turning the volume down. The images you will see on the screen will distract you from what you are trying to study. This is because it interferes with your ability to visualize the information you are trying to learn, understand, and remember, and visualization is the most effective learning tool in the world.

Music is also a distraction to the learning process because:

1. Music can make you visualize the words in the song when you should be visualizing the information you are studying.

2. Even without words in it, music can create an emotional response within us. Sometimes it bores us; sometimes it makes us romantic,

sometimes it makes us violent. Whenever you see a boxer going into a ring, listening to music, he isn't listening to Gershwin, he's listening to "Momma says knock you out." We need to be emotionally connected to what we are studying. Not to the music on the radio.

When it comes to learning information, we can't afford to miss a single word. That's why we avoid distractions. <u>Success is all about focus, which means to mentally and emotionally concentrate on what you are doing.</u> If you eliminate distractions like the television or the radio playing, you are more likely to mentally and emotionally focus on what you are studying, and absorb the information. In other words, "Turn off the television and then pick up the books."

This is a photo of Fire Chief John B. Stewart, Jr., (left), Richard Epps (right) and me (center).

Before I ever received a single promotion, I would call Chief Stewart around every six months and ask him for advice regarding my academic and professional career. He was always extremely helpful. During the first 10 years of my career, I did everything I could to be just like him. I failed. I had become a good man by the time I retired, but Chief Stewart has always been a great man in my eyes. As soon as I became Chief of the Department, I took the steps necessary to name a firehouse in his honor. It is company 14's and it stands at 25 Blue Hills Avenue in Hartford, Connecticut. It's name: "The Fire Chief John B. Stewart, Jr. Firehouse" of course.

Richard Epps (last man on the right of the previous photo) was the man who told me to "turn off the television and pick up the books." From the time that I applied for the fire department to the time of this promotion, he had been promoted to Deputy Chief and then Assistant Chief. There is no doubt in my mind that he could have become Chief of the Department if he wanted to.

These men and four other members of the Hartford Fire Department, Cecil Alston, Carl Booker, Frank Carter, Sr. and Nelson K. Carter, Sr., all had such an impact on me that in 1987 I wrote the following poem as a tribute to their careers. It is called . . .

The Squandered Inheritance

The times endured in the past were severe
Unbearable to some at best
These men were determined to make disappear
Or lay those conditions to rest

They strove to create a bright future for those
Who followed the path that was laid
With tools like persistence thus came to a close
The times of suffering did fade

Perhaps if those who followed the path
Found walls and mountains to scale
They would have avoided the sad aftermath,
This squandered inheritance tale.

Will tools like persistence strength and passion
Be bequeathed to those who feel
No need to excel in any form or fashion
Lives devoid of all zeal?

A change is need at once so it looks
Our time must wisely be spent
"Turn off the television and pick up the books"
I heard them say as they went.

The reader may see some of the Tools of Learning in this poem. Also, there is a very important question that appears in the third stanza: "Will tools like persistence, strength, and passion be bequeathed to those who feel, no need to excel in any form or fashion, lives devoid of all zeal?" This question was meant to compel all of us to ask ourselves the question, *Were all those sacrifices that were made for my benefit just a waste of time?* Only by our actions can we answer that question fully.

Part 2
Chapter 12

Launch Pad
1982

The day came when I got my letter from the city of Hartford in the mail. Not since the days of my GED exams have I looked in the mail box so frequently. When I got it, I refused to open it right away. I brought it to work with me so I could read it there. I wanted to do so just in case it was bad news. Reading it at work would be better, because if I wasn't successful, I still had a good job to raise my family. Even though it was raining, I went outside to read the letter. The news was good. I was so elated that if someone had seen me, they would have thought that I hit the lottery or that I had lost my mind. I was jumping wildly when suddenly I came to realize that I had to give my notice to Tony Broncato. He was so good to me and my family that I dreaded doing so. I had not been there for very long, so I thought that he had every right to be very upset with my leaving. I finally got up the nerve to go talk with him. After I told him that I was leaving he looked me in the eyes, and said, "If I was in your shoes I'd do the same thing." He then stood up, extended his right hand to shake mine and said, "Good luck, Charlie. Come back and see us sometime." The way he treated me made me realize that you can be the boss and still care deeply about your employees. I determined then and there that if I made it to Chief of the Hartford Fire Department, I would be the same kind of boss as Tony Broncato.

Through a variety of speeches, I have shared this experience with hundreds of people, including some United States Congressmen and Senators. The last time I shared it was during my retirement celebration, 28 years later. Tony was still around. In fact, he looked great for a man of his age or a man who is 20 years younger. He is seen here with his son-in-law Tommy Discipio. Just by coincidence, Tommy and I came on the job together. We learned of our connection through Tony while we were in Drill School learning how to become firefighters. I believe this connection helped us decades later. At that time, Tommy was the Union President and I was the Chief of the Department. We did great things together. I credit Tony with that.

This is Tommy Discipio and his father-in-law, Tony Broncato, standing next to me and my wife, Helaine. Boy, was I happy to see these guys. The reason I was so elated to see them is because I could never tell if Tommy had negative feelings about me as Chief when he served as Union President. I also had concerns about him sharing those negative feelings with Tony, a man I had great respect for. The fact that they were both at my retirement celebration proved that only mutual respect remained. Tommy and I had gone through hell together, but we remained friends.

"We should never teach anyone anything unless we have first taught them how to learn, understand, and remember that information."

— ., Sr.

Drill School
Summer 1982

In two weeks, I reported to the Hartford Fire Department's Training Academy. If I knew how much my new career would require of me, I would not have had the nerve to get out of my car. As I approached the Training Academy building, I got a little nervous. What if I didn't make it? What if I flunked out like I did with the New Careers program? As I got to the edge of the training grounds, I stopped, looked up at the Hartford Fire Department emblem on the side of the building, and remembered the words of Walter "Doc" Hurley who told me nine years earlier to "get an education, be of service and don't quit." With those words in my mind, I distinctly remember saying, "They may throw me out of here, but I ain't gonna quit." This was during a time when the training grounds were not paved, and the area I was about to step on was made of crushed stone. I looked down at my feet, took a step forward and walked toward the building. I can still hear the sound of my feet hitting those stones as the building grew closer.

The Hartford Fire Department emblem that I spoke of is shown in the picture above. This is a photo of the group of men who were promoted to the rank of Lieutenant in November of 1987. The emblem I spoke of is on the building. I am in the back row, second from the left.

This is that very same emblem now; it is not a duplicate. As time passed, the Hartford Fire Department changed emblems. As the old one was thrown into the garbage, I took it home and put it in my garage. It represented too much to me to be discarded. That's my last helmet at the top. I put it there the day I retired on April 9, 2010. It's still there today.

Meeting everyone in my drill school class was a totally natural experience. Since everyone hired was from Hartford, everyone seemed to know at least one person in the class. We were directed to go to our seats, which were easy to find because there were name tents on the table. The Deputy Chief of Training was Raymond McTeague, the Captain was Tommy Williams, and there were two Lieutenants: Cecil Alston and Andy Ouellette. I say their names because I wanted to make sure everyone knew who helped make a childhood dream of mine come true. Chief McTeague was always a no nonsense kind of man. If he ever had a good time at work, I never noticed it. The first time he addressed our class, he laid down the law. He told us, "I certainly hope some of you left your previous jobs on good terms because you're going back." Then he informed us that we were expected to maintain a 70 average. If we went below that, we would be dismissed from the program. Just prior to him making his presentation, I looked through the syllabus in our training manual. There were algebraic equations like "gallons per minute equals twenty nine point seven times the diameter squared times the square root of the nozzle pressure." There were also long chemistry definitions that had to be memorized and first aid information to learn. Because I used to go to the firehouse when I was a kid and I used to chase fire trucks to fires, I thought I knew what a firefighter did for a living. Apparently, I did not. So, of course I was very concerned when the Deputy Chief warned us. I had just quit my job as Plant Operator in the Thickening Area for the MDC waste treatment plant. I had two kids to support, and I knew that I could not go back to my previous job because while I was going through the transition from that job to firefighter, I kept the part-time job as the superintendent of the housing complex where I used to live. One of the tenants in that complex was trying to support his wife and two kids while working nights as a security guard. I remembered being in that position. So, I told him about the vacancy that I was about to create by leaving the MDC. I actually helped him to fill my old job and he was very grateful for it. So when Chief McTeague said, "You're going back," I knew I <u>had no job to go back to</u>. Also, I remembered my past academic failures, and I knew that I would not be given four chances to master the information like I had with Plan B Incorporated.

What I did not know is that the next few hours would serve as the foundation to my magnum opus, my major life's work, the creation of a system of learning, understanding and remembering information that would change not only my life but the lives of potentially millions of people in the years to come. Ingenuity was about to force the creation of the Tools of Learning.

During our first break, I went up to the first recruit I saw outside, Eddie Lopez, and I said to him, "How are you planning to get through this program successfully? Maybe we should get some studying groups together so that we can help each other pass training." He could have said something like, "What, are you stupid or something? I'm going to study like everyone else." Instead he said, "We don't need a study group. <u>I was in the military and they taught us how to remember information. He them went on to describe what they were taught</u>. It included a system of repetition and visualization of the information, to enhance retention. Upon hearing this, I was stunned. I said to myself, *You mean there is a <u>system</u> of remembering information?* Apparently there was.

I began to reason, *If this man knows a system of remembering information, then who else does and what other kinds of systems are there?* I decided to think back on the few positive learning experiences that I had in the past, and I experimented with ways to enhance my ability to retain information. I took lots of notes and followed each set of directions I wrote unless it became obvious that the method I developed was a waste of time. Within two months I discovered a total of six ways to learn, understand and remember information. Along with those six ways, I had the five ways that I learned before my training program began. I had not applied those five ways in the past, but I was ready to do so now.

When I finished training, I was assigned to a firehouse with several fire service-related publications in the office. <u>One of those books was titled *Orientation and Indoctrination into the Fire Service* by the International Fire Service and Training Association.</u> In that book was a system known as SQ3R. I obtained permission from the publishers of that book to use SQ3R in my program, and I added to SQ3R the following:

<u>Saying words you want to remember to enhance your ability to pronounce difficult words and phrases</u>

<u>and</u>

<u>Stating the words out loud so that we can hear what we want to learn. This is done because some of us learn audibly.</u>

Throughout my 10 years as Chief of the Hartford Fire Department, I could not find time to give presentations on the Tools of Learning. However, periodically I would visualize myself giving a presentation. I would give it in my mind's eye. I would then ask my Administrative Assistant, Jessylyn Fothergill, to print up a copy of the Instructors Guide to the program, and when she did, I would make the changes that I visualized. One of those changes included two additional R's: "Recent" and "Relevance".

I also determined that the word "Recite" from SQ3R was very useful when it came to learning long definitions, but it did not address the concerns I had about solving math problems. Simply stated, I could "recite" the way to solve a math problem, but that would not prove to me or anyone else that I could solve that type of problem. I also knew that, to paraphrase an old saying, "Reciting is the mother of all learning," but I needed a way to remember the information, not just learn it. Therefore, I decided to exchange "Recite" of the SQ3R system with "Repetition." My reason for doing so was based on the old expression "Repetition is the mother of retention." Therefore, SQ3R went from:

Survey, Question, Read, Recite and Review

To SQ5R:

Survey, Question, Read, Relevance, Repeat, Review and Recent

This change from "Recite" to Repeat" made it possible to still "recite" information if I wanted to because reciting is a form of repetition. However, it also reminded me to solve many math problems if I wanted to remember how to do so during a test or solving a problem.

Thirty-one years after I received written permission from the International Fire Service and Training Association to use SQ3R, I came to realize that SQ3R was not created by that organization, but by a man named Francis Pleasant Robinson. Although he is no longer with us, I thought it appropriate to give him along with Eddie Lopez credit for helping to develop the foundation to Tool #17.

TOOL #17
(Summer of 1982)
Dedicated to Eddie Lopez H.F.D., my determination to make it through drill school successfully, I.F.S.T.A., and Francis Pleasant Robinson

To be considered a true professional, you must memorize the taxonomy of your field.

Use SQ5R

SQ5R stands for Survey, Question, Read, Relevance, Repeat, Review and Recent. It is this tool more than any other that will assist you in <u>retaining information so that you can solve problems more effectively and efficiently.</u>

The word "survey" means read the objectives at the beginning of each chapter and look over the entire lesson. Also, get a general idea of its content and look at the:
- a. pictures,
- b. drawings and
- c. captions that accompany them.

A caption is a group of words that appear next to the pictures and drawings. Its purpose is to explain the picture or drawing next to it.

I cannot over emphasize the importance of pictures, drawings, and captions, because retaining the information displayed by them is usually beneficial. An author is an expert in her or his field. This person is capable of expressing their thoughts in writing, but they are not usually photographers or artists. Therefore, if they want to put a picture or a drawing in their book, they must go through the time and expense of hiring someone to create it. However, they will go through this time and expense because the pictures, drawings and captions are the author's way of:

1. helping you to "visualize" his or her written words and
2. reemphasizing essential written portions of the publication.

Some people are opposed to surveying the information because surveying information takes time. It may take 20 minutes or more to survey the highlighted sections of 30 pages. It is possible to read four pages in that amount of time. However, the goal is not to read the information; it is to remember what you read. Surveying the information enhances retention.

The word "question" means read the questions found in the chapter and write down any questions brought to mind during your survey, keep them in mind, and search for the answers as you read the material. You won't be able to answer them yet, but they will provide a set of goals as you read.

<u>Although reading is essential, it is too passive an activity to be considered studying. Reading is to studying what stretching is to sports competition. Once you have read the information, then it is time to study it.</u>

With that in mind, the word "read" means reading the material, taking notes and highlighting important sections as you read. As you read, you must understand everything. Periodically ask yourself, "What is it that I just read?" Without the ability to answer this question, you are wasting your time. If the subject you are studying is math, and you are having a particularly difficult time with it, try reading the section you are studying at least twice. The first time through, identify examples of the problem, and <u>how the answer appears</u>. Although you may not understand everything you read the first time you read this section, you will get a better sense of which portions you must pay close attention to as you read this section a second time. Also, ships behave the way people should; they have a port, a destination and a course. Reading through the section the first time, without having to understand it, helps you to identify the problem (the port) and the form the answer takes (the destination). Now all you have to do is identify the way to arrive at the answer (the course). That can be accomplished the second time you read it.

How you highlight as you read, is a matter of preference. If you prefer to use a pencil instead of a highlighter pen, one means of highlighting consists of:
a. Hash marks for important sentences   /
b. Underlining <u>important words and phrases</u>
c. Brackets around important paragraphs   [   ]
d. The letters "V.I.P." for "very important page", at the top of the page
e. An asterisk for essential or difficult to remember information   *

If the book does not belong to you and you must return it unmarked, highlight by reading the important sections into a recording device. Another way of highlighting when the book does not belong to you is to use sticky notes that point to or flag important sentences. If the paragraph is important, then write the letters "HTEOP" on the note. HTEOP stands for "Here To End Of Paragraph."

The word "relevance" means to relate what you are reading to the overall importance of the lesson, the course, the degree program or even the employment position you are preparing for. If you are relating the information to your employment, you must determine if you are preparing for a job, a career or a calling. This is necessary because a job is something you do just to make money. Relating the information to a job is important but not as important as relating it to a career. A career is something you do to distinguish yourself professionally. In a career, you may someday pursue a position of prominence like a supervisor. A calling is entirely different from a job or a career. Your calling is what you feel is the reason why you were born. It's your way of distinguishing yourself among the billions of people on this earth. If you are studying information in preparation for your calling, you must relate to the information in a deeply emotional sense. It is not just a cognitive process, or a thinking process, but an affective one, one that requires deep emotional reflection.

Also under the word "relevance", it is very common for a student to ask himself or herself and the teacher, "Why do I have to learn that?" For example, "Why do I have to learn y=mx+b? Where am I ever going to use that in real life?" The answers to those questions can best be explained in the following fashion: y=mx+b and all of the seemingly impractical lessons we must learn are part of the ABCs of the subject we are studying. A person can learn how to read without knowing his or her ABCs, but it would take a very long time to do so. Without learning their ABCs, most people who now read very well would never have learned how to read at all. Yet when was the last time you used your ABCs? Except to teach child, we never think of them consciously. However, subconsciously we do use our ABCs every time we pronounce a long word that is unfamiliar to us. For example, if we write the word "antidisestablishmentarianism", we can probably sound it out by pronouncing each syllable. To pronounce each syllable, you must know the sound each letter makes, and before you can learn the sound each letter makes, you must know your ABCs. So, we do use our ABCs for more than just teaching a child. The point is this: if you are going to learn the math it takes to someday become an accountant, auditor, computer programmer, doctor, psychologist or one of many other occupations, you must learn the ABCs of math. It is the foundational knowledge we will someday need to learn the practical math of our chosen fields.

Other than these things, you should know that no matter what your chosen field is, if it requires a college education, you will have to take a math test prior to being allowed to get into any good college or university. That test requires a mastery of problems like y=mx+b.

The word "repeat" is the step in which remembering takes place. Although "reciting" is the mother of all learning" and "fun" is the father of all learning, "repeating" is the mother of retention.

Repeating should be used when remembering the taxonomy of a subject. ***The taxonomy of a subject is the foundational knowledge associated with your field of study***. If you were studying chemistry, the taxonomy would be the periodic table. If you were studying United States law, the taxonomy would be the United States Constitution. If you want to be respected as a true professional in your field, you must memorize the taxonomy of that field. Repeating the information in the following fashion is the best way to accomplish this:

Those sections with an asterisk (*) next to them were developed by me during the summer of 1982.

a. Divide the phrase into smaller groups of words or sentences that make sense. *
b. Read the divided phrases to yourself.
c. Archimedes once said, "Give me a lever long enough and a place to stand and I can move the earth." Well, the Tools of Learning has a tool more powerful than the lever. It's called "visualization." The art of visualization cannot be overstated; it is the most effective learning tool known to humankind. Some of us can recall word for word portions of television shows we saw years ago because we can visualize them. With that in mind, raise your head, close your eyes and try to visualize each word in the phrase you've just read.
d. Reread the phrase to yourself.
e. Raise you head again and say the phrase out loud.*
f. Reread the phrase aloud to check yourself for accuracy. *
g. When you feel confident with the smaller phrases, consolidate them until you have memorized the entire phrase. *

Throughout these last seven steps (a-g), you will use as many of your five senses as possible to enhance your ability to remember the information. In step (c) you will see the information, and in step (e) you will hear the information. This is done because the more of the senses that we use while doing anything, the more likely we are to remember it. <u>There is an added benefit to remembering information word for word. It forces us to give precise consideration to the most important expressions related to our field of interest. After retaining these expressions we improve ourselves because "we become what we think about." (Napoleon Hill)</u>

Because remembering how to solve math problems requires practice, it is not as beneficial to recite the solutions to problems as it is to simply practice solving the problems repeatedly.

The next step of the SQ5R system of learning is the "review" step. It means to frequently perform a reading and reciting of the phrases until it becomes as easy to recall as the ABC's or the Pledge of Allegiance. (These things you don't have to practice anymore, but you can recall them because they are in a portion of the brain called the neocortex.) The SQ5R system of remembering information makes it possible to more effectively store information in the neocortex.

Use a pencil instead of a pen or magic marker when highlighting information. That way you can erase the highlight when you have retained the information and no longer have to review it. Also, remember to vary your means of review. In addition to your notes, use an audio recording device with the information you want to review on it.

Of all of the 5R's, the "recent" step is probably the most challenging to gauge. In the recent step, we organize the information so that we can recall it quickly, thereby making the information practical to use. For example, in the fire service, if someone comes to the window of a burning building and yells, "Help, I'm trapped," you don't have an hour or even minutes to figure out which size ladder you need. You've got seconds. Making quick, accurate decisions is possible only if the information we have learned is readily accessible, even during times of great stress.

Audibleize?
1982

I've made up the use of a word. Some say this word does not even exist. It's called "audibleize." The Tools of Learning teaches that if it is possible to visualize, or see information in your mind's eye, then it is possible to "audibleize," or hear information in your mind's ear. I once had a math teacher by the name of Mr. Howard who used to say, "Subtracting a negative is the same as adding a positive, and subtracting a positive is like adding a negative." I never saw this information in writing, so I cannot visualize it, but because I can imagine hearing him saying those words. I can "audibleize" what he taught me.

This is Eddie Lopez (left) and me (right) in drill school, summer of 1982

Photo courtesy of the Eddie Lopez collection

If it hasn't already, someday it will occur to the reader that you have only this moment to live this moment and then it is gone forever, never to be relived again. Being a firefighter means having many of these experiences. Sometimes it happens when you see someone lose his or her life, and sometimes it happens when you come close to losing your own   I had a few of these experiences before I got in the fire department, but I was not there mentally or emotionally to benefit from them.

Hearing from fellow recruit Eddie Lopez that there was a system of remembering information was the first experience of this kind that I had as a member of the great Hartford Fire Department. Before that conversation, I thought, *If you were smart you learned, and if you were not smart, you simply didn't.* Nothing could be further from the truth. I began to reason, *If this man knows a system of remembering information, then who else does? And if they do, did they learn it in the military or while they were in high school, and I didn't because I was not in the military and I didn't go to high school?* I decided to think back on the few positive learning experiences that I had in the past. Those experiences have already been stated in this book, and appear as part of Tool #13, and all of Tools #5, 1, 2 and 3. However, I experimented with ways to enhance my ability to learn, understand and remember information, and within the next two months, I discovered the following:

Tools 7, 10, 11, 14, 15 and part of 17 were all discovered while I was a recruit in drill school during the summer of 1982. I wasn't taking any chances when it came to passing that program. The following information is about each of them.

As I utilized the Tools that I already knew, my ability to recite definitions word for word got better. During one of our classroom sessions, I was asked by the Training Captain named Tommy Williams to define the term "ignition temperature." I gave the following response: "The minimum temperature required, to initiate or cause, self-sustained combustion independently of another heat source." That was the definition verbatim, and I knew it was. Upon hearing this definition, Captain Williams stated, "Very good Teale. What does that mean?" Since I had only memorized the definition, instead of understanding it, I could not answer his question at all. As some my classmates laughed at my predicament, I distinctly remember writing down in my notebook, "It's not enough to learn the information, you must understand it too." As I wrote this in my notes, Captain Williams told the class that understanding what we learn could someday mean the difference between life and death. I never made the mistake of just learning information again.

TOOL # 7
Examine Your Ability
Dedicated to Captain Tommy Williams.
Summer of 1982

"We are not tape recorders learning how to just recite information."
— Captain Tommy Williams

For you to be able to recite information verbatim does not guarantee a thorough understanding of the information. It only means you have learned the information. Understanding is a prerequisite to remembering. "If you want to prove that you understand something, say it in your own words."

I'd Rather Study
1982

At one point in our training experience, the Deputy Chief of Training, Raymond McTeague, was directing three recruits on the proper method of taking down a ladder from a building. The commands are very basic but coordinating the efforts of three recruits is not. They were new to the evolution, and having the person who is responsible for recommending or not recommending your being hired surely must have made the recruits very nervous. When the ladder is fully extended, it is in its most vulnerable position. A gust of wind can turn it from vertical to horizontal very quickly, and that is exactly what happened on this day. The rest of the class and the instructors (approximately 35 people) were not paying attention to this operation at all until we heard the Deputy Chief yell, "Butt that ladder, butt that ladder!" That means to hold the ladder steady with your right foot. If one of the recruits used his or her left foot instead, confusion will occur and no one will be securing the ladder. So, the ladder will rock from side to side as if it was walking. When that happens, it's dangerous because the ladder can fall on the people trying to control it or it can fall on spectators. When it appeared that this ladder was going to fall and the recruits could not control it, the Deputy Chief yelled, "Let it go!!!" That's when everyone in the class turned around only to find that the ladder, which was made of wood, heading right for a pile of wooden pallets. When it was over you couldn't tell the pieces of pallets from the pieces of ladder, and the Deputy Chief was beet red with his hands on his hips. The rest of us quickly looked away as if to say, *I didn't see that, so I could not have been responsible in any way*. At the end of the day, the Deputy Chief came before the class with a special announcement. First he told us all how awful we were when it came to learning our new professions. Then he said, "There are 30 people in this class, and 30 people out there ready to take your jobs." I thought heads were going to roll, but what he said was, "This is a holiday weekend coming up. I believe if you all go home and don't study anything over the long weekend we can start anew next week. So no one do any homework until then."

I was not about to follow that order. By then, I had been studying for about a month, and I had developed a system of review that kept the information fresh in my mind. I was deeply concerned that a three-day vacation away from the information would set me back. This led me to develop Tool #10.

TOOL #10
Give Yourself Homework
Dedicated to Deputy Chief Raymond McTeague
Summer of 1982

When you have some spare time, you should review difficult to remember information.

Not even the best teacher knows more about a student's academic weakness than the student. When a teacher fails to give out an assignment, it's time for the student to study those subjects he or she knows that they are having some difficulty with.

It is especially important to remember this tool when we go on summer vacation. Sometimes we are given a summer reading assignment. It is important that we complete that assignment. However, during this time, we should also study those things we know we have trouble with. For example, let's take math. We are sometimes taught a lot of math during the school year. If we don't review what we learned while we are on vacation, we will forget information that may have taken us the entire school year to learn. It's like taking three steps forward and three steps backward. No progress. Since reviewing is much easier than learning, why not make things easier for yourself and review while on vacation? Also, when it comes to math, never assume that because you understand what you are reading you will remember how to do what must be done during a test. To review math means to do math. Take out some paper and pencils and practice, practice, practice.

Rewrite
1982

After the deputy chief of training told the members of my recruit class that if we didn't maintain at least a 70 percent average we would be terminated, I immediately remembered being dismissed from the New Careers program a few years earlier. To help insure my success, I would take as many notes as I could so that I was able to review what was covered in class later. Back then, I would take notes in cursive. Because I was determined to write down everything that was necessary, I wrote very fast which meant that my handwriting was bad and difficult to read afterwards. Knowing that sometimes I couldn't read my own handwriting, I would rewrite my notes as soon as I had the time, after class. That way, I could remember what I wrote, even if I could not read my own handwriting. To my surprise, I received additional benefits to proceeding in this way.

TOOL #11
Rewrite Your Notes
Dedicated to my determination to get through drill school
Summer 1982

"We will forget 90 percent of what a speaker says if we don't take notes."
— Earl Nightingale

There are at least five reasons why we should rewrite our notes as soon as possible. They are:

1. If our handwriting is bad, we can remember what was said during class.

2. We can develop a legible record of what the teacher said. That way, we can review what the teacher said months and even years later, if necessary.

3.   We can recall some of the things the teacher said that we did not originally get in our notes.

4.   We are physically active while learning.   This is known as the psychomotor learning domain.   <u>The use of the psychomotor learning domain is recommended by the Tools of Learning only three times.   Here, Tool #13 and Tool #17.</u>

5.   Experience the presentation that the teacher gave a second time <u>through visualization, or audibleizing,</u> while all of the other students only heard it once.   This "second presentation" is reviewed at "mind speed."   The Tools of Learning differentiates between "mind speed" and "speech speed."   Some estimates indicate that we can speak at about 125 words per minute. However, some estimates indicate that our minds can study information at around 1,000 words per minute.   What this means is that if you are reviewing a teacher's presentation mentally, you can review each word she or he spoke for an hour in as little as eight minutes.   That's why it is better to take good notes than it is to record a presentation and listen to that recording again.   Which would you rather do, review your written notes for eight minutes or listen to a recording of the presentation for an hour?   Reviewing what was said mentally saves a tremendous amount of time.

(Caution: Some people say that "audibleizing" is not a word and others say that it is a word, but it does not pertain to the following meaning: Audibleizing is when you can imagine hearing what someone said in your minds ear.)

Also, if we take notes on Friday afternoon, we should not wait until Sunday evening to use this Tool.   That would be too late. <u>We should rewrite our notes as soon after class as we can.</u> If we make a habit of rewriting our notes as soon as possible after class has ended, we will be better able to recall what our teacher said during class and write it down accurately.

Although I am not inclined to tell anyone which of the 20 Tools of Learning is the most effective, I don't believe I can hide it from my audiences. This is the one that I appreciate the most because it yields positive results quicker than all the other Tools.

The PSG
1982

While studying for the various quizzes and exams we were assigned to take, I could not help but wonder if I truly remembered the important points that I had studied. I didn't want to wait until I got a test back with a bad grade on it to realize that I didn't know the information well. So, I created a "personal study guide" (PSG). A PSG is a notebook <u>every student should have</u> that is full of questions that that student finds difficult to answer. Every time I read or heard information that I thought might be on a test, I would write down a question that tested my ability to remember that information. Then, on the other side of the paper or a separate sheet of paper, I would write the correct answer to it. For example, if I wrote, "What is the definition of the word fire," the next thing that I would do is write on another sheet of paper, "A chemical reaction known as combustion which is rapid oxidation or chemical combination accompanied by the evolution of heat and light." I would not look at the answer until after I answered it. If I did <u>not</u> answer it correctly, I would highlight the question by writing an asterisk next to it (like this [*] but larger). I would then use the system of remembering information found in Tools #14 to 17 to improve my ability to answer it correctly the next time. I answered the questions in rotating fashion. By that I mean I would determine how much time I had to review the information in my PSG. That amount of time was usually 15 minutes. I would start on page 1 and review as much as I could until those 15 minutes were up. If I got to page 5, that would be fine. I would then take an additional 15 minutes to review those questions that had asterisks next to them. Of course, I named this step "asterisk review." I always kept track of where I finished so that the next day, I could pick up where I left off (for example, page 6). Wherever I left off, I would fold a few pages in half or write the letters "LO" which stood for "left off," and then I would write the date. That way, if something prevented me from reviewing for a while, I could tell where I finished my last review session.

TOOL #14
Write Questions
Dedicated to my determination to make it through drill school
successfully
Summer, 1982

Before you get tested, test yourself with your personal study guide.

Can you solve a particular type of math problem? Do you remember the difference between a noun and a verb? Doing your homework helps to prove that you can, but usually your homework just asks you to do problems of a particular type. For example, you may solve many division problems for your homework, but how good are you at adding? Have you forgotten the difference between a subject and a predicate? If we don't review, we forget. To determine how good you are at solving many different types of problems, take one question from each type of problem you must solve, and place it in your PSG. After you have answered that type of problem, go on to the next one. The problems in your PSG may be slightly different from other problems of the same type that you must solve, but the general rules are the same. Using this method, you will grow accustomed to solving several types of problems in a short period of time. That's how most tests are given. If you are having difficulty with a particular type of problem, place an asterisk next to it (*). Set aside additional time for a review of all the problems with asterisks next to them and review those types of problems more frequently than the others.

This method works for math, English, and other subjects as well, particularly definitions, but there is another application for this Tool that is beneficial.

Sometimes a person will have difficulty passing a particular test that he or she must take. Even after several tries, he or she just can't get a score high enough to pass. When this happens, either of the following is the likely cause:

1. The person is not studying.
2. The person is studying and thinks that he or she is studying the right information for the test. Unfortunately, without realizing it, he or she is not reviewing the correct information needed to pass the test.
3. The person is studying the right information but is not remembering that information when he or she takes the test.

If you cannot seem to pass a particular type of test and you are given several tries to do so, try highlighting the important facts of the information, and create a question for each important fact that you must be able to answer correctly before the test is given.

If you can answer the question precisely, then you know the answer. If you cannot, then spend additional time committing the information to memory using Tools # 14 to17.

Memory's Friend: The Mnemonic
Summer of 1982

A mnemonic is a memory aid. If you find it difficult to remember something, a mnemonic will help. One of the subjects we had to study while in training was hazardous materials. Within that subject is the term "BLEVE" which is an acronym that stands for "boiling liquid expanding vapor explosion." When I saw this correlation, I thought to myself, *Why not use a similar system to remember other lists of names?* In time, I discovered many acronyms and another form of mnemonic called an acrostic. Sometimes I made up acronyms and acrostics. Words like "CLARPH" started to appear in my vocabulary. CLARPH is not a word, but it is an acronym that I made up, and it stands for the six types of alarm systems: central, local, auxiliary, remote, proprietary, and household. These two types of mnemonics proved to be very beneficial during tests, presentations to my superiors, and to the general public.

TOOL #15
Use Mnemonics
Dedicated to Captain Tommy Williams, Lieutenant Andy Ouellette and Lieutenant Cecil Alston (BLEVE, etc.)
Summer, 1982

Learning mnemonics is good; creating them is excellent.

Please don't misunderstand this Tool. An education is not a bag of tricks. It takes hard work to get an education, which is why people are so happy at their graduations. However, there are ways to remember information that can make remembering some things easier to do. One example is a mnemonic, which is any learning technique that can be used to aid memory. Try this: You can use a mnemonic to remember the number of days there are in a month by using your fist. Start on the knuckle of your index finger. That represents January, which has 31 days. All of the other knuckles represent months with 31 days too. The low points of your fist in between the knuckles represent those months with less than 31 days. Low means less.

The Tools of Learning recommends the use of two types of mnemonics: acronyms and acrostics. An acronym is a form of mnemonic that is a word made from the first letter of a group of words. There are many examples, but my favorite acronym is the word H.O.M.E.S. In this word is the first letter of each of the five Great Lakes. The H is for Huron, the O is for Ontario, the M is for Michigan, the E is for Erie, and the S is for Superior. An acrostic is another form of mnemonic. Although there are many kinds of acrostics, the kind we will focus on is "making words from the first letter of other words." An example of this type of acrostic is "My very educated mother just served us nachos." Here, the first letter of each word in this sentence represents each of the eight planets of our solar system, in their order from the sun. They are Mercury, Venus, Earth, Mars, Jupiter, Saturn, Uranus and Neptune. Using mnemonics, like acronyms and acrostics, is probably the best way to remember a group of words or phrases. However, it must be remembered that the ultimate goal when it comes to mnemonics is learning and remembering how to create them for our specific needs. The potential use of mnemonics applies to every academic and professional field. To make a mnemonic like an acronym or acrostic correctly, you must anticipate the question that will be asked of you during an exam. For example, supposed you were asked, "What are the names of the eight planets in our solar system?" You could answer in any order you would like. But supposed you were asked, "What are the names of the eight planets in our solar system in their order from the sun?" Then you must not only remember the names of the planets, but you must also remember their order. Therefore, constructing the mnemonic must be done with a concern about the order of the letters in mind. Also, be aware of repeat letters like the letter M, which in this case stands for the planets "Mercury" and "Mars." In a case like this one, you must remember which "M" stands for which planet.

At this point, the reader should be advised that 11 of the 20 Tools of learning had been learned by the end of the second month of my fire-training program. That's five Tools before training and six while I was going through it. However, they are by no means the Top Ten Tools of Learning. For the rest and some of the most effective methods I discovered during my 28-year career, please read on. In other words, some of the best is yet to come.

As a recruit class we weren't doing that well. At one point in our training experience, some of us were doing so poorly that some were dismissed for bad grades, just like Chief McTeague said would happen. This time, I made it through. Thanks to the system of learning information that I had compiled, for the first time since I was 11 years old, I was not afraid of failing because of my grades. It was a system that was to take me to the top of the class of 27 recruits. I graduated from drill school with a 99.7 average. At our graduation ceremony, Deputy Chief McTeague announced that I had the highest average. What a welcome change of pace that was for me and my family. For the first time in my life, I was actually proud of my academic ability.

It was my drill school experience that caused me to make another addition to my formula regarding accomplishment. I now knew that it took more than the H which stands for Health and the D which stands for Desire, to accomplish my academic and professional goals. It takes a Strategy too. The equation now took on a form that would remain the same for almost three decades:

$$A=H+S+D$$

For the next 28 years, I would use this equation to direct my academic and professional pursuits, and whenever possible, I would share this concept with others.

Here's our class getting ready to graduate. Although the photo is not clear you can pick me out. I'm the one with the real wide smile. (Second row, second from the left). I did a lot of smiling in those days.

Photo courtesy of the Eddie Lopez collection

On the day of my graduation from drill school, I received a surprise party. Here I am at that party with my daughter Kathleen (photo above), and Charlie (photo below).

Chapter 13

Firefighter Teale
Summer 1982

I was assigned to a firehouse along with one of my fellow recruits named Benny Guzman. He is probably one of the youngest people to ever wear the uniform of the Hartford Fire Department. He, along with another recruit named Justo Marrero both came on the job at the age of 18. However, they were mature beyond their years. We were all very eager to prove ourselves. We didn't have to wait long. On my first day in the firehouse, NBC Channel 30 news reporter Lew Brown came to the firehouse with a cameraman. He asked me, "Are you the firefighter who graduated number one in your class?" I answered, "Yes." He then spoke with the Captain Lucien Theriault, the officer in charge, about interviewing and filming us while we simulated a training exercise. The captain agreed, and right in the middle of Lew Brown filming our mock training exercise, the alarm went off. I was so new that I hardly knew how to get on the fire truck, but somehow, Lew Brown edited out the awkward parts, and my company was filmed responding to my very first call. It was televised all over the region. I cannot tell you how many people called my home or approached me in my neighborhood to congratulate me on becoming a firefighter. Their kind words resonate within me to this day. They seemed to erase all of those incredibly difficult times that I had beforehand. Twenty-eight years later, Lew Brown was still as youthful as he was the first day I met him. Throughout my career and even after it, he was a constant source of encouragement. As I prepared to retire, I could not help but ask him to serve as the Master of Ceremonies for the event. He agreed to do so and did a great job as usual.

Lew Brown, my wife Helaine and me

I was assigned to Ladder 6, which was in a firehouse just three blocks away from where I lived at 146-A Stonington Street in Hartford. While walking to the firehouse one day, I decided to count all of the jobs I had in the past. Although some of them were just childhood jobs, like emptying garbage or caddying, if someone paid me to do the work, I counted it as a job. The number I came up with was 26 jobs. I had taken the long road, but I finally made it to the position of Firefighter in the great Hartford Fire Department!

The guys I was assigned to work with were the best coworkers I ever had. What made the experience particularly rewarding was my company officer, Captain Lucien Theriault. Captain Theriault was a legend in the department and the city of Hartford. He was a big man for the times (people were thinner in the early 80's than they are now), but he could run faster than almost anyone you could find. He was known to challenge collegiate track stars to a 40-yard dash while he held a sack of potatoes under each arm. He never lost, and he literally kept track of all the money he won. It was in the thousands of dollars. Aside from his off-the-job antics, he was inclined to engage in unusual conduct on the job too. It isn't that he broke the rules or anything. It's just that he was nearing the end of his career and as long as we weren't at an emergency, he sometimes took comical risks. The comical stories about him were numerous but because the first five years of my career were spent under his supervision, I could tell the best stories about him. However, at this time I'm not inclined to reflect on the comical stories about him at all, because he was more inspiring than comical. One day he told me, "If you do as I say and not as I do, someday you will be chief of this department." That wasn't the only time he said things like that either. This man was a constant source of encouragement to me. He also told me, "Someday when I go into the watch room, guys will have to stand and salute." Another time he told me, "You're a winner, and I know a winner when I see one." Because of Captain Lucien Theriault, I was off to a great start in my career.

There isn't enough space in the pages of this book to elaborate on all of the experiences you have when you start a career like firefighting. Sometimes you go from tedium to terror in just seconds. During the early part of the day, we would check our equipment and do housework (cleaning). I was kind of a nut about housework. Because I had worked as a janitor at the Wadsworth Athenaeum (an art museum in Hartford), I knew how to clean and thought every room I cleaned had to be pristine because someone would be making an assessment of me based on the work I completed. I even used to keep an extra uniform in my locker so that I could clean without worrying about my appearance afterward. I did this just in case we had to go out area surveying, which is a form of building inspection.

One day while cleaning, the alarm went off. I slid the pole and saw a different look in the eyes of the guys in my company. They were shouting things like, "That's a worker" and "We're first due" and "That's just past Park Street on the right." A "worker" was slang for a "serious fire" as opposed to a false alarm or small fire. One of the veterans named Vern Tyson looked at me with an expression on his face that was more serious than I can describe. He then said, "This is a worker, I'm sure of it. When we get there you stay with the Captain, **do you hear me?**" I nodded my head yes. Within an instant, I said to myself, *This is one of those times when you get to see if you emotionally survived all of the bad things that happened to you so far in life, and if you became a stronger person because of those experiences or not.* As we pulled up to the fire, it was burning so fiercely that I thought to myself, *Someone had better call the fire department.* Then it dawned on me: we were the fire department! I won't go into specifics because as fires go, it was quite common with the exception of one thing. There was so much smoke we couldn't find the source of the fire. So, at one point, the deputy chief in charge of the fire, Chief Edmond Kuresczka, decided that we were going to advance a line onto the first floor, extinguishing and searching for the seat of the fire as we progressed. I was on a ladder company, and we had already done our jobs of forcible entry, searching for victims, and ventilating the building. A ladder company did not advance hose lines so I thought to myself, *I'm sure glad I'm assigned to another company.* Suddenly, Captain Theriault shouted, "I've got a man for that line." And that man was me. He was trying to get as much experience for me as he could. As we advanced the line, the officer in charge of the company I was working with, Lieutenant Jimmy Ring, paced back and forth in front of us as we sprayed water on the ceiling. It was difficult to see him or hear him, but at one point, he started shouting, "Get out, get out, get out!" These weren't requests, they were direct orders from a superior officer. I was on probation and knew that if I disobeyed, it I could be fired easily. Besides, this was an experienced officer, and I knew a man like that could see danger while I was too new to sense it at all. I was still very new to the job, but I soon found out that Lieutenant Ring loved the job and the men he supervised, but he didn't show his emotions in a mild fashion. He was direct and gave orders so that you knew they were orders and not requests. The orders he gave on that day were no exception to that rule. We retreated and entered the building from another direction. After the fire, I returned to the area where we were ordered to get out by Lieutenant Ring. A few feet from where we were, there was a huge hole in the floor. Lieutenant Ring saw the hole because there was fire visible through it. That's when the strategy changed so that we could fight a basement fire. If he had not told us to retreat, we probably would have fallen through the hole and into the fire. He may have saved our lives. Everyone knew it, but he took it in stride like it was something he did every day.

I bring this account to mind to give the reader an idea of what it meant for me to be a Firefighter; not a Company Officer or a Training Officer or Chief of the Department, but a person who risks his life for a living while depending on the specialized knowledge of his superiors just to stay alive. Knowledge in this field meant more than money or authority; it meant survival.

I've Got the Watch
Fall 1982

One of the first things a person realizes upon becoming a new firefighter is that you must learn the entirely different language of the profession. One day, I was in the watch room of the firehouse, talking to some veteran firefighters. I was trying to learn the definitions of the new terms of my profession. As I struggled to learn it all in a short amount of time, one of the veterans said, "Don't worry about this. It usually takes a person about five years to learn most of it." Since I knew that lives would be on the line (including mine), I determined that that was five years too long. So, instead of learning through experience (which can be the worst teacher), I developed a strategy for learning the definitions to new words. That meant whenever I heard a word or a phrase that I did not know the meaning of, I tried to "sense" what the word meant based upon how it was used in the conversation. Just in case I misunderstood what the word meant, I wrote it down. As soon as time permitted me to do so, I would "search" for the definition of that word. Then I would memorize the definition. This was about 15 years before the Internet was available to the general public, so I relied on a dictionary and the glossary of any book assigned to me by my drill school instructors, or books that were in the firehouse. In this way, I quickly built up my taxonomy, or the foundational knowledge related to the fire service. Due to a lack of training, education and experience, I may not have been as capable as I wanted to be "yet", but I was able to comprehend what well trained, educated and experienced individuals were saying. That meant that I could learn from them quickly, and they appreciated my intense interest. Some of them started to say that the fire service was "in my blood." Also, having a wide vocabulary in the field, worked wonders during the promotional exams I would be taking in the near to distant future.

Although creating it began in 1982, it would be another 32 years before I could complete Tool #4. It was during a meeting of former members of the Greater Opportunity (G.O.) program. We had all been at The Hotchkiss School during that summer of 1971 (see Tool #1). At the meeting held in 2014, one of the Hotchkiss brothers, retired school principal Sadiq Ali, shared his system of how to improve your vocabulary. In addition to my methods of "sense" and "search" he had the idea that we should look for a synonym, use it in a sentence and then tell a story using the new word. As I listened to him, I came to realize that if I stopped memorizing definitions (which can become very time consuming) and used his methods of "synonym, sentence and story", a person would have a complete understanding of the meaning of a word if they used his method and mine combined. His method and mine combined created "the S times 5 system of building a powerful vocabulary" and it appears in "Tool #4" as follows:

TOOL #4
Dedicated to my determination to master the taxonomy of the fire service and Sadiq Ali
Fall 1982

Misunderstanding the meaning of one word can prevent us from understanding major portions of a an entire subject

Keep a Dictionary on Hand

This tool pertains to knowing the meaning of words and phrases
While going through the learning process, be extra alert when you see the words "always or never". They are not used often, but when they are, it is usually to drive home a very important point. That point in this case is, while in a classroom setting, you should never hear a word or phrase without knowing what that word or phrase means.

If we lack knowledge about words or phrases, we can use words or phrases incorrectly. Words like "conversate" or "oftenly", phrases like "with a fine tooth and a comb" or "for all intensive purposes" are not real words or phrases and using them can cause us to get bad grades in school and cause us to lose credibility as professionals. If we use a word or phrase incorrectly, it is called a "malapropism", and some people think those who engage in malapropisms are ignorant or uneducated, and sometimes funny to listen to. To keep this from happening to you, do the following whenever you hear a word or a phrase that you don't know the meaning of.

The "S times 5" System of Building a Powerful Vocabulary
  a. Sense
  b. Search
  c. Synonym
  d. Sentence
  e. Story

  a. Sense
Estimate what a word or phrase means when the teacher uses it. Determine how it is used in a sentence so that you can get a sense of what it means. However, don't assume that you know what a new word or phrase means yet. Even if you don't know how the word or every word of a phrase is spelled, write it down the way it sounds and correct the spelling when you look it up.

  b. Search
As soon as possible, look up the unknown word or phrase using
    i. notes or a memo application
    ii. a browser
    iii. a dictionary

Look up the word and phrase until you understand what the word or phrase means completely. There are over 600,000 words in the English language. Some of those words we use when we speak. Other words, we must know because we have to take exams that include those words. Words like "indubitably" which means "too apparent to be doubted; unquestionable." Most of us would never think of using this word, but if we want to score high on the vocabulary portion of exams we plan on taking, then we have to know the meaning of it.

c. Synonym

Think of a word or phrase that you already know, that means the same thing as the word or phrase you have looked up and are trying to learn. If you don't know a word or phrase that is like the new word or phrase, then memorize the meaning of the new word or phrase. Someday it will serve as the synonym you know.

d. Sentence

Use the new word or phrase in a sentence during a conversation with someone.

e. Story

Although this one is more time consuming, tell or write a story using the new word.

College, Round 3
Fall 1982

By the time I was assigned to a firehouse, I had grown accustomed to using a study schedule to insure that I learned something new every day. Those who saw me studying would say things like, "I've seen guys come on this job and be gung ho like you. Six months later, they wouldn't be studying anymore." To me, that was a serious warning! It made me more determined to "use a study schedule" throughout my career, and learn something new every day. One day, there was a discussion about who would become Chief of the Department in the future. Someone said, "The person with the most education." They then mentioned a firefighter on one of the other shifts named Kevin Sullivan who had a master's degree. I had a great amount of respect for Kevin, a respect that would last throughout my career. I knew I was on the right track when people started to compare me with him. Then someone turned to me and said, "You could become Chief if you had an education," and then that person said, laughingly, "but you can't do it with a G.E.D!" It was during that time that my captain, Lucien Theriault, spoke with me about going to college. I had tried two times before but failed each time. However, I still remembered the lesson I learned from Mr. Hurley about getting an education and persistence. Now that I had a system of learning, understanding and remembering information, I decided to try it again. While taking courses at the Connecticut State Fire School (now called the Connecticut Academy), I enrolled in Hartford State Technical College's fire technology program. Three months later, I would finish the course I took with an A+. I had a winning strategy for academic success, and every quiz, test and grade I received proved it!

Captain Cieri
Fall 1982

Firefighters in the Hartford Fire Department had to grow accustomed to a process known as "detailing." Detailing was a form of temporary assignment to another company, usually a company in another firehouse. This was usually done to fill in temporary vacancies. One day, Captain Theriault said to me, "You're not working here today; you've been detailed to Company 9's." This was a completely new experience for me, and like everything else about my career, I was eager to know what it was like working somewhere else. I gathered up everything I thought I would need (including my study books and equipment), and I headed out to Company 9's. When I got there, I was greeted by another great group of guys. I know the reader will probably think I'm exaggerating, but I firmly believe that firefighters are the best people I have ever met. The only time that I have ever had a negative interaction with one was when he or she had a very serious problem at home. Transference is when you take problems from one place and show the emotions, caused by that problem, someplace else. Well, I came to understand how that works the hard way. When I became a lieutenant in the Training Division, I had an interaction with a Company Officer who was having a terrible time at work. His attitude was awful. It was as if he didn't really care about his job at all. I got so disgusted with him that I complained to my superiors in the Training Division. Their response to me was, "He's been like that ever since his son committed suicide."

Since that day, I have never judged a person in haste.

Back to Company 9's. I quickly settled in to Company 9's. Because I was trained by Captain Theriault to always check with the officer when I got into the house, I went straight to the Captain and introduced myself. His name was Cieri. Captain William Cieri. He seemed to appreciate the fact that I respected his authority so much that I would approach him and ask for my assignment for the day. I checked the equipment that I was responsible for and had a conversation with the guys. Later that evening, I settled down in the bunkroom with my books and a rope for practicing knots. Being in the bunkroom before 9 pm was not common because it looked like a firefighter was sleeping when he should not have been. However, it was the only place I could study without distractions. My study sessions usually lasted six hours during the day and three hours during the night. After about an hour, Captain Cieri walked into the bunkroom. I know he was checking up on me to see if I was sleeping, but I had much more important things to do than that. When he saw me with that rope in my hand, while staring at a book, a relationship was started that I still cherish to this day. He looked at me and said, "Whatcha doing kid?" I told him, "Studying my knots." He said, "Show me what you got." I showed off. Bowline, backhand bowline, clove hitch, body hitch, the works, or at least so I thought. He then reached out his hand and said, "Give me that rope!" When this man got finished I thought I would have to buy a new rope. He did everything but rappel with it. At one point he tied a bowline behind his back. I stood straight up and said, "How'd you do that?" I didn't get much studying done that day but I accomplished a lot more. I just didn't know it yet.

Getting detailed to Company 9's was easy for me. Most of the guys in my house didn't like to go there because Captain Cieri demanded housework and a lot of it. Guys use to say, "I'm afraid to go anywhere in the firehouse without a mop in my hands," when they talked about how Captain Cieri ran his house. I didn't mind cleaning then and it doesn't bother me now. I believe it builds character as long as it isn't someone else's job. The next time I was detailed to Captain Cieri's house, I was armed with my best display of knot tying. I even showed him that I could tie a bowline behind my back too. It was my turn to hold the watch, so I went there with a history book about Hartford. The history of Hartford has been a passion of mine since my grandmother Pearl Woods-Smith used to tell me stories about how it was in Hartford when she moved here in 1913. But anyway, I was studying my history book in the watch room when a couple of guys in the company came in and said, "Whatcha doing kid?" I was starting to think that I wasn't going to get any reading done at company 9's because of that one question. I replied, "Reading about the history of the City of Hartford." Well, one of them grabbed the book out of my hands and said, "Let me see that!" The next thing I knew I was in the middle of a fascinating discussion about how Hartford was decades ago. Several of the members of the Department were World War II veterans at that time, so the stories they told would go back sometimes to when they were kids in the 1920's. This I found very entertaining when suddenly, one of them said, "There's the circus fire. The Captain was there." The reader may recall the details of what I wrote about this tragedy in Chapter 2 of this book. However, I'd like to write a few words as a reminder.

On July 6, 1944 the Ringling Brothers and Barnum and Bailey Circus came to the city of Hartford. During the performance, a fire was set. The top of the tent was waterproofed with paraffin wax that was thinned with gasoline, so the fire spread at a rate beyond imagination. More than 167 people were killed.

I was so shocked to hear that Captain Cieri actually responded to the fire, that when I was told "the Captain was there," I responded with "Captain who?" They looked at me like I had lost my mind, and said, "Captain who? The only Captain in the house, Captain Cieri, of course." I rose to my feet and started walking to where the Captain was. One of the men said, "He won't talk about it." I said, "Oh yes he will!" Somehow, I knew he would talk about it with me. As I approached Captain Cieri, he was filling out a

145

report. From the direction I approached him, I could see his entire face. He had a cigar in his mouth, and as I walked up to him I said, "Hey Cap, were you at the circus fire?" He replied with the words, "Yeah, I was there. Worst thing I ever saw." I won't go into detail as to what Captain Cieri said about the events of that day. Some of what he had to say is too graphic or sad to relay to anyone, but it left me with a sense of obligation to those who lost loved ones and to the memory of those who perished. Twelve years later, Captain Cieri, around 400 other people, including members of the Hartford Fire Department, and survivors of the circus fire gathered at the site of the fire to commemorate the 50th anniversary of its occurrence. Just to the west of where the tent stood there is a school named the Fred D. Wish School. Initially, we planned to hold it outside, but the temperature was so hot that we decided to go inside to the auditorium. The temperature was of paramount concern because several of the attendees suffered burns in the fire, so extensive that their bodies could not perspire. High heat would have made matters unbearable for them. Almost as soon as we got started, the air conditioning in the auditorium broke down, so a ladder company was called to the scene to provide ventilation by way of smoke ejectors. One of the members of that ladder company was a man by the name of Jeff Powell who later became a member of the Chaplain Corp of the Hartford Fire Department when I was Chief. The efforts of that company made a huge difference.

Twenty-three years after that conversation with Captain Cieri about the fire, the entire community, including the Hartford Fire Department, turned out for the dedication of a memorial to those who perished. Over 750 people contributed so that a memorial could be built 61 years after the fire. Although it was a solemn occasion, many people said that "it was the last unfinished business related to that tragedy." A committee was formed to accomplish this task, and I've never worked with more dedicated people. So impressed was I with their efforts that I decided to include their names in this book. They are:

Ronald Basto, Kathy Spadda-Basto, Retired Fire Captain William Cieri, Retired Lieutenant Rick Davey, Brad Davis, Honorable Maria Lopez Kirkley-Bey, Don Massey, Antonio Matta, Honorable Kathleen Palm, Nancy Spadda (a survivor), Retired Fire Chief John B. Stewart, Jr., Chief Charles A. Teale, Sr., and Mary Alice Weissenborn.

Everyone on the committee had their motivation for building the memorial. Mine included the victims, their survivors and those firefighters who responded on that day. I cannot imagine how they must have felt, knowing that so many people were lost, and some of them were so very young. If there was a lesson to be learned from this experience it is this "time <u>does not</u> heal all wounds."

Although Captain Cieri helped us to get our start on building the memorial, he died before its completion. His name appears on the memorial along with the rest of us who would not give up the quest to build a final tribute to those who were lost.

Once in a while, I'll take a rope out and tie a bowline behind my back. It reminds me of a man I came to love and respect. He was one of the great ones that I miss every day.

This is Captain Cieri on October 23, 2000, the day I was officially sworn in as Chief of the Hartford Fire Department. I'm sure he was providing me with advice that I surely put to good use. As you can probably tell, I was listening very carefully to him. I always did. In the background of this photo are Assistant Chief Michael A. Parker and Jessilyn Fothergill who later became the Administrative Assistant in my office. Both Assistant Chief Parker and Jessylyn Fothergill were excellent beyond my ability to describe.

Michael A. Parker and me on the day of my promotion to Chief of the Department, October 23, 2000. He was there from the beginning of my administration to the end and was immensely valuable. I told him publicly and I'll say it again, I couldn't have made it without him.

Assistant Chief Parker was also the retired Chief of the West Hartford Fire Department. His experience helped me throughout the ten years that I served as Chief. He even stayed after I retired so that he could help the new Chief, Edward Casares, transition into the position. Chief Parker is officially the only man in the more than 220-year history of the Hartford Fire Department to have served as a chief in West Hartford and Hartford. He is also the last veteran of the Vietnam War to serve as a member of the Hartford Fire Department.

I'll Drive
1983

As a firefighter, it was necessary for me to learn all of the streets in Hartford. Because I was born and raised in the city, I did not expect a problem, but I was assigned to a part of the city that I did not know as well as where I was raised. If I didn't know my streets, my officer would not let me drive the fire truck, and I desperately wanted to do that. Each engine company officer carried a notepad in his shirt pocket. He did this so he could get information from the resident when the company responded to a call. I used to keep a notepad in my shirt pocket too. However, I also kept a list of "things to do" (TTD) in it, and I used it to write down new things that I learned like words and phrases. Well, some of the guys I worked with told me to write down all of the streets I had to learn on that pad. They then told me to study those streets whenever I had a chance to do so. This method worked so well that I decided to apply it to other subjects that I had to study. As technology improved, I found myself writing notes into a smartphone with a notes or memo application. I can honestly say that this system of learning, understanding and remembering information has gotten me through the most difficult exams and professional challenges of my life. What I find most impressive is all you need is a pad that costs around $2.00, and you are on your way to learning information that can literally help you to save lives.

That is why Tool #16 became part of the Tools of Learning.

TOOL #16
Dedicated to the men of Engine Company 1 and Ladder Company 6
Group 1
1983

The more you look at information that is difficult to understand and remember, the easier it will be to learn, understand and remember.

Use Short Periods of Inactivity Wisely

Everyone finds themselves with brief periods of time on their hands and nothing to do with it. Some good examples are waiting for the bus or standing in line at the grocery store. Instead of just waiting, use a pocket-sized note pad or the "notes" or "memo pad" application of your smartphone and write the information you find most difficult to remember in it. Take this information out and study it. <u>You will find the more you look at information that is difficult to learn, understand and remember, the easier it will be to learn, understand and remember it.</u>

When I look back on the times that I spent as a firefighter without supervisory responsibility, I can honestly say that they were the most enjoyable years of my career. I came on the job with a love of history and a love for the Hartford Fire Department. If the reader can recall, I met my first firefighters when I was a small child of 5. I never forgot the kindness they showed me when I was in school and the bravery I saw in them when they responded to emergencies in my neighborhood. Therefore, out of a sense of appreciation for those who served before me, I was compelled to seek higher positions. The higher positions were more fulfilling in some ways, but nothing ever beat the excitement of being a true fireman for the Hartford Fire Department.

After a year of serving in the Department, the guys in my company called me to the kitchen. I wasn't inclined to be among them because I was either studying or working out, but they understood me, and I could sense it. To my complete surprise, there was a cake and some gifts for me. Somehow, the city had forgotten to provide me with a helmet shield. I don't know how this happened, but I went without one for a whole year. Among the gifts they gave me was the first helmet shield of my career. I never forgot that gesture, and I kept the shield. (Department policy states that you turn in your helmet shield when you get transferred. I didn't have to turn mine in when I got transferred because the men, not the city, gave it to me.) This one gesture more than any other served as a reminder to me that no matter how many promotions I got, I still owed the guys. I'd like to remember them now by printing their names along with the a picture of the gift that they gave me.

June 1983
Hartford Fire Department
Group 1
Ladder 6
Captain Lucien Theriault, Ladder Driver Richard Stebbens, Firefighter
Thomas McMahon, Firefighter Jack Doherty, Firefighter Charles Teale.
Engine 1
Lieutenant Al Lawrence, Pump Operator Vern Tyson, Firefighter John
Donahue, Firefighter Richard Yagmin, Firefighter Michael Thomas
My first helmet shield, courtesy of the Brothers.

The next four years were very similar to the first one. I applied myself at work very consistently because I developed a reliance on my Tools of Learning schedule. Essentially, every day started with doing the things that were required of me. I learned while working at the Wadsworth Athenaeum that if you do your work before you are ordered to do so, it doesn't feel like you are being forced to do it, and it feels like you are doing it because you want to. To insure consistency when it came to doing my work, I created a page in my notepad entitled "Things to Do" or TTD, which I mentioned in the previous section. I would start each day by looking at that list and doing what was written on it. Every day began with checking the equipment I was assigned to use at an emergency, interacting with the officers and other company members, housework and special assignments for the day like area surveying (A.K.A. inspections) or training at the Department's drill school. Some may find it surprising that I would include "interacting with other Company members" in my list. This was not only an enjoyable part of my schedule, but it was necessary to let guys know that they were more important to me than my studies. I believe that it is better to be a good fit with a group of employees than it is to be a knowledgeable professional. Besides that, when it comes to being a firefighter, you can never tell who will be in a position to save your life someday. You don't want a bunch of strangers watching your back!

As long as I didn't have an emergency to respond to, housework, company training, or area surveying, I could do whatever I wanted. I knew from past experience that I had to accomplish something every day that I worked (see Tool #2) and that habits were hard to break, so I got into the good habit of using my list of TTD, which included the duties of my position. However, if time permitted, I would study and workout too.

Most of the time I was studying. I actually broke the studying time down into two segments consisting of:

a. Review
b. Learning

In this way, I enhanced my ability to remember the information that I learned. I reviewed the more difficult to remember items more frequently than I did the easy to remember items. This process is part of Tool #18 of the Tools of Learning.

At the conclusion of my first semester at Hartford State Technical College, I knew that I had been doing well because of the grades I received on quizzes and tests. However, because my previous experiences with college were so negative, I still wasn't sure that I would receive a good grade until I received it in the mail. I had aced the course. The following semester I had the same results. I even surprised myself by getting excellent grades in my emergency medical service courses. During this course, I discovered that I had an appreciation for patient care that I did not know I had at all. I started thinking that I could have done well in the medical field if I had chosen that profession instead of the fire service. One day, I woke up in the firehouse and went to the washroom to prepare for the day's events. As I looked at myself in the mirror, I distinctly remember saying, *You finally figured it out. You now know how to succeed in school. With that knowledge, you can become anything you want. Well what is it? Do you want to become a cardiologist or the Chief of the Hartford Fire Department?* After I said these things to myself, I imagined hearing the expression **Grow where you are planted**. I took that to mean that since I was already in the Fire Department, I should work at becoming Chief. That's exactly what I did.

New Berth
1985

Around two and a half years after I became a firefighter, I went to work only to find out that I had been transferred. Initially, I was saddened by this news but suddenly I felt relieved. During those two years a lot of changes had taken place on our shift. Several of the guys, including the officers, were assigned to other houses, and the place didn't feel the same. It's strange to say this, but somehow, I imagined that everyone I started working with would be on the job when I retired. This wasn't practical thinking because some of them had been on the job for 20 years already. Obviously, they would have been retired long before my time came. But the two officers I initially worked with were at the new house that I was assigned to. By this time, I was heavy into the books. I had developed a schedule that would prove to be quite rigid in the sense that as long as I wasn't under orders to do something else, I would be either studying or working out. This left very little time for interacting with the guys, and in the new house they were not as understanding. Sadly, I don't believe I ever developed the same close relationship that I had with the guys at the new house as I did with the guys that I first worked with. I also kept hearing in my mind's ear the words of one of the guys I first started working with by the name of Vern Tyson. It was Vern who upon seeing me study said, "I've seen guys come on the job studying and within six months they weren't even interested in the books." This statement still concerned me. Vern was one of the guys that had been on the job for decades before me so he had seen a lot. I decided to learn from his experience and to remember that complacency was right around the corner if I did not continuously apply myself. So, as I started working in my new house, I became more determined to make professional and academic progress. I never meant any of my new coworkers offense, but I think some of them were not pleased with the amount of time I spent away from them. Sadly, going to the firehouse started to feel like going to any other job. This time, I studied and worked out to get away from everyone else, and I did a lot of both.

The discomfort that I felt in the new house came to a head over my newfound responsibility of driving the fire truck. The truck I drove was a tower ladder and it was 46 feet long. I wasn't the usual driver because someone was permanently assigned to that position. I became the acting driver. However, because I had never driven anything that size, the first few times that I got to practice, I was not good at all. The permanent driver took the opportunity to tell me how bad I was in front of everyone including some firefighters who were working overtime from another house and shift. After he expressed his words of criticism, I turned to him and said, "That's okay. I didn't come on this job to drive; I came on this job to become Chief!"

Eventually, I mastered the ability to drive too. I learn; I just learn slowly.

A Brush with History
1984

My love for history continued, and some of the literature I studied on a daily basis consisted of history. Thanks to all of that reading, the recollections of the men I worked with and some retirees, I was developing a complete awareness about the Hartford Fire Department, and it was happening very, very, fast. I learned about the positive and the negative, but I decided to stay focused on the positive. I did this because I had a great deal of pride in our department, and I simply enjoyed reading more about our accomplishments, than I did our failures. To insure that I could study without distractions, I found a table in the firehouse, and I put it in the locker room. Once the shift began, no one went in there so I had complete solitude. One day, I was in the locker room studying when Dave Whalen, one of the members of the company I was assigned to, walked in. He wasn't there to see me; he was just going to his locker. We struck up a conversation anyhow. As we talked I came to realize that Dave was a third generation member of the Hartford Fire Department. His father and his grandfather came on the job before him. His grandfather joined the department after moving here from Ireland in the 19th century. I had read about these men and the way they professionalized the Hartford Fire Department. The year we had this conversation was 1984, and Dave had been on the job since 1948. Prior to this conversation, Dave and I never talked to one another, but upon hearing that I had a love for the history of the Hartford Fire Department, our relationship changed in an instant. He shared his family history with me, and, as you can imagine, I was fascinated by what I heard. He then said to me, "I'm surprised that you don't go to the Connecticut Historical Society to learn more about this." I replied, "The Connecticut Historical Society? Where is that?" He told me, "One Elizabeth Street. You will know that you are there because there's a big bell on the front lawn." I later came to realize that that bell was the old fire bell that was used to tell firefighters where a fire was. I went there the next day not knowing that I would be starting a relationship that would last for the next 30 years at least. Among the many reasons why I came to appreciate this organization so much are the following:

1. I learned the true and complete history of the Hartford Fire Department there.

2. Whenever I felt discouraged, I could go there and learn about the sacrifices made in the past, so that I could have the career that I had. Reading about their level of commitment inspired me.

3. When I was emotionally devastated by an incident, I could go there and read about men who had suffered much worse. Through the examples of men who had served almost 200 years before me, I learned how to recover from my negative experiences.

I owe a lot to that organization, and, in time, I became a member of its board of trustees. I even had the honor of serving as the board's president for a term. Upon returning from a trip to France, my wife Helaine asked me if France is the best place I had ever been. After giving it careful thought, I looked at her and stated honestly, "My favorite place to be is the Connecticut Historical Society." I meant every word of it.

When I first became Chief of the Hartford Fire Department the second time (I will explain later), I helped coordinate an event through the Connecticut Historical society called "Celebrating Hartford's Heroes." Several hundred members of the Department and retirees attended. It was my major statement to the Department that we were going to pursue a standard of excellence on my watch because we owe it to those who served before us.

And to think it all started with Dave Whalen.

There was one other thing related to my interaction with Dave Whalen that I wanted to share. Although I wasn't one to interact with the guys in my new house, I did eat dinner with them. It was during dinner that I had a conversation with Dave. To get a full sense of how meaningful this conversation was, the reader must also know that Dave Whalen was in the Navy during, and shortly after the Second World War, another group of men whom I have great respect for. One day after dinner, Dave said to me, "When I got off the boat after serving in the Navy, I bought something, and the person I bought it from gave me change with a coin that had a colored guy on it." Dave then asked me, "Have you ever heard of such a coin?" I replied with astonishment, "No, I've never seen or heard of such a coin, but I would love to see it. Can you bring it in?" Dave replied, "Yes, I will." The next day we were scheduled to work, Dave brought the coin to the firehouse. While everyone was having dinner, he displayed it. It had the likeness of Booker T. Washington on the front, and on the back it said, "From Slave Cabin To Hall Of Fame." I had never even heard of such a coin. I've always had a love for this country, and to see that it dedicated a coin to the life of an African American decades ago was simply overwhelming. I looked at Dave and honestly stated, "I have no idea how much this coin is worth but if you ever want to sell it, I'll buy it if I can afford your price. Whatever it is." To me, it wasn't just the coin but the meaning of it. Dave was special. His history with our nation and the Hartford Fire Department was very meaningful to me. Those things coupled with the emotional value of that coin was enough for me to want it for inspirational purposes. Upon hearing my desire for the coin Dave said that he would consider selling it, but in a joking fashion he said, "It's worth a lot of money." I simply told him that I would try to meet his price. I didn't know how much the coin was worth but I was willing to pay what I could for it. I've never been one for material possessions, but this was no material thing. I didn't know what purpose it would serve if I owned it, but I knew that it would serve a practical purpose.

Weeks went by. With all of the guys in attendance, I reminded Dave of my desire to purchase the coin. He replied, "I still don't know how much to charge you for it, but I'm giving it some thought." More time passed by. As we were finishing up a night shift and going home for the next three days, Dave looked at me and said, "Hey Charlie, do you remember that coin that you were interested in?" I replied very excitedly, "Yes." He then flipped the coin across the room in my direction as he said, "Here." I caught it and said, "How much?" He said, "Keep it, it's yours," and then he left. All I could think to say was "Thanks." That coin was with me during all of my promotional exams. It was with me as I graduated from every college or university I attended. It was with me during all of the press conferences I attended, not as a good luck charm but as a source of inspiration. When getting ready to retire as Chief of the Department more than 23 years later, I called Dave Whalen. He had retired many years earlier. As I planned to make my exit, I tried to catch up on all unfinished business. One such business included updating the Department's website which held the photos of all of the Department's retirees. I created this page out of respect for their contributions. Although I had sent a letter to Dave asking him for photos of his father and grandfather, I had not received one. After asking him to send me photos of these men I mentioned the following: "Hey Dave, do you remember that coin that you gave me with Booker T. Washington on it?" He replied, "Yes." I then told him, "I still have it." Dave said, "I know that. That's why I gave it to you."

That's the Dave Whalen I knew.

Among the retirees at the Connecticut Historical Society event was retired Chief John B. Steward, Jr. I used to tell people that during the first 10 years of my career, I did my best to emulate him. His example helped get me to the top of my profession.

Close, but No Cigar
1985

In the fire department where I worked, you had to be on the job for three years before you could take a promotional exam. I studied every day and every night that I worked in anticipation of that day when I would become "eligible" to take my first test. The positions that I would be able to test for included a job called Deputy Chief's Aide. The job had many responsibilities, including relaying the orders of a Deputy Chief to the Captains and the Lieutenants. I thought it would be the perfect next step in my career. I studied with my mind focused on that objective every day for two years, 11 months and one week. As my third-year anniversary approached, I got more and more excited. My studying intensified, particularly the review portion of it. One day while sitting in the kitchen of my apartment, the phone rang. It was one of the firefighters at the firehouse. He was laughing so hard that I could not understand him. In essence he told me that "the test for Deputy Chief's Aide had been announced." I stood straight up. I missed being eligible by three weeks. I was devastated. I felt like my entire career had come to an end, and that someone wanted "me personally" to fail in my quest to become Chief of the Department. I complained to everyone who would listen to me. The next day, I worked, and the hour came when I would usually be studying. However, instead of studying, I sat down to watch a movie. I had decided that I would stop studying and start "enjoying" my time at work more. This idea did not last long. When the movie was over I stood up, and said to myself, *That was a complete waste of time.* I went to my study area and did what had now come naturally. I hit the books. I haven't stopped since. Apparently, habits, both good and bad, are hard to break.

The TEE's
1986

During the first couple of years after I became a firefighter, I maintained my part-time job as the superintendent of the housing complex that I lived in. It was still providing me with a rent-free apartment and a salary. However, it was not possible for me to continue in the position because sometimes I had to be in the firehouse when I should have been available for the tenants. Although I still felt that I needed to supplement my income with a part-time job, I knew it was time to get a different one.

In addition to getting an education at Hartford State Technical College, which raised my level of education, I also took courses to raise my level of training at the Connecticut State Fire School in Meriden, Connecticut. This organization now exists under the name Connecticut Fire Academy, and it is now located in Windsor Locks, Connecticut. My goal was to become a State Certified Instructor at the school. During one of the classes I took there, one of the instructors by the name of Ed Amatrudo asked the class, "When you have 20 years on the job, will you have 20 years of experience or one year of experience 20 times?" He went on to explain that just because you have more time on the job does not mean that you are more knowledgeable or capable. With that question in mind, I began documenting everything I learned at the calls that I responded to. That way, I could review what I learned and grow from my experiences. In rotating fashion, I was working on my training, education and experience (the TEE's). Working toward my Instructor Certification also introduced me to administrators like Wayne Sanford and Jeff Morrisette. They provided me with the direction I needed so that one day I would become a State Certified Instructor. One semester, I did not go to college. However, during that semester I took a course at Hartford Hospital to become an Emergency Medical Technician (EMT). Upon passing that certification, I started working as an EMT for one of the local ambulance companies. Although the experience of responding to medical calls was beneficial, I lasted only a year because I had completed the training necessary to become a State Certified Instructor for the Connecticut State Fire School. I applied, and I was hired as an Instructor. It now became my responsibility to teach what I had learned so far, statewide.

MCC
1990

My efforts to acquire an associate's degree continued. At one point, I needed a literature course to finish up. However, that course was not scheduled to be given at Hartford State Technical College for quite some time. I spoke with my advisor about the matter, and she said, "You may go to another college, take a literature course there and transfer the credits into this school." I took her advice, and the next thing I knew, I was attending classes at Manchester Community College. I had taken a few courses there around 12 years earlier, and I failed them all. I was depending on the Tools of Learning to get me through this time. The school was great! Teachers and students were very friendly, and I could have made it my permanent school if I needed more credits, but all I needed was three. As class began, I quickly came to realize that I was the only person from Hartford in the room.

For me, this created a type of pressure that some people can relate to. I had to excel. If I did not, I thought that people would think people from Hartford are not that smart. My past failures started to haunt me.

In spite of all my concerns, I completed the course with an A. The Tools of Learning made my return a huge success. I felt redeemed.

The Home Stretch
1987

During this time, I read the most current information related to my profession. Some of it was printed in a newsletter that included a story about General Julius W. Becton. General Becton was the head of the Federal Emergency Management Agency (FEMA). I wanted to know what it took to receive such a high public safety office. I also wanted to know what it took to be respected in that position. The article explained it in this fashion: "technical knowledge, human relations skill, and economic development ability." That means that if you are to be a truly respected public safety administrator, you have to know your profession (training), know how to interact with people from all walks of life (human relations skills), and you had to know how to handle large sums of money (economics). Since the first letters of each word spell THE, I created an acronym that was unforgettable. That was important because it was to direct my educational pursuits for the next 13 years. I named it "the education triangle".

After my brief encounter with indolence and apathy, I got busy preparing for the next promotional exam. With five years on the job, I would be eligible to take the lieutenant's test. It seemed like too much to hope for. After all, the last test was announced just three weeks before I was eligible. What if it happened again? Would I once again be laughed at because I had prepared so hard for a test that I would not be able to take? It never once escaped my notice that half of the guys in the department were just as smart as I was and the other half were smarter. How was I going to get a better grade than them on the test? Then it dawned on me that many people half-heartedly apply themselves because they have no guarantee of succeeding after they have given so much effort. That's why they don't give it their all. If I applied the Tools of Learning and gave it my all, my chances would be excellent. So, I started studying even more hours than before. At one point, I was bringing books into the firehouse in milk crates because there were too many to carry in my hands alone. I did this through the back of the firehouse when no one was around because I knew the ridicule I would face from those who thought my actions to be foolish. One day, one of the guys saw me executing my book transfer system. He looked at me and said, "When you flunk that lieutenant's test I'm going to buy you a rope because you're going to want to hang yourself after doing all that studying." I told him, "Keep your rope because I'm passing that test." I didn't say that I was going to get promoted. That would have been cocky.

I watched the bulletin board where promotional exams were posted almost hourly. I knew it was coming because the vacancies in the position of Lieutenant were mounting. Four vacancies is a cause for concern but we had over 10. I kept studying. On the day that I became eligible to take the lieutenant's test, I held a private celebration and I celebrated by increasing my study schedule. Shortly after my fifth year anniversary, the position of Lieutenant in the Firefighting Division was announced. I don't know if I can describe how focused I was. By this time in my career, I was studying the words of "the Dean of Self Improvement" Earl Nightingale who is probably best known for saying, "Successful people come in all ages shapes sizes and colors, but they all have one thing in common, a winning attitude." I decided to put this and all of the other things I had learned from Earl to practical use. This was also when I worked part-time as an instructor for the Connecticut State Fire School. I appreciated the job very much because I knew if I could teach those subjects, I must know the information well. However, in preparation for the lieutenant's test, I stopped doing everything but my job with the Hartford Fire Department, so that I could have more time to study. I even stopped exercising, which in hindsight was not a good idea. By this time I had mastered the Tools of Learning and was using it exactly as written. I figured if this system could get me through my training program as number one in my class of 27 people, and help me pass college courses that I once failed, it could help me pass the lieutenant's exam.

While studying, there were some subjects that were fairly easy to remember, and then there were those that were close to impossible to remember. To review those subjects that I found difficult to remember, I would use a system of highlighting the information. This system went like this: I estimated that just 10 percent of all the information that I studied was something I could actually use for doing my job or passing an exam. So, whenever I read information that fell into either one of these categories, I would highlight the information, not with a highlighter but with a pencil. I would use either a hash mark, an asterisk, or a series of asterisks. If a statement had an asterisk next to it, it was either very important or very difficult to remember. Some statements had several asterisks next to them. This meant that the information was important or difficult enough for me to review more frequently than the other highlighted statements. Every day that I studied, I would start out with an asterisk review, or a review of those statements with asterisks next to it. I would do this for 15 minutes, and then I would review the other statements for an equal amount of time. Then I would study the new information. This system worked very well because after you review essential information, it strengthens your foundational knowledge. When your foundation is strong, it becomes easier to learn new information. Eventually, information that was difficult for me to remember became as easy to recall as anything else. In 28 years, I only came across one statement that warranted five asterisks. Although I haven not reviewed that statement for 27 years, I can still recite it verbatim. This system led to the development of Tool #18:

TOOL #18
Dedicated to the Effort I Put into Preparing for my First Promotional Exam
1985

Organizing

Information that has been learned and understood, must be organized according to subject and date to help insure long term retention

"Repetition is the mother of retention."   — Old expression

Short Term:
Sometimes the number of books we have to read during a semester is so great that by the time we finish reading the end of one book, we will have forgotten what we read in the beginning of the same book.
We must organize the information we have learned but find difficult to remember, even if it is for extended periods of time. This can be done in the following fashion:

1. Using a pencil, highlight the information that you think is very important or is difficult to remember as you read. Use a consistent system like:
a. Place a hash mark next to important sentences
b. Underline important words and phrases
c. Place brackets around important paragraphs

d. Place the letters "V.I.P." (which stands for Very Important Page) at the top of pages that must be reviewed entirely

e. Use asterisks for those sentences, paragraphs and pages that are vitally important or extremely difficult to remember

2. Review the highlighted sections of important and difficult to remember information that you have read for about 15 minutes. Notes that were taken during a class (see Tool #11) must be reviewed during this time too. Review those notes that are of the same subject as the highlighted sections of the book you are reading. This simply means that if you are reviewing sections of a book on the different parts of speech, for example, then you should review your notes on the different parts of speech. In order for us to review our notes at the same time that we review highlighted portions of books that we have read, we must write at the top of our notes the subject covered.

3. If you are still having problems remembering those sections with asterisks next to them, use Tool #16 and place the information next to the asterisk in a small notebook or electronic device. Look at that information as frequently as necessary until it is as easy to remember as the ABC's.

4. Once you have mastered the information and feel it is no longer necessary for you to review it, erase or cross out the highlight. Once again, erasing will be possible if you highlighted with a pencil.

5. Math is best learned and reviewed in order, from the foundational level to the advanced level. However, some subjects can be learned and reviewed with no regard for order. An example of this would be famous sayings. If you place an asterisk next to those sayings that are vitally important or extremely difficult to remember, you can take extra time to review those sayings in any order you'd like, before you do a basic review.

6. After you have reviewed information in a book or in your notes, put the date when you last reviewed that section on the page. That way, you will be able to tell where you left off the last time you reviewed. The following method works: L.O. 5/29/15. This will tell you that you left off on this particular page May 29, 2015. The next time you review, this is where you will begin. In that way, eventually, you will review all of the information that you know you must review.

Long Term:
Studies show that as of 2013, adult education students who passed the general educational development (GED) exam were capable of passing a test that more than 40 percent of high school graduates could not pass. Although statistics regarding the new test implemented in 2014 were not available as of this printing, I strongly believe that that 40 percent figure will be greater now. This means that students who pass the GED exam are in an ideal position to be successful college students. The problem is that many of those very same students will assume that they no longer have to study the information that helped them pass the GED exam in the first place. Throwing away information that helped us to succeed is a formula for failure. Once this is done, we have made an error that can decrease our ability to succeed at the next level. It's like giving away a very dependable car that we need to get to work. A continued review of the information necessary to pass the GED exam is necessary until that information is mastered. That information that helped you to pass your test (s) -- the books, notes and handouts -- all must be organized by subject and date so that they can be reviewed as often as necessary.

The Home Stretch (Continued)
1987

I calculated how many hours per day I was studying, and it varied depending on whether I was scheduled to work in the firehouse that day or not. On my days off, I averaged 16 hours per day. I would wake up, start studying, eat breakfast, study, eat lunch, study, eat dinner, study and then go to bed.

As the test day drew near, I found myself wishing for just three more weeks. When the test was announced, a list of the books used to create the test was given to every applicant. If you waited to see that list before you started studying, you waited too long to pass the test with an excellent score. Although I had read most of the books that were on the list already, I had not read all of the books that were on the list. However, test day was coming and I was going to have to take it without mastering that set of information. During this time, my children Kathleen and Charlie were excellent. They seemed to understand how important this promotion was to me. During all of the professional and academic transitions I experienced, I never forgot that the reason why I chose to run into burning buildings for a living was to provide for my children. I thought becoming a Lieutenant would help me to improve in that area of my life. Unfortunately, my wife and I were growing apart.

I didn't have to wait very long before I actually found myself in a chair with the exam in front of me. Over 250 men showed up to take the test. I had two items with me for inspiration, a watch that my uncle Manuel Pina used to wear, and the coin Dave Whalen gave to me. My Uncle Mal had been deceased for several years, but I somehow, inherited his watch. I used his watch because of the incredible knowledge of history he had and that he would share that history with my brother Rocky and me. I can still remember him saying something related to history, and when we were shocked to hear it, he would say, "You didn't know that?" I used the coin given to me by Dave Whalen because it reminded me of two things: Dave's family history in the Department (which I found inspiring) and the accomplishments of Booker T. Washington. When the test moderator announced that it was time to begin, I checked my Uncle Mal's watch, and I placed the coin I got from Dave sharply on the desk I was sitting at. I took the time to realize how important that moment was, and I got so nervous that I had to remind myself that I had an excellent job and that if this didn't work out for me, then I would be just fine where I was. Otherwise, I would have been too nervous to proceed.

In time, I received my written examination score. I received the highest score of anyone of my rank. Only one person scored higher than me, and he was already a Lieutenant in the Training Division. It was Kevin Sullivan, the man everyone in my first firehouse thought would someday become Chief of the Department. Throughout my career, I could depend on scoring number one as long as he was not taking the test. However, when he scored higher than I did, I was proud of him because I know he must have worked very hard.

The overall testing process consisted of more than just a written exam. Like most fire department exams, there was an oral interview too. I spent more time preparing for the oral examination than I did for the written exam because I knew that an oral exam was very subjective. No matter how good you are, one of the evaluators may misunderstand your answer and give you a bad score. I used my system of learning methodology to memorize long definitions so when questions were asked of me I could answer them word for word. I can still remember the look of shock in the eyes of one of the evaluators as the question was asked, "What is your definition of the term 'size up'?" As I pretended to ponder the question, I took a breath and answered the following:

"To understand the term 'size up', you have to know that the safe, effective, efficient protection of a community from hazardous processes or conditions is a continuous cycle of strategy development, tactics implementation and evaluation. Strategy development is the creation of written policies defining fire department deployment procedures, tactics implementation consists of the application of resources which uses existing strategies to meet fire ground objectives, and evaluation is synonymous with the term size up. Simply stated, size up is your estimation of the situation which determines your course of action."

That's a quote from the International Fire Service and Training Association. This is the organization that published most of the books we had to study for promotional exams. It has been almost 28 years since that test, and I can remember my answer verbatim because it is in a portion of my brain called the neocortex. The neocortex is where all of our long-term memory is stored. That's why we can recite the ABC's or the Pledge of Allegiance without practice. When I gave that answer, it also proved that I did not cheat to pass the test. Oral interview test questions are put together a short time before the actual test is given. No one that I know could have prepared me to answer that question, that definitively, in less than a month. I knew I had aced that oral examination the second I saw the look of astonishment in the eyes of the evaluators. After all, if I was wrong, then the book was wrong.

Chapter 14

New Lieutenant
1987

In a few weeks the results were out. We all received our ranking in the mail. I had not come out number one but number four overall because I had only a few months of seniority points to add to the overall score. Fortunately, I had been in school, so I had points to add for courses taken. I was elated. Chief Stewart decided to promote 16 people to the rank of Lieutenant. I was not sure he would promote me because I had only five years on the job. Most of the men who were promoted had closer to 20 years instead of five. I felt like a child among men, but I took my promotion with pride. I became the person with the least amount of seniority in the history of the Department to make Lieutenant.

Here I am seated next to Anthony Milner. He and I were promoted to Lieutenant together. When I served as Chief of the Department, he was one of my Assistant Chiefs. His contributions to my administration were so significant that when the mayor directed me to give him the names of three people who should be considered for the position of Chief, I could only come up with two. Anthony Milner was one of those two.

Here I am with Kathleen and Charlie on the day of my promotion to Lieutenant, November, 1987. I really miss them at that age. Fortunately, they became even better adults.

Here I am with my first officer, Captain Lucien Theriault. If I wrote all of the things that he did to insure my success, this book would be 25 pages longer. He covered all of the bases, including: getting me started in college a third time, telling me how to act like a leader before I became one, and telling me how to get important things done on the fireground while looking after my own safety.

Although the day was filled with great joy, that joy would not last for long. As I would do time and time again, I had accepted a job with a lot of responsibility and not everyone would be happy for me.

It started almost immediately. Although I had many friends and family who were proud of my accomplishments, there were those who now despised me. As I tried to look at my success from the perspective of others, I came to realize that the more I succeeded, the worse some of those who could not succeed must feel. There wasn't a day that went by when I didn't sense their displeasure with me. I came to realize that if you are willing to work hard there are only two ways that someone can make themselves look as good as you do: they can work as hard as you do or they can tear you down. (More on that later.) I can't count the number of people who chose to do the latter. I just kept hearing from supporters, "Watch your back." It was a refrain that I would hear until I established myself as Chief of the Department. After that point, everyone came to realize that I was not the kind of person who you wanted to try and harm professionally. I had come too far, and a professional attack was always met with nothing short of retaliation. If I did not get even, eventually they would mistake kindness for weakness, and a weak person cannot lead. By the way, the best way to get even is to get ahead. To me, that meant getting a college degree to go with my new promotion. This line of thinking began when I served in my newfound capacity of Lieutenant. As I look back on that time, I now realize that it was too much. If I had relaxed during this time, and not been so much on the defensive, I would be able to look back on it with a sense of fondness, but that was not how it was. One particular incident more than any other summarized the entire experience.

I was tending to my duties, which included office work, when one of the men in my company shared with the others present that he didn't think that a person with five years on the job should be a lieutenant. He thought that the minimum amount of time should have been 10 years. Since this man had more than 20 years on the job, I took this to mean that he should have been promoted instead of me. I immediately took offense. Since I expected challenges to my expertise, I studied everything related to this man's job, including the fire truck he had been driving for several years. In reply to his statement about it being too soon for me to serve as a lieutenant, I said, "I don't think it should be a matter of time on the job but what you have done with that time. If a person knows more, then he should be promoted." To this the man said, "If you have been on the job longer, then you know more."

This is exactly what I wanted to hear. I then said, "The fire truck you have been driving is something that is new to me, but if we take out the specifications regarding it, and both of us had to answer questions about it, I will give you a dollar for every question I get wrong if you give me a dollar for every question you get wrong. By the end of the day, I will own all of the money you earned this week." Once I said this the man looked deflated. I could have made my point without offending him or diminishing the sense of pride he had in the job, but I didn't. The next thing I knew, he had requested a transfer and was working at another house. His replacement was a great improvement, but I have always felt badly about the way I treated this man and many of the people I interacted with during that time period. During the Company Officer training that I received when I was promoted to Lieutenant, there was a psychologist present who informed us that stress creates a chemical change in the body and the brain. Although I didn't know it, I was suffering from stress that caused me to make many bad decisions about how to treat others. That included treating people harshly when another form of treatment would have sufficed. However, I got along well with everyone on my shift and in my firehouse.

These are the members of my first company. The firefighter who said that a person should have at least 10 years on the job before becoming a lieutenant had transferred to another house by the time this photo was taken. The names of those present are, L to R: myself, Pete Hennigan, Eddie Kureczka (on the truck) and Al Russo. Not present in this photo is Firefighter Vincent Graves. Tragically, we lost both Pete and Eddie when I was Chief of the Department.

These are firefighters Michael Booker (L) and Eugene Cieri (R). When I got hired, I sent Mike a case of Heineken Beer because he was the one who told me about Plan B Incorporated, the organization that prepared me to take the written exam. A few years after this photo was taken, Mike was dead.

Eugene Cieri is the son of Captain Bill Cieri, the man who responded to the Circus Fire. Eugene became my Executive Officer when I was Chief, and he literally created a mobile data computer system that received an international award. He retired as a Deputy Chief.

Throughout it all, I maintained my focus on the learning experience. Something deep inside of me kept saying, "Keep going," instead of what I used to hear: "Quit before they fire you." I'm sure it was the words of Mr. Hurley, the pain of losing a job due to bad grades, moving in with my in-laws or the depression that followed, but I knew that I didn't want to ever quit when it came to my education again. Even when learning seemed impossible, the Tools of Learning made it inevitable. At one point, I was scheduled to take a computer course called B.A.S.I.C., which stands for Beginners All-Purpose Symbolic Instructional Code. I had no idea what I was doing. To make matters even worse, every student in the class was given a password so that they could access the schools computer and practice what we had learned in class. For some reason, I didn't receive my password until three weeks after the rest of the class did. I knew the teacher, and my children would go swimming where he worked during the summer. Our relationship was always friendly, and it frustrated me that he would let me go so long without a password. However, the day came when I got one, and when I gained access to the schools computer, it was like it landed on Earth from Mars. I was totally lost. I went to my advisor to determine what I should do. At this point I was seriously considering dropping the course because I was so far behind the rest of the class. I also, wanted to master the information because I sensed that computers would someday be important to the fire service. My advisor informed me that perhaps I should try using a tutor to get caught up. My first response to this statement was, "I can't afford a tutor." Her response was, "Tutors are free of charge to college students." I couldn't believe what she was saying. If I had known that when I first went to college, I would have at least tried using a tutor. Perhaps that alone could have prevented failing all of those courses. By this time, I had struggled with a few of my math courses, and if I had known that I could have received a tutor free of charge, I would have gotten one then too. I took my advisor's advice and got a tutor. I never mastered the computer course (meaning I didn't get an A in it) but I did pass it with a B.

Tutor Teale
Summer 1982

My first attempt at tutoring someone came when a friend of mine was in drill school with me. He was having a very difficult time keeping his grades up, and I knew nothing about it. Then, one Friday, he told me that he had been warned. He was told by the administration that if he failed one more test, he would be dismissed from the program. We were scheduled to take a test in three days, so I told him, "Let's get together and study Saturday and Sunday. That way you will be ready on Monday." He told me that he had something urgent to do on Sunday and could only make it on Saturday. So, we studied for eleven and one half hours on the only day he had available. After he took the test on Monday, he had a meeting with the administration. He needed a 70 but scored in the high 60's. He was fired. As I think back on this experience, the reasons for his failure were obvious.

1. He failed to set priorities. Unless it was an emergency, he should have made himself available that Sunday.

2. He waited too long before he got a tutor. A tutor is not a miracle worker. It takes time to learn some subjects. One day will not do.

TOOL #6
Dedicated to my mother, Francisca L. Smith, and my struggles with B.A.S.I.C.
1987

Expecting trouble? Get a tutor before the course begins!

Get a Tutor

Thousands of years ago, one of the many responsibilities of a tutor included accompanying a student to school. Well, in a figurative sense, that still is the purpose of a tutor today. A tutor does not literally accompany the student to school but he or she figuratively brings that student to a place where he or she can learn, understand and remember information.

College teachers must assume that a student arrives in the classroom with a certain amount of knowledge. They seldom have time to make an assessment of each student's level of knowledge individually. However, some students do come to the classroom with a lack of some of the basics. Unless you received a score of 100 percent on each test that you had to take in your previous coursework, you probably lack some of the basics necessary to master the next level of study. That means that there are holes in your foundation. A tutor can make an assessment of a person's specific level of knowledge and teach that student the basics they somehow missed but should have learned. Then the student can get caught up with the rest of the class.

The methods used by the tutor vary from person to person but the Tools of Learning can be utilized to accomplish this task.

When the tutor has done his/her job correctly, then the teacher can teach the student the new information that the rest of the class is learning.

Also:

Many college students won't get a tutor because they think they cannot afford one. Well, many colleges provide tutors free of charge. Therefore, if you feel as though you will need one, get a tutor ASAP. This is particularly true if you think you are going to have a real difficult time with a course. If that is the case, get a tutor before the course begins. In that way you are more likely to get a good grade on your first exam, instead of failing your first exam. This will eliminate trying to work your way out of a hole in a difficult subject.

A Meeting with the Dean
1987

My quest to master my academic and professional goals took many forms. I knew that if I was to succeed in getting the position that I wanted, I would have to make sacrifices. I gave up watching television so that I could find more time for studying. I also chose not to buy a car. This meant that I had more money to pay for courses that I wanted to take. Therefore, I found myself trying to get to work and school via bus or walking. At this time, work was at a firehouse named Company 2's which stands at the corner of Main and Belden Street in Hartford, Connecticut. On my days off, I would also visit the gym which was around three miles from where I was working at the time. On this particular day, I really needed some exercise so I walked to the gym. As I walked, I listened to a tape that was sent to me in the mail. The tape was entitled *The Essence of Success*, and it had the teachings of Earl Nightingale on it. As I walked, I listened to this tape. Anyone who knows Hartford knows Scarborough Street and the beautiful homes that are three blocks to the west of that street: Terry Road, Westerly Terrace and Prospect Avenue. I had had an appreciation for these homes since the age of 11. While listening to this tape, the words of Earl Nightingale with his booming voice said, "Successful people come in all ages, shapes, sizes, and colors, but they all have one thing in common; a winning attitude." These words hit me so hard that I literally stopped in mid-stride. I then played these words over and over until I looked up at the house that I was standing in front of. It is easily one of the largest homes in Hartford, and it has a beautiful black and gold gate. I found myself asking, "Do the people here have a winning attitude? They are obviously very successful." I said this every time I arrived at another house. By the time I got to a house that was once occupied by the world-renowned former director of the Wadsworth Athenaeum, Arthur Everett "Chick" Austin, Jr., I came to realize that it was true. Successful people do come in all ages, shapes, sizes, and colors, and they do have one thing in common: a winning attitude. I was so impressed with this revelation that I decided to purchase the rest of the tape set. I also received as a gift, Earl Nightingale's book by the same title. Within these tapes and the book, I found the inspiration for Tools #8 and #9. My interpretation of what Earl shared with the world is found in the following Tools:

TOOL #8
Dedicated to Earl Nightingale and Rudyard Kipling
1987

There is no such thing as a passive learning environment.

Ask Questions

The poet and author Rudyard Kipling once wrote:

I Keep six honest serving-men

(They taught me all I knew);

Their names are What and Where and When

And Why and How and Who.

If you are going to stay alert and learn in a classroom, you must ask questions. There are only two types of students who don't, they are:

1. Those students who know all the answers. (If they know all of the answers, then why are they students?)

2. Those students who don't understand anything that is being presented by the teacher and are afraid to let anyone know that they don't understand the information.

If you don't understand something your teacher is presenting, then there is a good chance that other people in your classroom don't understand it either. Unfortunately, when some of us don't understand something we start thinking to ourselves, *I'm the only person here who doesn't get this. This is embarrassing.* This line of thinking only makes matters worse because you are now thinking these negative thoughts when you should be <u>focusing</u> on what the teacher is saying. This creates anxiety, and anxiety is the number one reason why we find it difficult to learn. Also, while you are thinking these negative thoughts, your teacher could be saying something that would clarify everything. Therefore, don't be afraid to tell your teacher if you don't understand something. When you tell the teacher, "I still don't understand it," someone else in the classroom is probably saying to himself or herself, *I'm sure glad he/she said that because I don't get it either.* Maybe now the teacher will discuss it in greater detail so that we <u>all</u> can understand it." Also, when you ask questions in the classroom, you are telling your teacher that you "value" the information, or that you see the importance of the information so much that you are asking for help understanding the information. If you don't ask questions, your teacher won't know if you are paying attention or just pretending to listen while you think of something else.

If you find yourself not understanding anything that the teacher is presenting, don't give up. Take action by consulting with your teacher during class or after school. Usually, consulting with your teacher is all that is required. However, you may need some additional help, like a tutor, to keep yourself from failing the course. (See Tool #6.)

This does not mean that a student should constantly ask questions that the student <u>should</u> know the answer to. If a person asks questions that they should know the answer to, it shows a lack of the prerequisite knowledge they should have before taking the course. An example of this would be someone who did not do their homework. Also, it shows a lack of initiative if a person keeps asking questions related to definitions. In other words, although you want to ask questions, you cannot keep asking your teacher, "What does that mean?" For the way to address this challenge, see Tool #4.

I have an experience with this concept I'd like to share with you. While working on my master's degree I took a math course called Quantitative Analysis. During this course, I sat next to a student whose major was engineering. His father was also an engineer. Engineering students are usually excellent at math, so he did not expect to have any problems with the course. Whenever the teacher would present a problem that was too difficult for us to understand, he wouldn't ask questions. Instead, he would say, "My father is an engineer. I'll ask him how to do this when I get home." One day we got our midterm exams back. I got a B and he got an F. In fact he got a 40. Also, by the end of the semester, half of the class had dropped the course. None of those who dropped the course asked questions. I thought that they did not ask questions because the course was easy for them. This taught me that some people in the classroom don't understand the information, but won't ask questions because they are too proud or afraid to look like they aren't as smart as the other students. Those students who learned from experience the value of asking questions eventually learned. But they learned from experience, a very expensive teacher. Students of the Tools of Learning don't have to learn from personal experience. They have the experience of this author to rely on.

TOOL #9
Dedicated to the Chinese and Earl Nightingale who said that, "Visualization is the most powerful learning tool in the world." 1987

To help insure understanding, you should visualize a classroom with you teaching the information you want to learn.

Be the Teacher

To examine your ability to understand a particular concept, use the art of visualization to imagine a person or group of people listening to you explain the information you are assigned to learn. Can you explain it to them adequately? If not, you probably lack a total understanding of the information.

The theory behind Tool #9 is best expressed in the ancient Chinese proverb, which says: "The best way to learn is to teach."

One of the most difficult courses that I have ever taken included the subject trigonometry. It was over 25 years ago, but I can still sense the fear my fellow students and I felt when we saw our instructor, Mr. Howard, walking toward our classroom. He was a very tall man and he always wore a bow tie. As he explained the homework we were assigned to do, he would frequently exclaim, "There are many roads leading to New York." This was his way of telling us that there were sometimes several ways to get to the right answer in a problem. I never expressed this verbally, but every time he said, "There are many roads leading to New York," I would think to myself, *Please just give us one road because by discussing all of them, you are confusing the heck out of me.* This course was so challenging that one night, I started doing my homework at 9:30 pm, and I didn't finish it until the sun came up. I had not developed the foundational knowledge necessary to pass that course, but because of the following, I did pass it.

TOOL #12
Dedicated to my study of trigonometry at Hartford State Technical College
1990

You should do difficult homework assignments ASAP after you rewrite you notes

Complete Quickly

If you do your homework, a teacher will review the easier to understand information during the beginning of a class, and then cover the newer, more advanced and therefore more difficult to understand information during the class's closing minutes.

Sometimes, this means that a student did not spend enough time on the new information to totally understand it. The best thing to do when this happens, is to bring your books and notes to a study area as soon as possible and try to enhance your understanding of this information. The longer you wait to do your homework, the more difficult it will be to finish it. Do your homework ASAP after you rewrite your notes, and then review your homework until class begins. Show up for class early. If you are on time, you are late; if you are 20 minutes early, you are on time. When you get there 20 minutes early, do a last minute review before the class begins. Mathematical concepts commonly create this type of situation, and when they do, you must also solve as many of the problems as necessary until you feel capable of completing this assignment.

Chapter 15

Serving as a lieutenant in charge of my own company was as stressful as it was rewarding. At one factory fire, my company was ordered to cut a hole in the roof to release the smoke and heat from the building. This makes interior operations safer. Thanks to a book I read on firefighting tactics by Emanuel Fried, I always brought a roof ladder to the roof even when the roof was flat. As two men carried the ladder, two other men walked ahead of it. As we walked across the roof, one of the members walking ahead of the ladder fell halfway through the roof. Fortunately, he had the presence of mind to hold his arms out to the side so that he didn't go through it completely. If we had run over to help him out without that roof ladder, we would have all fallen through. However, we slid the ladder over to where he was, walked along the ladder (which distributed our weight over a wider area) and pulled him out of that hole. As he waited for us to get him, all I could see were the faces of his wife and children. I thought to myself, *How am I going to look them in the eye and tell them that their loved one is not coming home ever again?* I was a courageous (and sometimes reckless) firefighter, but supervising firefighters was much different. I was extremely concerned about the safety of the members of my company. Just how different supervising firefighters was came to light on that day. I decided to make a change in careers. I was heading for the Training Division. Although I would still be a lieutenant, it was in another division. So, I would have to take another promotional exam. Using the Tools of Learning, I came out number one.

The head of the Training Division at that time was a man by the name of Tommy Williams, and he was the Deputy Chief of Training. Chief Williams was the Captain of Training when I went through drill school as a recruit. He was the officer whose words inspired the entire section in the Tools of Learning on what it takes to understand information. He was a huge supporter of me and of my career, so I looked forward to working for him as a lieutenant. There was one major problem. Chief Williams was diagnosed with cancer, and due to his illness, I didn't get a chance to interact with him very much. However, I did get to see him sparingly while assigned to his division. I started out just before a new group of firefighters arrived. I was going to help train a group of recruits and I could not have been more excited.

The Tools of Learning Debut
1989

Just before the arrival of the new recruits, the Chief of the Department, John B. Stewart, Jr., called a meeting with the members of the Training Division Staff and some representatives of an insurance company's human resource department. Chief Stewart was concerned that so many recruits had been terminated in the past due to bad grades. As we met, ideas were exchanged about how to address this problem. Suddenly one of the insurance representatives said, "We have the answer to your problem. Lower your standards. Your tests are too difficult, make them easier." The members of the Training Division staff were stunned when we heard that. We knew that if we lowered our standards and somebody got hurt because they were not properly trained, we would be to blame. Our group was at an impasse. Due to his illness, Chief Williams delegated the responsibility of attending this meeting to his Captain of Training, John Chemiliewski, and his Lieutenant of Training, Bobby Williams. The two men and I left not sure what would become of this matter. That night, while lying awake in my bed, I heard the words, "What about this?" I then sat up and envisioned myself teaching the new recruits my system of learning methodology called the Tools of Learning. Since it had worked for me throughout my training program and on a promotional exam, why wouldn't it work for the new recruits?

The next day, I shared my idea with the Captain of Training, and in time, I received permission to present my information. It would be the first presentation of this information I ever gave to anyone. I had 30 minutes to talk about something that I knew should take three times as long, but I was excited to be sharing it at all. I wrote out the various Tools in the form of a National Fire Protection Association lesson plan and prepared to present it. It was the first subject the new recruits received. **That's the way it should be done!** At the end of their training program their grades were so good that no one was dismissed due to bad grades. In fact, they had the highest average on record, 85 percent. So good was their average that I was ordered by Captain Chemielewski to obtain in writing why they did so well. Overwhelmingly the answer they gave was, "It was the system of learning methodology that Lieutenant Teale taught us." One recruit even wrote, "If I had learned this in high school, I would have gone on to college."

I knew I had a winner, but those words confirmed it!

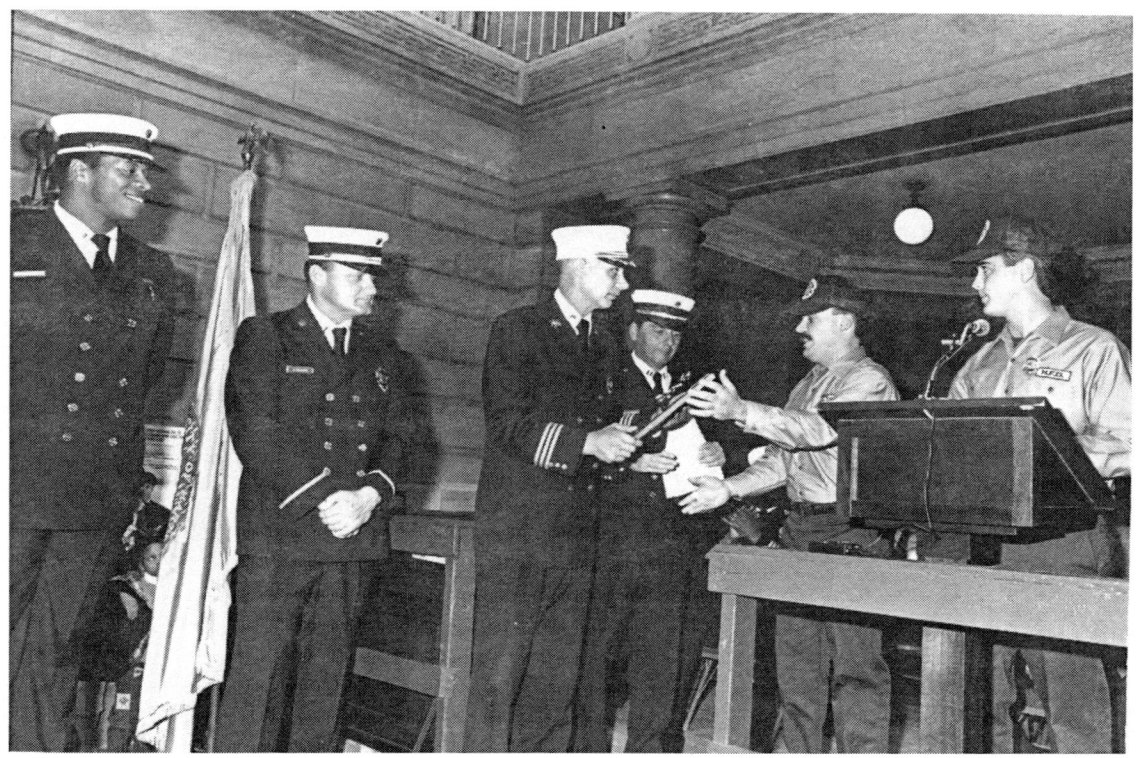

Here is Deputy Chief of Training Tommy Williams (center) in 1990 receiving a plaque from probationary firefighters Brian Buckley (left) and Daniel Kolavage (right) at their graduation ceremony. The other personnel are (from right to left) Captain John Chemiewlewski, Lieutenant Robert Williams and me.

Farewell Chief Williams
1990

Shortly after the graduation ceremony of the class of 1990, the health of the Deputy Chief of Training, Tommy Williams, worsened. He had been a constant source of encouragement to me for years. I even heard him say great things about me when he didn't think I was listening. His contribution to my career and the Hartford Fire Department would have been enough, but his contribution to the Tools of Learning has benefitted everyone who has listened to one of my presentations. I truly believe that people will continue to benefit from this dedicated man of the fire service for many years to come, and I never fail to mention him when I get to the section on "understanding." He had the potential to become Chief of the Hartford Fire Department and much, much more, but one day we received tragic news. Deputy Chief of Training Tommy Williams had died. He was just 49 years old.

My time in the Training Division was not long after that, approximately one year. Soon, I received word that my job as a Lieutenant in the Training Division would be unfunded. Although this news did not come from a superior in the fire department, it was from a reliable source. I began to think about going back on the line, working in the firehouse again. If I requested the house that I wanted at that time, I had a good chance of getting it. However, if I waited until the position was unfunded, and I was sent back, I could be assigned to a very uncomfortable house and shift. I decided to go back and get the house and shift that I wanted. The house that I was sent to was different from the one that I left, and it was considered a slower house. To the younger members of the Department, that was a bad thing, but to me, it meant that I could find time to do more of what I wanted to do while I was at work. Since I was about to finish my associate's degree, and had plans to obtain a bachelor's degree, I decided that I would put all of the time I could find into getting an education.

In the year 1991, I graduated from Hartford State Technical College with an associate degree in Fire Technology. I had been working for nine years on that degree. Sometimes I took just one course per semester because I was also working full-time as a firefighter, and part-time as either the superintendent of my housing complex, emergency medical technician, or instructor for the Connecticut State Fire School. I even took additional classes through the Commission on Fire Prevention and Control, which made it possible for me to reach their highest level of certification as a Company Officer and as an Instructor. However, even with all of these activities, I would not quit when it came to my education. I finished the first of three degrees that I planned on getting, the technology degree. Although I still had the human relations and the economic development degrees to obtain, I had finished one side of the "education triangle," and at last I was a college graduate.

Here I am getting my first college degree from Collin Bennett. Collin Bennett was an icon in the city of Hartford. His contributions were legendary. Among the many things that he did was serve as a constant source of encouragement and direction to those of us who did the best we could.

Here I am with my brother Rocky at my first college graduation. You may notice that I had on my fire department uniform underneath. I did that for each of my college graduations as a tribute to the organization that made it all possible. When this photo was taken, I was too excited to think about the bad times that I had in high school, but I cannot help but feel a tremendous sense of gratitude to Rocky now. He never gave up on me getting an education, even when I had given up on myself.

UConn
1992

After acquiring my associate's degree from Hartford State Technical College I decided to keep going, so I got started on my bachelor's degree at the University of Connecticut in West Hartford, Connecticut. I knew that the Human Relations degree was next, so I got started on a bachelor's degree in General Studies. Although this does not sound like a Human Relations program, school administrators assured me that I could choose some of the courses that I would take and that those courses could cover the human relations field. Also, during this time, I had a concern about transportation, so I had to find a school that was close by or on the bus line. Since this school was in a town next to Hartford, it was convenient. However, unfortunately it did not fit my needs completely. I was trying to get an education that enhanced my human relations skills and although this degree was excellent in many ways, it simply did not provide what I was looking for. With the three sides of the education triangle in mind, Technical Knowledge, Human Relations, and Economic Development (THE), I finished out the semester and transferred to Springfield College's School of Human Services in Springfield Massachusetts. It was much further away, but I knew what I needed for an education, and they had it in abundance; a knowledge of "human relations."

Springfield College
1992

My next school of choice was selected because of their mission statement. It was Springfield College's School of Human Services, and they were opposed to all of the "isms." The next two years of my academic life were filled with oral and written presentations. Initially, all of the new students in the school were told to draw an animal that was most like themselves. I cannot draw a barn, but I did the best that I could and chose to draw a horse. We were then told to place our drawing on the board in the front of the room, and give a presentation on why we thought we were most like that animal. When I put my drawing on the board, some of the students exclaimed, laughingly, "It's a race horse!" I said, "No, it's a plow horse." I then went on to explain, "I may not be fast, but I get the job done eventually." This was my way of emphasizing the importance of hard work and persistence when it came to learning, understanding and remembering information. However, there was one experience that stood out more than any other. During a course named

"Issues in Research", my classmates and I were directed to think of a group project that we could work on and receive school credit. I immediately thought of the Tools of Learning, and so I made a presentation to the students in my class. My idea was to accomplish the following:

1. Determine if any schools in the Hartford area taught their students a system of learning, understanding and remembering information.

2. If they did, what did this system consist of?

3. Make presentations to determine if there was an interest or a need for the program.

There were two students in my class who were interested in working with me on this program. Their names were Bruce Whitaker and Randy Wilson. For the next three semesters, we were to conduct research, meet and present information on this system. The results were astounding.

Foremost among the experiences we had, were the result of visits to several schools in the region. I personally went to the Silver Lane School in East Hartford, Connecticut, a private school in the Hartford region, and several public schools in the city of Hartford. The Silver Lane School was visited because, at that time, it was considered one of the top eight elementary schools in the nation. During my visit, I was shown a book that taught children how to picture information in their mind's eye. I believe this was the only time I have seen a reference to "visualizing information" which was also one of the Tools of Learning. It was the method that I learned from Eddie Lopez, the recruit who served in the military. After that, I had the experience of going to the private school that I referred to earlier. The person in charge informed me that they did teach their students a system of studying information, and that it was the first course their students took before taking any other classes. I asked if I could see this information and was flatly refused. I was told that it was for their students only. I also visited several schools (a sample determined by my advisor) in the city of Hartford. None of these schools had any system of the sort, at all. After this experience I found myself wondering, *Why did the private school have a system, the public school in the suburbs have a system, but the public schools in the city did not?* It was this experience that made me promise to take the Tools of Learning into the cities of our nation. After all, in 32 years, I have never seen a program nearly as good as the Tools of Learning.

Falling Isn't Failing
1992

Time passed by, and before long, I was eligible to take the test to become a captain. I never stopped studying, so I was almost ready to be evaluated. The one thing that I had to do was increase my rate of review. My review system caused me to be able to recall the most difficult information that I would likely be tested on. I applied myself according to the steps spelled out in the Tools of Learning. As usual, there was great excitement leading up to the test. A captain fills in when a deputy chief goes on vacation, which means that periodically a captain is in charge of several companies at an emergency. That makes it a very responsible and respected position. Also, if you do the job well and you pass the next test with a high score, your next uniform will have a gold badge instead of a silver one. When the test was given, I applied my test taking strategy on how to calm myself down when being evaluated. This made it possible for me to remember the things that I had memorized. At last, the test was finished and the results were sent to us. I scored number one on the written exam. Even I didn't expect to score as highly as I did. I assumed that I would pass the written and began studying for the oral before the written exam results came out. I was not being cocky or presumptuous; I was being proactive. If I had waited for my written exam results to come out before I started studying for the oral interview, I would not have been as prepared for the oral interview. I say these things because I am hoping the reader will consider applying this strategy. The worst thing that could happen is that I studied for the oral, and did all that studying for nothing. The reader should know that <u>there is no such thing as "doing all of that studying for nothing."</u> That line of thinking causes us to apply ourselves halfheartedly when we need to exert ourselves completely. Even if you cannot use the information for your intended purpose now, someday, the information you learn will be of benefit.

The oral interview seemed to go as well as any that I had ever taken. However, the results were not good. For some reason, I received a score so low that I would not be considered for a promotion for that position for quite a while. I went from being number one to number 11 because of a bad oral interview score, and there were just four jobs available. I never fully understood what I said that took me from number one to number 11, but I vented by writing a poem to express how I felt at that time. It is called . . .

Forever Undaunted

Hard work and sincerity equal success
But this time the adage has failed
To prevent the unwanted, an ugly digress
From a course once endless...curtailed

To follow a plan used by mentors and those
Who changed the world in their quest
Yet fail in your try to win, I suppose
Could be the ultimate test

With questions to answer that comes from within
Like;
Did I wisely invest the past years?
Or should I "relax" and engage in its twin
"Indolence, the bane of careers?

The answers depend on the words that you choose
To recall in this time of dispute
Choose the wrong ones, in the end you will lose
A chance to find worth absolute

Until that day when you've reached your goal
Remember these words that are true
Doing your best is an honorable role
That's all that a person can do.

Charles A. Teale, Sr.

Dedicated to my grandfather

Candido Pina

It was during this time that things got increasingly worse in my household between my wife and me. We were both thought of as good people by everyone we knew, but we had grown apart. It would be several years before I fully understood this, but once I did, we were able to establish a friendship. I know that I have said, "This is not a book about my personal experiences, but it is a book about my learning experiences." Well, this and the following personal experiences are exceptions to this rule that I must pass along to the reader. They made me acknowledge the negative effect personal challenges can have on the learning experience.

A Time to Mourn
1993

Shortly after my wife and I separated, my father, Charles Edward Smith, died. Although initially it was difficult adjusting to his presence when I was a teenager, it became better when my daughter Kathleen and my son Charlie were born, when I was in my early 20's. It was around the time that my daughter was born that my father had a triple bypass operation. When he died, 16 years after his operation, I thought to myself, *He lived to see his grandchildren, and to see him and me become like father and son again.* I could only ask for one more thing at that time. Our family had financial challenges when he died. I prayed that I would be able to succeed professionally so that I could take care of all my family members. That prayer was answered positively, and I have helped everyone who has needed my assistance ever since.

Renewed Determination
1994

Based upon the words of the previous poem, I was obviously upset but not discouraged. I still remembered Doc Hurley's words "don't quit", and persistence had become a habit. Several months passed by and another captain's test was announced. This time it would be in the Training Division of the Department. I had worked in the Training Division before as a lieutenant, but I knew that my position was about to be eliminated when I was there. This was a chance to return at a higher rank. It was great working under the supervision of Deputy Chief Tommy Williams, but sadly, he was gone. Although I was not sure that I would take the job if I was offered it, I took the test anyway. To my surprise I scored high enough to be offered that position before the firefighting captain's position became available. I took the job, and in time, I was offered the captain of firefighter's position twice. However, I decided to stay in the Training Division.

Here I am being promoted by Fire Chief John R. Vendetta (far left). Chief Vendetta was a source of great inspiration to many members of the Hartford Fire Department including me. Also present are (from left to right) my daughter Kathleen, my son Charlie, and my uncle William "Rab" Smith.

Chapter 16

Persistence Pays
1993

During my personal and professional challenges, I stayed with school. I tried to keep something in mind that would keep me enthusiastic (see Tool #2). If something was going wrong with work, I always had school; if something was going wrong with school, I always had work. When my quest to become Chief of the Department seemed to stall, I focused on my studies. While working on my bachelor's degree, instead of taking one or two courses per semester, like I did during my associate's degree program, I took four courses. When I was scheduled to work at night, I would leave the firehouse in the morning, eat breakfast at a restaurant, go to the library, study all day, get something to eat and go back to work that evening. Within two years, I had finished the second side of the "education triangle" by acquiring a bachelor's degree in Human Services from Springfield College in Massachusetts.

Two down one to go!

50th Anniversary of a Disaster
1994

Possessing a love and respect for history has many benefits. Even a negative occurrence can motivate someone to pursue a standard of excellence never seen before the occurrence. Such an experience was the circus fire spoken of earlier in this book. Although some may find this not relevant to my learning or professional development experiences, I truly beg to differ completely. Allow me to explain. My knowledge of history served as a reminder that the 50th anniversary of the Ringling Brothers and Barnum and Bailey Circus fire of 1944 was near. With that anniversary fast approaching, via chain of command, I informed the Chief of the Department, John R. Vendetta. I requested that the Hartford Fire Department put together an anniversary ceremony that would honor the more than 167 people who died in the fire and bring comfort to the many survivors who were still living at that time. Chief Vendetta was 100 percent in favor of the idea. For someone in middle management to come up with an idea that the entire department will be working on is comforting. It makes you feel like your rank is more than just a title. The work leading up to the event was extensive, but at the time, I was Captain of the Training Division and the department had recruits that wanted to help in any way that they could. I served as the master of ceremonies of this event, so I started making the necessary contacts, which were many. Due to the phone calls that I received, I knew that this event would receive national attention. I could not disappoint those in attendance, or those who viewed the ceremony through the eyes of the media, so I scripted every little detail. Using the Tools of Learning, I memorized what I wanted to say verbatim from the start of the ceremony to the very end of it. In attendance were some of the people who distinguished themselves 50 years prior by rescuing people, people who helped those who were badly injured, and even those who assisted people who had lost loved ones in the makeshift morgue. Even the man who discovered the identity of one of the unknown victims was there, retired Lieutenant Rick Davey. Along with Don Massey he coauthor the book *A Matter of Degree*, which I believe is the most accurate account of what happened before, during and after that great tragedy. The youngest attendee was my son Charlie who was 14 years old at the time of the 50th anniversary. With the eyes of the nation upon us, everything went exactly as planned, until I got a nagging sensation within me. I had been reciting every word that I spoke from sheets of paper that I had at my seat. Close to the end of the ceremony, I started asking myself, *You have been empathizing with the survivors of this disaster since you were 9 years old. Why are you so afraid to say what is on your mind and in your heart?* Then it happened: I rose to my feet to conclude the ceremony, and I said exactly what I felt. When I finished speaking, I could hear the response from the audience of around 400 people. They were deeply moved by what I had to say and that's what I wanted. My goal was to comfort them during a very difficult time of reflection, and I did. It was on that day and at that precise time that I became a public speaker.

I mention this in a book about academic and professional development to illustrate a very important point. If a person longs to be successful in any endeavor, he or she must be able to speak in front of an audience. The steps of becoming a public speaker consisted of the following for me: picture yourself saying words that you want to be remembered for saying, live by those words, think ahead of your voice (Bawby Gomes), and then speak from the heart.

Although there may be other ways to accomplish the task of becoming a true public speaker, please remember that this one was learned under the most trying of circumstances, and it has enhanced my ability to be of service to others many times.

This is Just a Test
1995

While serving as a captain in the Training Division, I knew that I was getting experience as an administrator. That meant that I was learning about how to handle a budget, which was the "economic development" side of the education triangle that I had been working on throughout my career. Although this was experience and not a formal education, it consisted of information I couldn't learn in the firefighting division. It wasn't like controlling the 26 million dollars spent by the entire department, but I did learn how to make wise decisions related to department finances. I also got to represent the department at meetings with division heads from other departments, and sometimes I even got to interact with other department heads. This experience was about to come in very handy.

Chief Stewart had retired, and the person who replaced him left within a year. John R. Vendetta, Hartford's Fire Marshal had been serving in the capacity of Acting Fire Chief for the past 13 months. Chief Vendetta was one of the most respected men in the fire service statewide, but he was about to vacate the position of Acting Fire Chief. He wanted to return to his position as Fire Marshal. Because the city had begun the process of searching for a permanent fire chief, someone was needed to serve as Acting

Fire Chief for two more months. I applied for the job. Because I was such a long shot, I didn't want anyone to know that I was applying. It would have been laughable to most, and I was not in the mood to be laughed at when it came to my profession. I met with Deputy City Manager Henry Langley who asked me many questions about my interest in the position. Foremost among his questions were the ones related to my education. He wanted to be certain that I had a college degree. I assured him that I actually had two.

Note: It is during an interview like this that a candidate must express why his or her college degrees makes him or her more qualified for the position they are applying for than someone who does not have one. Essentially, there are three reasons why a college degree makes you more qualified. First, having a college degree shows that you are sincerely interested in your field. No one goes through the time, effort and expense of getting a degree in a particular field if he or she is not truly interested in that field. It's too much work. Second, it shows that you can finish what you start. You must be persistent if you are going to get a degree. If you are not persistent, then you won't graduate. The ability to finish what you start will help you as a student and as a professional because it takes persistence to succeed in anything. Persistence is successes most common ally...(Earl Nightingale). Third, it shows that you have the ability to learn, understand and remember information. If you did not have this ability, you could not pass the courses necessary to graduate.

Now back to my interview with Henry Langly.

During those days, I never told anyone that I did not graduate from high school. I thought that that information might ruin my chances of getting the job that I wanted. If someone asked me, "When did you graduate from high school?" I would simply say, "I was a member of the class of 1973." This was telling the truth. I was a member of the class of '73 until I dropped out of school at the age of 14. In any event, after being interviewed by Deputy City Manager Langley, I was offered the job of Chief for two months. The next day, it was in the newspapers and not everyone was pleased. Some of the deputy chiefs were outspoken in their opposition. However, one man did indicate that I was an excellent man but that it was too soon. In the midst of all the commotion, that was reassuring. Most people don't get to "sit in the big chair" until they have been on the job for around 30 years. I had 12 years on the job.

During those two months, I was present physically, mentally and emotionally for everything and anything that was even remotely related to the position of fire chief. I wanted to extract whatever I could from the experience so that I could determine what the job really required. At one time, I met with the head of the Department of Human Services, Calixto Torres, in his office. On one of the walls in his office was a diploma. Mr. Torres had earned a master's degree in Public Administration from the University of Hartford. What an impressive professional he was, and his diploma was impressive too. I looked at that diploma and discussed it with him on several occasions. Through my interaction with him and the head of the personnel department, Patricia Washington, I determined that if I was going to someday become Chief of the Hartford Fire Department and do the job excellently, I would need that degree. It was to be the third side of the "education triangle," the last degree necessary to obtain the technical knowledge, human relations skills and economic development ability (THE) every true public administrator needs. That year, I applied to the University of Hartford in my pursuit of my next learning objective. I had been living my life as a single man for a couple of years by this time, and starting to realize that success is nothing without someone special to share it with. She didn't know it, but I was about to ask my girlfriend Helaine to marry me.

So You Think You Are a Professional
1995

My two months as Acting Chief went by very quickly, and there were many challenges along the way, including a fire that took the lives of three people. During the aftermath of that fire, there were questions from authorities that the Hartford Fire Department had to answer. I did not feel comfortable attending a meeting like this alone, so I asked the Fire Marshal, Chief John R. Vendetta, to attend that meeting with me. Also, representing the Department was the Deputy Fire Marshal, Willy Barrow. During this meeting, several attorneys raised their concerns about what transpired on the fire ground. Although I felt capable of answering questions related to strategy and tactics, I was not prepared to address their legal concerns. However, Chief Vendetta was. Time and time again, he would answer their questions, and they would respond in astonishment with words like, "I believe he just recited the law word for word." They were all amazed at his level of knowledge, and so was I.

When the meeting was over, Chief Vendetta, the Deputy Fire Marshal and I got on the elevator to return to headquarters. I looked at Chief Vendetta and said, "That was the most impressive display of professionalism that I have ever seen. How did you know so much about those laws?" Chief Vendetta took a copy of the Connecticut General Statutes from under his arm and pointed to a law. He then said, "Do you see that law?" I replied, "Yes". He then turned the page, pointed to another section and said, "Do you see that law?" I said, "Yes." he turned to another page and again he said, "Do you see that law?" Again I said, "Yes." He then replied, "I wrote those laws." It is during times like these that even the most dedicated professional must look themselves in the mirror and simply ask, "How committed am I to my profession, what have I done so far, and what contribution will I make before this is all over?" That's exactly what I did on that day. I knew then and there that it was time to kick this career into high gear!

I handled everything to the best of my ability, and at the conclusion of those two months, Deputy City Manager Henry Langley told me, "If I had known you were going to do such a good job, I would not have hired someone else!" Those words made it all worthwhile. However, my time as Chief of the Department was up, and I was heading back to the Training Division as a Captain.

Kathleen and Charlie with me on my first day as Acting Chief of the Hartford Fire Department in February of 1995. It saddened me to read about those who were not pleased with this temporary assignment, but I understood. I only had 12 years on the job. It takes most men 30 years to sit in "the big chair."

I look back on those days now and wonder where I got the nerve to try the things that I did. I now believe it was because my desire to succeed far outweighed my fear of failure.

By August of that year I was a married man again. Helaine and I started working on everything we were determined to accomplish over the next 20 years. Because Helaine had two children before we were married, I got another son and another daughter, Jason and Ileah. Although I have not elaborated on the effect the Tools of Learning had on all of my children, it can be summarized very simply. Whatever the adults in a household do is a lesson to the children. Although I periodically shared specific information about the Tools of Learning with them, they learned some of it by simply watching me use it.

If the adults in a household don't have an education, then they probably don't have a strategy for learning, understanding and remembering information. That is one of the reasons why I share the Tools of Learning with adult education students. Every student receiving a Tools of Learning presentation is encouraged to share this information with his or her children. Throughout the 32 years that I spent developing and presenting this program, I tried to maintain its original academic level. It was written by a person with a GED, and I never saw a reason to make it more difficult to understand. The goal has always been to keep it at a ninth grade reading level. That way, parents who have learned it can teach their children the Tools of Learning.

Leave More Than You Take
1995

When I stopped serving as the Acting Chief of the Hartford Fire Department, things got financially challenging. They weren't bad, but I was starting to lack the money needed to continue working on my master's degree at the University of Hartford. I knew the information related to economics in this program would be beneficial, but I was concerned that I would be placing an economic hardship on my household if I continued. Although I received tuition reimbursement from the city of Hartford throughout my academic career, it didn't cover the entire cost of courses if the amount exceeded $800.00. At the time, courses at the University of Hartford cost $1200.00 and sometimes I took two courses in a semester. With concerns about how I was going pay for school on my mind, I went to the store to buy something on the way home. I cannot recall what it was that I wanted to get, but it could not have been much. I had only $5.00 in my wallet and nothing in the bank. I was living from paycheck to paycheck. As I approached the store's entrance, a man walked up to me and said, "Sir, I haven't had a bite to eat in three days. Do you have any change you can spare?" As I looked at this man, I could tell that he had nothing. Whenever I see someone like that, I imagine that it could have been my brother or my son or some other loved one. All I had was the $5.00 that I spoke of earlier, but I thought to myself, *Five dollars isn't going to make much of a difference in my life, but it will make a huge difference in his.* I opened my wallet and gave him what I had. He thanked me emphatically and walked away. Since I had no money left, I went back to my car and drove home. The next day, I went to work still wondering how I was going to get the money to go to school. If the reader is thinking that I could have used the $800.00 tuition reimbursement and then charged the rest to a credit card, then I'd like to inform you that all lines of credit were maxed out. As the day progressed, the Deputy Chief of Training (my superior) came in to my office and announced, "We're getting a recruit class of 45 people. It's time to get ready!" Preparing for the arrival of a recruit class is an exciting experience. There are many things that go through your mind like the chance to help a group of people start careers that they have dreamed of doing. Some of them have longed to become firefighters since childhood. But I was excited about the start of this class for another reason too. A recruit class also meant overtime pay, and I was in dire need of money so that I could keep going to school.

Ever since that week when I gave my last five dollars to a man who appeared to need it more than I did, I have not longed for money. I haven't been rich, but if I needed it, I have had the money I needed since 1996. I know this sounds superstitious but somehow, extending that kindness has paid off many, many times.

I know that some people think that the act of giving money to strangers is a foolish move. I have had people tell me "strangers who ask for money will only use the money for drugs." For all those people who think this way, I have the following account to share with you.

After serving as a Captain for a few years, I became the Deputy Chief of Training in 1996. During the time that I served as a Captain, I got several raises in a couple of years' time. The same happened when I was promoted to the rank of Deputy Chief of Training. Also, the city of Hartford had a system called "College Incentive Pay," so within a short amount of time, I received several raises for academic and professional accomplishments. The raises were so frequent that I lost track of when I should get one. I was just grateful to be receiving what I was getting paid. However, one week, something told me to carefully analyze my pay. I cannot recall exactly what compelled me to do this, but upon completing this analysis, I came to realize that my pay was very short. What was most astonishing was that it had been that short for about two years. When I finished my calculations, I came to realize that I was owed several thousand dollars. I was speechless. The steps necessary to get the money owed to me were many, and took several months. However, in time, the money came. I spent it responsibly for the most part paying off credit cards that were maxed out due to tuition costs. However, on my way home that night I went to a restaurant in Hartford called "New York Style Chicken and a Biscuit" on Farmington Avenue. As I entered the restaurant, I noticed a man pacing frantically by the cashier. The man saw me come in, and said, "Hey, Chief, today is my son's birthday, and I haven't got anything I can give him. I was hoping to buy him a chicken dinner, but I don't even have money for that. Can you help me out?" With that I took out a 50-dollar bill, and I told him, "Give this to your son and buy both of you any dinner you want on the menu. It's on me." He couldn't believe what I was telling him but he thanked me emphatically and placed his order. At this time, the reader must remember that I dropped out of high school at 14 and received a GED when I turned 20. Because of this, for the past 15 years, I have had the honor of serving as the keynote speaker at adult education graduation ceremonies throughout the city of Hartford. Several years after I gave this man the 50-dollar bill and the dinners for him and his son, I gave another speech at a GED graduation ceremony. When the ceremony was over, a man approached me and said, "Hey, Chief, do you remember me?" Unfortunately, I did not and I said, "No, but it's great to see you anyway." This was my standard reply to people I didn't remember. Well, he said, "We met at New York Style Chicken and a Biscuit. I told you that I needed money for my son and you gave me fifty dollars and two chicken dinners for my son's birthday. I brought everything home and gave it to my son. After saying that he grabbed a young man by his graduation gown, pulled him over to where we were, and he said, "This is my son. Will you tell him that it was you who gave me that money and the dinners? He never believed me." I may have told the young man what had happened or I may not have. I was too stunned to talk.

So to those who claim that it's a waste to give money to someone who asks for it, keep these stories in mind. Seeing that young man and his father, and hearing them both say "thank you" made all the donations I have ever made worth every single red cent.

This is my son Charlie and me at a graduation ceremony for a recruit class. Charlie was in the Air Force serving as a firefighter, and I was the Deputy Chief of Training. Charlie agreed to be our keynote speaker and did such a great job that he literally got a standing ovation.

Chapter 17

Kindness Is Not Weakness
2000

In March of 2000, my wife Helaine and I were on a two-week vacation. I had finished my master's degree 10 months earlier, and for the first time in 17 years, I had no tuition bills to pay. Times were great financially, and we planned to be in Newport Rhode Island one week, and then we were going down to Florida. After finishing the Newport trip, we came home to prepare for the next week. This was before the days when everyone had a cell phone so I answered the voice messages left on my house phone. One of them got my attention completely. It was the City Manager of Hartford. She stated that the Chief of the Fire Department had suddenly resigned, and she was wondering if I was interested in serving in the position. She even stated, "I hope you are because I already told the media that you would be the next Chief." The reader may not be able to relate to what it is like to hear such a message, but I will try my best to explain it. All at once, I felt like the challenges of the past were about to become just that, the past; like it was time for me to distinguish myself in ways that I could only dream of until now; like this was my opportunity to show how much I appreciated everyone who, as Mr. Edmonds told me 27 years earlier "spent their lives, risked their lives and sometimes gave their lives so that I would have the opportunity to succeed."

Although I wanted to serve as Chief, in Hartford, the position comes with many additional responsibilities. Years ago, the major decisions of city of Hartford's Fire Department were made by the members of the Board of Fire Commissioners. However, in 1947, Hartford decided to disband that organization. A close personal friend of mine by the name of Billy Dwyer told me that he worked for the Chief of the Fire Department at that time, and the Chief used to say boastfully, "I can hire, I can fire, I can promote and demote." Although this sounds like a good thing in the sense that you would be free of many bosses, it is actually a tremendous amount of additional responsibility. I thought briefly but thoroughly about taking the job of Chief, and decided I was up to the task. I immediately told my wife the news. She responded most favorably, and the next thing I knew, I was on the phone with the City Manager, telling her that I would accept the position. Our vacation ended, both literally and figuratively. The next few days were a blur of media attention, congratulations from well-wishers, and desperate attempts on my part to comprehend the entire matter. I had 17 years on the job.

Sadly, Henry Langley, the man who interviewed me before I became the Acting Chief, had died five years earlier. His level of prominence was great for a man of his age, and all of us who knew him were truly saddened by his passing. During his funeral, his widow Denise told me, "He had such big plans for you!" Less than a year later, she would be dead too. Henry's loss meant that I would not have someone to provide me with the formal and informal advice that I needed to be successful in City Hall. I knew my Department, but I would have to figure out how to interact with all of my peers and superiors by myself. Sometimes my lack of political experience showed.

For a while, I had a "honeymoon" when no one approached me with major issues until one day an old friend of mine came up to my office and told me that someone was at a social gathering of members of the fire department. It was during this gathering that this person stated, "Teale is going down." After making this comment, he had everyone's attention, but he was not stating anything particular. Upon hearing about this, I thought, *What could it be that I've done wrong that would lead to such a strong statement as "Teale is going down?"* I thought, *Could it be that he found out that I dropped out of high school, and there's something illegal about hiring high school drop outs as department heads?* I just had no idea what would prompt such a response until I received a memo from Assistant Chief Parker. In the memo, he stated that the union had brought a matter to his attention. This matter had to do with the practice of Fire Department personnel working after hours for surrounding fire departments. These surrounding departments would use the fire department's training academy for training purposes, and they would pay the Hartford Fire Department personnel directly. In Assistant Chief Parker's memo he stated that he felt that the practice was illegal. This entire matter seemed very strange to me. After all, I knew that others had engaged in this practice before me. Why is it an issue now? If it was illegal then, why didn't someone say something about it years ago? The next few weeks proved to be nothing less than hell. First, I received calls from the media and then City Hall. Foremost among the media were reporters from our regional newspaper. To be in their newspaper was a great honor for me -- at least, up until now.

The articles printed during this time period were damning. Many thought that my career was over. The entire matter came to a head with one front page article that read "Acting Chief Admits that He Took Payments." The truth of the matter was that I got paid for work that I did. That's not the same as "taking payments." Outraged and disgusted, I called the supervisor of the reporters who wrote the article. He agreed to meet with me and discuss the matter in my office. During our meeting, I came to realize that the practice I was involved in started as far back as 1964. That's when I was 9 years old. I could not help but wonder, *Why did they not know about this "wrongdoing" when I was a child, a teenager, or a young man? Why did they learn about it when it was my turn to serve as Chief? What about the others who committed the same offense? Why aren't their names in the paper?* Eventually, I stopped being angry and became determined to redeem myself, in spite of those who obviously wanted to keep me from succeeding. To resolve the situation regarding the controversy I did the following:

1. Admitted that I engaged in the practice that I was accused of
2. Apologized for what I did
3. Paid the city of Hartford all of the money that I received and repaid the city of Hartford all of the money that people under my supervision had received. That kept their names out of the paper.

Throughout it all, my true friends and family stayed with me. Even the members of the Hartford Fire Department were on my side. A couple of friends were especially supportive. My pals Manny Liebert and Billy Dwyer were two very elderly men who I had befriended years before this occurrence. Although they are no longer with us, I will always remember these guys. Every time that I think of them, I know why they were called part of "the Greatest Generation!"

Several months later, I was named the permanent Chief of the Hartford Fire Department. Integrity had won out again. I wish that I could say that no harm was done, but the truth of the matter is that some of my family members were deeply wounded by the negative press. I thought that I could take legal action against those who wrote lies about me in print, so I discussed the matter with one of the city of Hartford's attorneys. He informed me that the laws regarding libel and slander are not the same for public servants as they are for the general public. In essence, this attorney informed me that a person can say anything they want about a prominent public servant as long as they can prove that they didn't know it was a lie when they said it. If they can prove that they did not know it was a lie when they told a lie about me, I had no legal right to complain.

This realization changed everything. I was reminded of a time when I trained fire recruits. Just prior to their graduation, I would call all of them and all of the instructors into the main classroom. Although this was not official, it was quite formal in the sense that I wanted everyone to know how important taking the oath of office was before they took it. They were becoming part of a great tradition, and I wanted to share some lasting last thoughts with them. Among the things that I had to say was the following:

"Not everyone is going to be pleased to see you become firefighters for the city of Hartford. Some will sense that you are in some ways better off then they are. They won't like that. There are only two ways that they can make themselves equal to you. They can work as hard as you have and rise to your level, or they can tear you down. Working as hard as you have took years. Tearing you down will take just money and or minutes if you let them. "

With that, I told them to safeguard themselves against such people. After I read the articles that I saw in the newspaper, I knew that someone had tried to tear me down. This was hard on some of the members of my family. Even now, as I approach my sixth decade of life, I ask myself, *Do I want to be the same source of discomfort to my family at 60 that I was at 16?* The answer is a resounding no! But somehow I must balance my concern for my family members with my life-long obligation and sense of gratitude to the city of Hartford.

Let's Solve This Now!
2000

As stated earlier, prior to serving as Chief of the Hartford Fire Department, I developed an appreciation for Emergency Medical Response. Part of it was due to the training that I received while I was in Drill School. Also, by the time I had three years on the job, I had pursued training at Hartford Hospital to become an EMT (emergency medical technician). Soon after obtaining this training, I started working part-time for one of the local ambulance companies. Although this didn't last long (around 12 months), this experience led me to believe that the Fire Department should become more active in the emergency medical field. At that time, circa 1985, the Hartford Fire Department was not the primary first responders to emergency medical incidents. We only responded to EMS calls when an ambulance attendant or a police officer asked for us. The final straw came when, while serving as a

Lieutenant on Engine Company 16, we received a call to a home that needed forcible entry. A woman lived there alone and no one had heard from her for a while. She was a cancer patient. When we arrived at the home, a police officer, the woman's brother and the woman's son were waiting for us even though it only took us two minutes to get there. My company forced entry only to find the woman, obviously dead, lying on her bedroom floor. There is nothing quite like the cry of someone when they first realize that their loved one is dead, and we heard that cry immediately. I took all of the negative feelings, including the rage I felt, home with me, and the results were not anything that I would ever write about. On that day, I became determined to make the Hartford Fire Department the primary first responders to emergency medical calls and to help develop an employee assistance program that worked.

These were my thoughts as I took the reigns of the Hartford Fire Department. I got to work accomplishing as much as it could during my administration. I met with division heads, deputy chiefs, and through the department's health and safety committee, I met with leaders of the local firefighters union. During all of these meetings, I used a system of solving problems that became Tool #19. This method made it possible for us to accomplish 87 major things in the department, and it consists of the following:

TOOL #19
Dedicated to the Deputy Chiefs, Division Heads and the Hartford Fire Department's Health and Safety Committee, 2000-2010

Solutions to problems are like medication for an illness; there may be side effects that must be managed

Using Knowledge to Solve Problems

Among other things in this program, we have covered the subtopics of "visualizing, teaching what you know", and "using information for academic, professional and business success." If we master information to this level, getting A's and B's in that subject will be easy.

Although the Tools of Learning helps students and professionals to pass tests, the passing of tests is not the ultimate goal of the program. The ultimate goal of the Tools of Learning is to use the knowledge we have retained to solve problems.

Use of the information to solve problems is the ultimate goal of the Tools of Learning. Some people believe that it only takes critical thinking to accomplish this task. Unfortunately, the definition to the term "critical thinking" varies from one expert in the field to another. It is troubling to this writer when someone knowledgeable about critical thinking attempts to diminish the importance of learning, understanding and remembering information. Whenever we encounter this type of response, we should simply consider the following:

If an attorney has excellent critical thinking ability, can you rely on that attorney to perform open heart surgery? Obviously not, because he or she has not learned, understood or retained the information necessary to do the job at all. The point is this: even though critical thinking is essential, the retention of information related to your field of expertise is a prerequisite to critical thinking. Much like multiplication should be mastered prior to attempting algebra, a person should have retained information prior to engaging in critical thinking. Otherwise chaos will occur. It is the belief of the developer of this program that the Tools of Learning and critical thinking are two sides of the same coin.

The implementation of change in an attempt at improving something does not count as an accomplishment, unless you "manage" that change. Although there are many problem solving models, the Tools of Learning recommends that you:

1. Recognize that there is a problem
2. Separate the emotions from the problem
3. Define the problem
4. Collect information about the problem, especially its' history. "Whereof what's past is prologue," is a line from the play *The Tempest* by William Shakespeare. Prologue is an event or action that leads to another event or situation.
5. Analyze the information
6. Develop several solutions to the problem
7. Choose the best solution

8. Implement the solution
9. Analyze the results
10. Manage the solution

Of these steps, the most important is number 4, "Collect information about the problem", and the most important information we can collect is a "history" of the problem. Knowing a problem's history prevents us from implementing solutions that have been tried (and failed) already. Also, since "the past is prologue, " the past may give us a sense of what we can expect at present and in the future.

The second most important of these steps is #10, "Manage the Solution". The solution to a problem is like medication for an illness. The meds may cure the symptoms of the illness but that very same medication may have side effects. Those side effects must be managed.

The Tools of Learning provides for management of its solutions through its publication *Chief Teale's The Tools of Learning: From GED to Masters Degree and Beyond,* and through presentations on the subject. This publication serves as a constant resource for those who want to solve the most common problem we face as a nation when it comes to academic and professional success: a lack of strategy.

The following information is a system of solving problems the Tools of Learning calls "situational analysis", and it shows how progress can be made completing major projects with limited resources and a strategy for doing so.

The "Tools of Learning"
Situational Analysis

Are you:

1. Standing Still

2. Going Backward

3. Moving Forward

4. Completing the Project

Every positive person or organization wants #'s 3 and 4, fears #1 and can't tolerate #2. However, can you tell which of these categories you or your organization fit in? The answer can be determined by using a system known as "situational analysis", and every person in an organization should know what it means and how important #s 3 and 4 are. The problem we have is "determining how to insure progress".

Here is how it works:

First, determine which things you would like for you or your organization to accomplish. This list can be changed any time you want so don't get writer's block. Just write what you want to get done and place a title above these items called "things to do" or TTD for short.

Next, place the name or group of names of the person or persons responsible for completing this task.

So far your "situational analysis" chart will look something like this:

TTD (Things to Do)

Research and Development of Mobile Data Computers (Deputy Chief Cieri)

Installation of Knox Box equipment (Superintendent Smith)

Public Education/Vial of Life (Captain Taylor)

Next, you want to create four additional columns:

Standing Still - Going Backwards - Moving Forward – Completed

(These are just my titles. Anything comparable that you would like will do).

At every meeting, this chart must be used and everyone should know that it is being used. No one wants to have a TTD mentioned with his or her name mentioned after it and a grade of "Standing Still" or "Going Backwards" listed. Everyone wants to hear "Moving Forward" or "Completed." A description indicating where the project stands is better than simply stating "moving forward." It is up to the CEO to mark the project as "standing still" etc.

It is not necessary to use a lot of writing with this system. On some lined paper, just place the initials of the headings:

TTD

	S. S.	G.B.	M.F.	C.
R & D of MDC (D/C)				X
Inst. Of Knox Box (Supt.)				X
Public Ed/Vial of Life (Capt.)				X

If the person using this system can readily access a computer, it will work better than paper and pencil or pen because information can be easily deleted or added without a concern for space. Complaints receive a grade of G.B.

There is just one more thing. Every completed project results in a change in resources or procedures. Therefore, when a project makes its way to the last column of the chart, "completed", then a written policy must be developed defining the change in procedure or resources. This policy must be reviewed by everyone responsible for completing projects. In other words, if your name appears next to any TTD, you should have the opportunity to review a proposed policy before it becomes an official policy of the organization. This is done to insure that the new policy does not make someone else's job more difficult. If this step is not taken, an uncoordinated effort will occur. This will create misunderstandings that will lead to hard feelings and chaos. In some organizations, lives may be lost if this step is not taken.

All completed projects are solutions to problems, and solutions are like medication for an illness; they have side effects. Those side effects and solutions must be managed, and that's one of the reasons why CEOs are necessary. They facilitate the creation of solutions through the use of methods like "situational analysis", and then they manage those solutions. Because even the best policies can be forgotten, each policy must be read frequently by the CEO to insure that the organization is complying with its own policies. This can be read in a rotating fashion, for example, two policies per day (depending on the number of policies that must be reviewed).

Engine Company 16's, 1992

It was with this company that I came to realize the need for solving some major problems in the city of Hartford. The following are the members of the company: Cornell Murray (kneeling), Pete Miller (standing), Anthony Napoleon (on the apparatus) and me (in the white hat).

It would be another 10 years after I received my emergency medical training that I began attending community meetings with an organization known as HART, which stands for Hartford Areas Rally Together. One of the concerns expressed by the members in attendance was the infrequency with which a "first responder" arrived at the scene of a medical emergency and the amount of time it took to respond. At the time, I was serving as the Deputy Chief of Training, and I did not have the authority to commit the Hartford Fire Department in any way. However, we began working on addressing this life-threatening matter as far as we could without approval from the Chief of the Department. In time, HART became convinced that having the fire department serve as the primary first responders was the right thing to do. Coincidentally, I was on my way to becoming Chief of the Hartford Fire Department.

Just 10 months before I became Chief of the Hartford Fire Department, I got my master's degree from the University of Hartford. I always felt badly when I had to go from Acting Chief back to Captain in the Training Division. However, if I had become Chief first, I would not have had the time for school, and this day may not have happened. On this day, the third side of the "education triangle" was completed. Economic Development.

Here is my son Jason and my daughter Ileah at my graduation. My daughter Kathleen and my son Charlie were in the Air Force and unable to attend this one, but they were at the first two.

Here is my wife Helaine and my mother Francisca Smith at my master's degree graduation. I didn't ask, but I wondered how my mother felt seeing me accomplish this goal after all that I had put her through when I dropped out of high school.

I started serving as Chief of the Hartford Fire Department a second time on March 26, 2000. There are many things that I could write about, but my primary focus right now is how Tool #19 entitled "Use Knowledge to Solve Problems" came into existence. The ultimate test of this tool was when the Hartford Fire Department went about the process of becoming the primary first responders to emergency medical calls. As beneficial as having the fire department respond to these calls might seem to the average citizen, there was resistance from some individuals.

As usual, it took persistence to get this program off the ground. When that day came, I sat down with my Assistant Chiefs and the union's side of our Health and Safety Committee. The word from City Hall to the media was that the fire department would have this program up and running in three months. It seemed like an overly ambitious goal at the time, but we were determined to make the best of it. If we failed to reach the deadline, we would be blamed. If we met it, we would be bonafide heroes. We met weekly, and in some weeks more than that. Not a stone was left unturned. I wish I had said more about how much I appreciated our ability to put our differences aside so that we could reach this goal. On May 1st, 2001, when the end of three months passed, we held a press conference at Engine Company 14's, just a couple of miles from the firehouse where I first determined that the fire department should be the primary first responders. As the press conference was held, a call came in sending the first company to an emergency medical incident under the new system. It was a heart attack and the patient survived. As we had our next Health and Safety Committee meeting, Union President Tommy Discipio looked at me and said, "We've done that. What's next?"

Now you know why Tool #19 is named partly in honor of this committee. It's not enough to learn about a subject. You've got to solve problems with what you know. After all, knowledge is like faith: without works, it's dead.

Chapter 18

A Return to Bowles Park
2000

While serving as Chief of the Hartford Fire Department, I was informed that there were plans to hold a reunion in the project where I lived as a teenager, Bowles Park. The main person organizing this event was my good friend Robin Bell. The reader might recall that I had a terrible time adjusting to the place when I moved there at the age of 11. I was totally opposed to attending the reunion. I knew that there would be people there who hated me 30 years before, so why should I attend? The last thing that I wanted to do was show up and argue with someone who I didn't get along with when I was a kid. The words of Dr. Victor E. Frankl came to mind: "The last of the human freedoms is to choose one's attitude under any given set of circumstances." So, I changed my attitude from a negative one to a positive one and decided that I would attend. I wanted to see everyone so that I could put the negative past behind us. My wife Helaine (another former Bowles Park resident) and I got involved in the planning process and contributed financially too. Then the big day came. I prepared myself. I expected to receive the most negative treatment imaginable. Since I was so indolent regarding my schooling, I even sensed that I deserved whatever ridicule was coming my way. However, the best way to describe the day can be expressed through my interaction with one former resident and classmate. Her name was Kimberley Taylor. She was in my class during the sixth grade and I remembered clearly the experience of being around her. She and her friend Leonora Nelson used to persecute me. If they weren't laughing at the size of my feet, they were laughing at something else about me. There was no hiding from them. On the day of the Bowles Park Reunion, I had no intention of hiding from anyone. I saw Kim from a distance and I walked right up to her. Our embrace was so genuine that I literally picked her up off the ground. There were over 300 people there that day. Everyone was just as loving and just as glad to see me, and I was equally glad to see them. What a difference a few decades and a positive attitude make. The next day that I could, I called Robin Bell and thanked her emphatically. To this day she is one of my favorite people.

Here I am with my daughter, Staff Sargent Kathleen Rene Teale. She was home on leave, and visiting her Pa.

You may notice that I was not one to place a lot on my walls. By the time this photo was taken, I had enough plaques to cover my office walls and some walls at home. However, what I displayed were photos of the Hartford Fire Department's history. In the background are the photos of four generations of Kellehers. The Kelleher family symbolized the pride some people had in the Hartford Fire Department. Their photos were a constant reminder to me to give it all that I had. Just like the Kellehers.

The Ultimate Test
2003

Of all the chapters of my life and career, the following is the most difficult to relay. At least since 1985, our department had responded to the Greenwood Convalescent home regularly. This was a nursing home that held elderly and handicapped individuals. False alarms were routine. February 26, 2003 would be different. Around 2 am, my pager went off which meant that I was being notified by the dispatch center of a multiple alarm fire. It was a second alarm at the Greenwood. Under normal circumstances, I would have gotten out of my bed and responded. However, on this day, I was unbelievably sick. I decided not to respond and have one of my Assistant Chiefs take command of the fire. Several minutes after I was notified by the dispatch center, I got a call from my Executive Officer, Eugene Cieri. He informed me that the fire had taken the lives of several people. With that, I responded. Before it was all over, 16 people had died. Prior to this time, the Hartford Fire Department had grown accustomed to receiving international recognition for going an entire year without losing a single life to fire. Losing 16 was inconceivable. No member of the Hartford Fire Department was on the job when the Hartford Hospital Fire took the lives of 16 people in 1961. During one of the meetings held in the Mayor's Office, the question was raised, "Who will tell the loved ones that their relative has died?" I agreed to do so, and I returned to the scene of the fire. Just prior to beginning the process of informing the loved ones of those who perished, I had a conversation with my executive officer, Captain Eugene Cieri, and my aide, Lieutenant Frank Carter. They were nothing less than incredible, and I knew that I could not even attempt what I was about to do without their assistance. Before the process began, a major from the Salvation Army asked me if I could use his assistance. His exact words I do not recall, but when I said "Yes," he thought that I was asking him to inform the loved ones of their loss! I could never have asked anyone for such assistance because it was simply too much to ask. However, this major informed several of those loved ones, which relieved me of having to do so. It was at that time that I came to realize if you ask someone from the Salvation Army for help, you will get it in full measure. I don't have the ability to state how much I appreciated his assistance on that day. However, I was left to inform some of the family, and I did so with as much compassion as I know how to display. Armed primarily with the quality of empathy, I approached the family members of the deceased to inform them of their loss. It was the most difficult thing that I have ever done...bar none.

That Explains A Lot
2006

I would be Chief of the Department for more than six years when suddenly the Mayor at that time, Eddie Perez, contacted all of the department heads and told them that he wanted us to take a week off and report to the Hartford Graduate Center to attend seminars. The description of this program sounded like so many that I had attended in the past, and I was not in the mood to engage in theoretical exercises designed at making me a more effective efficient administrator. I knew what I had to do in those days, and all I needed to do was spend more time doing what had to be done. I was certain that these seminars would be a waste of time, and that they would interfere with my ability to get my work done. However, I wasn't being asked by my boss; I was being ordered.

One of the tasks that had to be completed prior to my beginning this seminar was to fill out a set of questionnaires. The answers that had to be given were personal in nature, in excess of 500 questions, and it took me several hours to answer them. Although I had to stay up half the night to fill out all of the answers, I finished them in time for the seminars. As you can imagine, I showed up sleepy and not in the mood to sit in a chair all day. The seminars were pretty much what I expected until each department head was directed to meet privately with one of the psychologists giving the seminar. Although I was appalled by what I felt was a waste of time, I gathered the positive attitude necessary to proceed. I met with a psychologist named Beverly and she was from Bridgeport, Connecticut. As I sat down, she looked at my filled-out questionnaire and stated, "Ohhhh, I get it. You're a savior." I then said, "What?" She then said, "The reason why you are so successful at your career is because you like coming to the rescue of other people. You like saving them from harm of all types, not just fires. Look, it's all in the books and movies you like." As soon as she said that, my mind ran through a series of experiences I had had when I tried to help others. I even flashed back to a time when I was just 7 years old. Sometimes I tried to help others and completely failed. I suddenly felt tears running down my face. Beverly said, "Do you need a minute?" I said, "I sure do." She left the room for a while. While she was gone, I wondered if I was still the person I was before I joined the Hartford Fire Department, if I still longed to be of service or if I had traded it all away so that I could succeed in my profession. When she returned, she asked me what my plans were in life. I responded, "I want to work for a total of 50 years in the Hartford Fire Department and then I would like to retire. I'll be around 77 at that time." She said, "I don't doubt that you can do that if you want to, but if you do, you will not feel fulfilled at the end of your life." With that she told me that I am an INFJ, which stands for Introverted, Intuitive, Feeling and Judgment, and that less than one percent of all people in the world fall into that category. With those words, I knew that my career was soon to be over. I just had to find out what I could do with such an unusual personality type. I found myself asking a question that I had not asked in 25 years: What goal should I be aspiring to in my life?

Health Challenge Round 3
2008

I had experienced so much in the eight years since I was promoted to the rank of chief of the department. Sixteen-hour days were commonplace. Some days I would work all day, go home for a night's sleep and be awakened in the middle of the night because of a multiple alarm fire. Eventually, I began to wear out physically. One day my wife Helaine looked at me and said, "What's the matter with your eye?" I hadn't heard that question since I was 19 years old. One of the signs that people saw in me when I was diagnosed with myasthenia gravis was back. So much had changed in the years since my diagnosis. I was now at the very top of my profession. My kids were grown, and I had distinguished myself academically. I had developed a stellar reputation for being of service in the city of my birth. I felt accomplished beyond my wildest dreams and no longer feared losing my health. My only concern was for my loved ones. So, upon seeing the signs that I had not seen since I was 21, I went to a neurologist. He informed me that it could be myasthenia gravis or it could be a brain tumor.

I took tests to determine the presence of myasthenia gravis and the results were negative. I then took a test to determine the presence of a brain tumor and that test was negative also. In a couple of weeks the signs were gone but one thing did remain. The question in my mind was, *What is causing this reoccurring problem?* I started to sense that I had better get everything I have the potential to accomplish done as soon as possible. My career in the fire department was great. I became a good man thanks in large part to that organization, and I had made it to the top of my profession. However, somehow I sensed that there was a place beyond the top, and to get there I would have to help others to succeed.

To accomplish that, I would need to focus on myself and not the department.

Suddenly it dawned on me. It was time to retire.

Chapter 19

In Remembrance
2008

The next couple of years were filled with even more accomplishments. Everyone in the department worked together like a finely tuned machine. We had our disagreements, but at last, we learned how to respectfully disagree with one another. The final confirmation that it was time for me to retire hit me on August 8, 2008. We were graduating the largest recruit class in the history of the Hartford Fire Department. One of the graduates was my second cousin, Kevin Bell. I had already hired a second cousin on my father's side of the family by the name of Antoine Smith, and Kevin was to be the family representative on my mother's side of the family. In addition to hiring the best candidates for the job, to me, it was a way to maintain representation from both sides of my family, even after I had retired. I just sensed that my grandfathers on both sides of my family would be proud to see their great-grandsons as members of the Hartford Fire Department. At Kevin's graduation ceremony, I gave the oath of office the way I always did; from memory, no notes. Usually I included the words, "...and that I will faithfully discharge according to law, my duties as a <u>firefighter</u> for the city of Hartford." However, this time I said the words, "....and that I will faithfully discharge according to law, my duties as a <u>member</u> of the Hartford Fire Department." The reason why I said "member" instead of "firefighter" is because I knew that I would not be there to promote any of the new firefighters to any other rank, so I gave them an oath that would last them for the rest of their careers. Tragically, that career would not be long for Kevin. On October the 7th, 2014, he was killed in the line of duty fighting a fire. The reader must pardon the lack of description here. I haven't been able to come up with the words necessary to describe how devastated my family, the department and the community all were when this happened. He was the first Hartford firefighter killed in the line of duty in over 40 years.

Dear Mr. Mayor
2009

I called the director of Human Resources, fellow department head Santiago Malave. I wanted to be certain that I made a decision that my wife Helaine and I could financially afford. As Santiago and I sat down, I mentioned that I was considering retiring. He didn't believe me. His first question was, "Are you serious?" I said, "yes," and he performed the necessary calculations. Suddenly Santiago looked up at me and said, "You know what you're doing!" I asked, "How so do you mean?" He said, "It does not matter how much longer you stay in your current position; you cannot get any more pay or benefits. So, if you are seriously considering leaving, this would be the ideal time to do so." That settled the matter. I went home and discussed it with Helaine. As usual she said, "I'm ready to support you no matter what you decide." I then made arrangements to speak with the Mayor. My meeting with the Mayor was the beginning of a very rewarding and meaningful experience. We discussed possible successors. I presented to him two names, and we both agreed that one man in particular would be ideal. It was Fire Marshal Edward Casares, and he would be the first Hispanic in the history of the Hartford Fire Department to serve as Chief. I gave a six months' notice. Now I was ready to retire!

Just prior to my retirement, I was asked by representatives of the Connecticut Historical Society to serve as the President of the Board of Trustees. I had served on the board for several years and had a deep appreciation for the institution for the past 25 years. I accepted the position with pride and gratitude. During my acceptance speech, I told everyone in attendance about how "history saved my life." By that, I was referring to the words spoken by the counselor at Greater Hartford Community College, Bill Edmonds. It was Mr. Edmonds who asked me the question, "Do you know how many people spent their lives, risked their lives and sometimes gave their lives so that you could have the opportunity to succeed?" Upon hearing these words, I thought about the history lessons my grandparents used to give me as a child. It was during that conversation with Mr. Edmonds that I developed the connection between the suffering of my ancestors and the need for me to succeed. My life had come full circle, and I was convinced that a knowledge of history helped make my academic and professional success possible. It was appropriate for me to serve in this capacity because history was still my passion. It became so because when things got really bad in my career, I visited the Connecticut Historical Society and studied how the old-time chiefs survived their challenges. Signs of my appreciation for history were everywhere in the Hartford Fire Department during those days, particularly at headquarters, which was at 275 Pearl Street. Thus Tool #20 was created, and it serves as a way to enhance a person's appreciation for his or her family, profession, community, state, and our nation. It also helps some students get through the most difficult history courses they will take in school. Overall, this is still the greatest country in the history of the planet. We just need to focus more on the positive things that have taken place in it.

So, I decided to include "History" in the Tools of Learning. It covers the need to know our national, state, city, employment organization, and family history. It is also the final Tool among 20. The grand finale!

TOOL #20
Dedicated to my grandparents, Pearl Woods-Smith and Benjamin Smith, Mr. Bill Edmonds, and the Connecticut Historical Society

The Positive History: Learn, Understand and Remember Your Positive History
1962, 1973, 2010

F.A.B. (Focus, Attitude, Behavior)

National

Unfortunately, very little history is taught to students in the classrooms of our nation until they get to college. When they get to college and take a history course, the information presented can be offensive to them. That leads to a bad attitude in the classroom, which can lead to bad grades.

To keep this from happening, think of the acronym F.A.B. when you study history, which stands for focus, attitude and behavior. If we focus on the positive people and occurrences of the past, it will change our attitude, and it is attitude that determines what our behavior will be. Of course, we want the kind of behavior that leads to good grades in history.

Knowing that there were people from all walks of life throughout history who made sacrifices for us will help motivate us to learn that history. If we know who made those sacrifices, we will be more inclined to apply ourselves academically and professionally out of a sense of gratitude to them. Also, as Booker T. Washington once said, "You measure the size of the accomplishment by the obstacles you had to overcome to reach your goals." When you take into consideration the obstacles that our nation had to overcome, you have to say that it is the greatest country in the history of the world.

State and City

Because some cities are the size of some neighborhoods, it is important to be flexible in this matter. People who know the sacrifices others made so that their state and city governments could exist, make better citizens, and knowing those sacrifices enhances your desire to be a better citizen too.

Employment Organization

The supervisors of where we work usually have a great appreciation for our place of employment. One of the reasons they appreciate it so much is the positive effect that organization has had on their lives. They were able to provide for themselves, and their families because of that organization. In some cases, they were able to prove their value to society through that organization. When this happens, they feel like they owe the organization a great debt of gratitude.

Seeing a new employee take an interest in the history of that organization shows a deep sense of appreciation for it. It's one of the signs that an employee is grateful for the opportunity to serve in that organization, and most people will confuse gratitude with class every time.

Family

It is wise to remember those students from cultures who typically receive excellent grades in school. When asked why they do so well, some of them reply "because I don't want to bring dishonor to my ancestors." Those of us who don't know our ancestors sometimes don't have that level of motivation. But we should, because even though we don't know who they were, they lived and sacrificed for us. So, we still owe them.

From the Top to Beyond
2010

I believe that the process of retiring from your chosen profession should be a time of great reflection. It should be a time when you pause frequently and ask yourself if you gave it all that you had. You should also be able to say that you are leaving because you have nothing left to give. But more than that, it should be a time when you look forward to doing something else. Within the next few years, I would hear it expressed best by a school psychologist at the Hartford Adult Education Center in Hartford Connecticut named Mr. Thomas Blake who said, "We don't retire from something. We retire to something else." I knew that was true, but what was it that I was retiring to? One of the men whose words I had studied for the past couple of decades or more was Earl Nightingale. It was him who said, "When a man stops doing the thing that he has to do and starts doing the things he wants to do, the character is revealed." Of all the things that I wanted to do, giving presentations on the system of learning methodology I had developed called the Tools of Learning was the most important. It had been 10 years since I last gave a presentation, but during that time I constantly visualized the process of presenting the information to audiences of people both small and large. As I visualized, I made changes to the program. The major question remained: *Is the need for a system of learning, understanding and remembering information as necessary as it was when I first developed it for myself, the Hartford Fire Department and the general public?* The answer to that question was about to be given to me in a most surprising fashion.

For this special occasion, I brought my plaques in from home and took a photo. When times got hard, I would look at them and remember that some people still appreciated my service. On the wall to your left is a flag that my daughter, Staff Sargent Kathleen Rene Teale, gave me. She said it flew with her on September 11th while she was serving in the Air Force. The three men under it are my uncles, Charlie, Manual and Jack Pina. They served during the Second World War.

April 9, 2010

Finally, the day came when I was to have my last day as Chief of the Hartford Fire Department. I had been planning this for years. Strangely, I found myself perfectly balanced emotionally speaking. I was leaving, but I was not in a hurry. I knew that there were many other things that I wanted to do with my life, but I had an overwhelming feeling of gratitude about the previous 28 years. The Hartford Fire Department had made my life meaningful and rewarding, but it was time to go. Some of the things I will never forget was getting on the radio and saying goodbye to everyone with a radio who wanted to say goodbye to me. It was truly moving.

As Chief, I found the photos and drawings of all of the chiefs of the Hartford Fire Department with the exception of three men. I vowed not to place my photo alongside the other chiefs until the day of my retirement. The following photograph is of me hanging up my photo among the other men who served as Chief of the Hartford Fire Department since 1789. It was another very moving experience. One that will stay with me for the rest of my life.

There were several people in attendance who will tell you that as soon as I hung up my photo, I paused, reflected and left the third floor for the last time as a member of the Hartford Fire Department.

Below are the other members of the Hartford Fire Department who served as Chief since 1789. Out of the 35, only seven made it to the 10-year mark. I was one of them. I'm the only one to have served twice. I looked at these pictures every day I reported for work. I never had the desire to put my photo there until the day I retired. I didn't want to see a picture of me every day that I came to work.

I always knew that I stood on "The Shoulders of Giants." Here are some of them. The others are in the previous photo.

Part 3

This is the final part of this book. Part 1 consisted of the first 27 years of my life, Part 2 consisted of my 28 years in the Fire Department, and the time period following my retirement is Part 3, which has yet to be completed. However, I have every intention of making Part 3 more productive than Parts 1 and 2 combined.

— C.A.Teale, Sr.

Chapter 20

In Conclusion
2010

During my transition from chief to retiree, I remembered the words of Socrates who said, "An unexamined life is not worth living." So, I began examining my life by writing down every event throughout my life that I thought had some effect on who I became as a person — the good, the bad and the very ugly. It was at this stage of my life that I modified my formula for accomplishment again. During this time of reflection, it became apparent that "A", which stood for "Accomplishment", should be changed to "Attainment", which means to reach a major goal. "Attainment" is the result of "Accomplishing" many things. Also, it became apparent that Health, Strategy and Desire were not required in equal measure. All of the things that I experienced as Chief proved to me that Desire is twice as valuable as either Health or Strategy, and that it is as valuable as Health and Strategy combined. Therefore, the formula for success was changed to the following:

$$A= (H+S)\ D$$

Since that time, it has stood for "Attainment equals Health plus Strategy times Desire." In essence, this means if you want to reach any major goal, you must have a certain amount of physical, mental, and emotional Health and you must have a Strategy. However, Desire is as valuable as Health and Strategy combined.

Ideally, the values of each are as follows:

Attain 100 = (Health 5 + Strategy 5) Desire 10
Once you have added the value of Health to Strategy (10), you multiply that sum times the value of your Desire (10). Both sides of this equation have equal or "proportional" meaning. The greater your value on the right side of the equation (100), the greater your ability to reach your goals.

This formula proved to be so effective that it became the mission statement of the company started by my son Charlie and I called "Teale Ink, Inc."

238

Since my retirement, I have continued to be of service but in a different way. To accomplish the task of enhancing desire for academic and professional success, I found it necessary to write books that inspire.

By the time the book you are now reading was published, I had written my mother's family history and the story of her life in Wareham, Massachusetts during the Great Depression and World War II. The name of her book is *I Remember Wareham* by Francisca L. Smith, and the poetry included in her book, entitled *Random Thoughts* has been published and is being read as far away as Boston, Massachusetts. On my father's side of the family, I wrote my uncle's story of his family history and his life growing up and living in Hartford called "I Remember Hartford, by William "Rab" Smith. It is now being sold in the Hartford, Connecticut area and has sold as far away as California. I also wrote the autobiography of my former gym teacher and mentor, Mr. Hurley, entitled *The Making of a Legend: The Life and Times of Walter J. "Doc" Hurley*.

To address the "S" or strategy portion of A=(H+S) D, I have taught the Tools of Learning to over 1,500 students, educators and administrators throughout the state of Connecticut.

Requests for presentations that I could not give due to scheduling challenges and a request from the superintendent of CREC (Capital Region Education Council) for a train-the-trainer course, compelled me to write this book, which includes my system of learning, understanding and remembering information. With this book and the Tools of Learning Student Workbook, any nationally recognized teacher or instructor can teach the Tools of Learning to his or her students.

Although I will always feel the need to "be of service" in the city that I live, I am mindful of my obligation to make a nationwide contribution. Therefore, it is my aspiration to share the information contained in this book throughout the United States of America. I will succeed if persistence has anything to do with it.

The Appendix

This is my son Charlie and me at the first paid presentation of the Tools of Learning presented to a group of Capital Region Education Council (CREC) administrators, teachers and tutors. After seeing me struggle during this presentation without one, Charlie created the PowerPoint presentation currently referred to in the Tools of Learning Student Workbook and even created the name of the corporation that makes all of the books, history tours and the Tools of Learning possible. The name he selected was Teale Ink.

Appendix A

The Tools of Learning Activities

"An unexamined life is one that is not worth living."   — Socrates

Confirmation of Need
2010

During the first year of retirement, I was asked by the Hartford Foundation for Public Giving to serve as an interviewer of high school students to determine if they should receive college scholarships. I agreed to do so. They informed me that I would have to take an orientation session before I went into the field to conduct interviews, which I arranged to do. In the middle of their power point presentation, the following statement was shared by the presenter with everyone in attendance: "In the year 2000, the United States of America was number one in the world when it came to sending its citizens to college. In the year 2010, we are number nine." Initially, upon hearing and seeing this statement, I was stunned enough to interrupt the program. I asked, "Is that accurate?" Everyone in attendance looked at me as if to say "didn't you know that?" It suddenly dawned on me that our nationwide decline had taken place during my tenure as Chief. I was so busy working on matters that involved saving lives and protecting property that I saw nothing else. I had no idea that we had declined to such a level, and I had to ask, "Why? What changed in the last ten years?" I began to wonder what else had I missed. Also, that year I began teaching foundational reading and math at the Caribbean Resource Center. I also presented my Tools of Learning there. It was during this experience that I learned this statistic: Of the 124,000 residents of the city of Hartford, 40,000 of the adults did not have a high school diploma. I could not help but remember a time when I struggled to get my GED and failed two times at my first attempts to get a college degree. If it had not been for my GED, I would not have become Chief of the Hartford Fire Department because I would not have been eligible to become a firefighter. Also, if I had not become a firefighter, the information needed to write this book would not have been learned. Both empathy and a desire to be of service caused me to give careful consideration to these very important facts. I could not help but realize that if the challenge of 40,000 adults without high school diplomas exists in Hartford, then something similar or even worse probably exists in other cities throughout this nation. Could it be that we as a nation can increase the number of college graduates by sending more adult education students to college? At the risk of sounding boastful, I believe that we can, and the Tools of Learning can make this possible. I am proof of that fact!

This experience reminded me of the time that the members of the Training Division were approached by Chief Stewart and Assistant Chief Kehoe about the poor grades of our recruits. The Tools of Learning saved the day then, and I saw no reason why it could not save the day now.

I started retirement by giving presentations to several organizations including the Caribbean Resource Center in Hartford. For two years, I was assigned to teach foundational reading and math there. During this experience, I interacted with the directors, Dr. Carol Johnson and Edgar Johnson. At one time during those two years, I was informed that the GED was about to undergo a revision. It would be more difficult to pass the test and some people, who otherwise might pass, would fail. I sensed that the Tools of Learning could help every student who heard a presentation. This compelled me to seek a larger audience, which I found at the Hartford Adult Education Center on Washington Street in Hartford, Connecticut. With the approval and support of Dr. Tina Jeter, beginning in October of 2012, the Tools of Learning was taught to English-speaking students seeking their G.E.Ds. The program was very positively received by the administration, teachers and students of that learning institution. This culminated in an award presented to me during the graduation ceremony of 2013. In March of that year, a meeting was held among the following personnel of that school: Mr. Alpha Nicholson, Ms. Sandra Crews, Dr. Henry Haye, Ms. Miriam Levinson, Mr. K. Lewis, Ms. Marcia Rodriguez and this author. During that meeting, it was decided that "activities" were necessary to further enhance the ability of the students to fully benefit from the program. During a follow-up meeting between Mr. Nicholson and me, it was decided that those activities would cover:

1. Use of a study schedule
2. What should I put in my notes?
3. How do I remember what I learn?

With the help of Assistant Director Ms. Jacquelyn Mann, the subtopics of these activities were established and presented starting in April of 2013.
The contributions of everyone who recommended the following activities were all greatly appreciated and in a literal sense, noteworthy.

Activity 1

How to Create a Usable Study Schedule

Now that you have received a presentation on the Tools of Learning, it is time to put into practice some of its most effective recommendations. The first of these is actually the first Tool we learned entitled "Use a Study Schedule". Some of the things we discussed during this portion of the presentation included:

- 1. A study schedule keeps you from doing anything but studying, when you should be studying
- 2. Where to place your study schedule
- 3. Time spent on TV and other forms of media
- 4. Placing your schedule on your favorite electronic device

Although these recommendations are beneficial, some people will not be able to apply them until they have received this presentation entitled "Activity for 'Use a Study Schedule'". During this presentation, the student will learn how to create a study schedule that will enhance his or her ability to succeed academically and professionally. Although there are perhaps many more things that could be taken into consideration, the following are the top 10.

Let's begin:

1. No more fast food

I'm sure that many of you might be thinking that this is about staying away from fast food restaurants, but that is not what this is about at all. What this is referring to is our society's belief that we can get what we want without investing enough time to get it. I believe that this attitude got its start through the use of fast food restaurants. At first, they were just convenient. You went to one when you didn't have the time to fix a meal or the money to go to an expensive place to eat. Then they became a national pastime. Although the term is not used anymore, they were once called "fun food". Although the food may have been fun to eat, there were problems created by the use of this kind of food: it was sometimes not nutritious, and in other cases, it was actually unhealthy. Well, so it is with the learning process.

Many of us are under the impression that we invest enough time studying and we do not.

It is important to determine how long we must work at earning an education. For example, some students work at earning their GED after spending three years in high school and some students (like me) work at earning their GED with only six months of high school. It stands to reason that one person will probably take longer to finish than the other. Well, we don't want to come up short when it comes to our education. We want to spend enough time getting an education so that we can be successful students, and so that we can become successful professionals.

In addition to studying long enough, you must be persistent. That means being consistent or continuing with the studying process until you are finished. If you stop studying for a few months because you got a job or for some other reason, when you go back to school, you won't start where you left off. You must start from the very beginning. That's because time will erase most or all of what you learned before you stopped. Once you start, don't let anything tempt you into stopping. Finish up strong so that you will be better prepared for your next step!

2. Grow with the info.

Some students start school, and they get good to excellent grades. Suddenly, their grades start to decline. There are possibly many reasons why this happens so frequently, but one of them is the level of the information. Learning sometimes gets harder because the information gets more advanced. If a student does not expect this, then that student will not be prepared for the future. A lack of preparation causes failure.

Within a couple of years, the level of the information a student must learn can change from writing a paper on "how I spent my summer vacation" to "describe the different parts of speech." It can change from "adding and subtracting" to "algebra and geometry." Suddenly, we have a much bigger opponent to defeat. The information becomes more difficult to understand, and therefore, more difficult to remember. If we can't remember the information, then we cannot pass the quizzes and tests that we must take.

3. How much studying is enough studying?

We must also determine how much time is enough time for studying. It's important to realize that the difference between being a good student and being a bad student is often directly related to the amount of time you invest studying. If your grades are not good and you think it's because you are not smart, then you won't try to do great things with your life. You will think *well, I can't get good grades, so there is no sense in me going to college.* The truth of the matter is, we can succeed if we <u>spend</u> less time on media (TV, cell phone, social media, etc.) and <u>invest</u> more time in studying. However, the major question is *how much time is enough time for studying?*

Before you sign up to take a course or a group of courses, find out from the school how much studying it will take to get excellent grades in the courses you plan on taking. The most commonly used figure is 1:3. That means for every hour you spend in the classroom, you are expected to spend an additional 3 hours studying. Let's see how that works out mathematically:

If you are in class 15 hours per week that's 3 X 15 = 45 hours.

That's 45 hours of studying that should be done if you are in a classroom 15 hours per week, and you expect to get excellent grades in all of your courses. If you are not willing to invest that much time, then take fewer courses, but do not commit to taking courses that you will not study for.

4. Determine how many hours per week you have available for studying.

Although the 1:3 figure works well for some students, 45 hours per week is not the amount of time that the average adult education student has.

Here's why:

We all have 168 hours in a week. If we sleep eight hours per day then that takes up 56 hours, leaving 112. Many adult education students are employed full-time. That takes up an additional 40 hours per week plus transportation to and from work. That leaves a maximum of 72 hours. We also have to eat three times or more per day. At around one hour to prepare, eat a meal, and clean up afterwards. That leaves around 51 hours. Then, some of us have spiritual needs, family obligations and physical exercising (which are all important). These last three can only be determined by the student because they vary greatly from person to person. But even if you spent just two hours per day among these last three, you would find yourself with a maximum of 37 hours per week to do whatever you want to do. Now you could spend that time watching television or you could invest it studying. But even if you invested it all studying, you would be short by eight hours.

$$37 - 45 = -8$$

If the number of hours you have available is less than the number of hours you should study, do not get discouraged. You can still get good grades if you use vacations, snow days and holidays wisely.

5. Practice placing the time available in a chart.

a. Add up all of the hours you need for sleep, work, food preparation, eating, spiritual needs, family obligations and physical exercise. There will be other categories that you can add if you would like.

b. Take the total of that amount and subtract it from 168.

The Tools of Learning Hours Available for Studying Chart

Activity	Hours Per Day	Days Per Week	Approximate Number of Hours
a. Sleep/Rest			
b. Work			
c. Food Preparation, Eating and Cleaning Up			
d. Attending Classes			
e. Spiritual Needs			
f. Family Obligations			
g. Physical Exercise			
h. Miscellaneous			
i. Total Number of Hours	X	X	
j. Subtract Line (i) From 168	X	X	168
k. Hours Available for Studying	X	X	

c. Take the "Hours Available for Studying" and place them in the following schedule.

d. Fill out the subject section when you are certain of the courses that you will be taking.

Note: Under the activity "Miscellaneous", some people put the time they spend traveling. They do this because they don't believe that they can study while going from one place to another. If you remember the SQ5R system of studying, you know that reviewing is part of the studying process. Well, you can review information while traveling. An example of this would be taking the bus to and from work and school. While on that bus, you can listen to recordings of information that you think might be on the test. Even if you are driving a car, you can listen to a recording of important information.

In essence, motivational speaker Zig Ziglar said it best: "If you are sitting down you should be reading. If you are moving you should be listening to tapes."

The Tools of Learning Study Schedule

Schedule the completion of homework A.S.A.P after class

Day of the Week	Subject	Time
Sunday		
Monday		
Tuesday		
Wednesday		
Thursday		
Friday		
Saturday		
Revise the above for holidays, vacation days and snow days		

If you contribute a small amount of time to studying, you will get little rewards.

6. Prior to signing up to take a class or group of classes, determine the level of difficulty you will have in the course or courses you are going to take.

If you think that you are going to have a very difficult time with a course that you must take, then just take one course. This is especially true if you don't have as much time as you would like to have because of other activities.

7. If you don't have enough time to study during the week, then use other spare time.

Some countries send their students to school six days per week, and there is no such thing as summer vacation. "When we are studying, they are studying and when we are on vacation, they are studying," says Dr. Carol Johnson, who was noted earlier in this book. The only way to help offset the obvious academic advantage this gives them is for us to study on holidays, while on vacation, or on days when we have inclement weather (snow days, etc). Even though you have the day off from school, you don't have the day off from studying. Since we will not be in the classroom on these days, we will have additional spare time, which we can use for studying. Use the last row of your "Study Schedule" as a reminder to study additional hours during these times and as a way to increase the total amount of time you can study for your current diploma program.

8. Place this schedule in a prominent location.

Any place you go by frequently will do. If necessary, place it on the screen of your television set. In this way, you won't watch TV until after you have studied. Your cell phone is another place. Since it is with you all the time, place an alarm on it that tells you when it is time to study.

9. Notify all family and friends so that you can avoid interruptions.

This one is self-explanatory. One of the most challenging distractions a person can have to the learning process is family and friends. Some students even receive text messages from their friends when their friends know they are in class. To prevent this from happening to you while you are studying, you must tell everyone you normally interact with when you are studying, and inform them that unless it is an emergency, you would appreciate it if they did not contact you during these times. Otherwise, you may not get any studying done at all.

10. Aspire

"Aspire: to think of and to reach for a goal that excites you."

— C.A. Teale, Sr.

An aspiration is like both the rudder and the engine of a ship. If you don't have a rudder, you won't go to where you want to go, and if you don't have an engine, you are going nowhere.

Why are you studying? What are you hoping to do with your education? These may seem like simple questions, but some people have not given them any thought at all, so many of us don't have an aspiration. We just have not taken the time to think about what we eventually want to do with the training and education that we are pursuing.

As soon as you can, right now if possible, determine your aspiration. Write it down. Make it one that is so powerful that it will get you out of bed even when you have every reason to feel depressed enough to stay in it. If you wait until you need it, it may not work. That may be too late. Also, It should not be someone else's idea of what you should do with your life. It should be your goal that is so meaningful to you that it keeps you moving in a positive direction when everyone else around you is stalled. Think of that aspiration just before you study, and it will increase the desire you need to succeed. Remember, shoot for the stars.

Also, some people are reluctant about aspiring to a particular goal. They think that if they choose a goal, they will be obligated to stay with it for life, or they think that it will be kind of embarrassing to change goals once they have chosen one. This is entirely false. If you aspire to any positive goal, it builds enthusiasm and it improves study skills as you pursue that goal. Doctor Jonas Salk is a perfect example of how this works. He started out studying law in college and changed his goal to medicine. Eventually, he became a Nobel Peace Prize winning doctor because he discovered the cure for polio.

I certainly hope that this presentation has clarified that portion of my presentation on the activity for Tool #1 called "Use a Study Schedule" and that it will help to insure your academic and professional success.

Before starting the following activity, determine if the students have in mind a goal worth aspiring to yet.

Activity 2

What should I write in my notes?

As a result of the original Tools of Learning presentation, you should know the benefits of "rewriting your notes, A.S.A.P." (Tool #11 of the Tools of Learning) However, what should we write in our notes in the first place? The following information is designed to address this subject head on.

1. G.Y.S.T.

Some of you may remember reading about mnemonics during the presentation on the Tools of Learning. Well, a mnemonic is any memory aid, and one of the memory aids commonly used is called an acronym. An acronym is a word where each letter in the word represents another word. In this case, the word is GYST, which stands for Get Your Stuff Together.

The "stuff" that is being referred to in this case, includes the following:
a. Notebook
b. Pencils or Pens
c. Respect

There are students who show up to school without any of these.

    a. Notebook

A notebook is not just an object that holds sheets of paper. It is a means of holding all of the notes you have taken and keeping them together so that you can access them readily. If you are writing notes on sheets of paper that are not attached to anything, then you will likely misplace them and end up spending time searching for your notes when you should be studying them. That's a waste of valuable studying time. You might not find them at all.

Therefore, one of the wisest things that a student can purchase is a three-hole punch. If you have one, you can take your notes or a teacher's handout and put your teacher's name on it along with the date and the subject. Punch holes in it and place it in your notebook.

These notes should be in the same notebook as your personal study guide (PSG), close to your questions. That way, you can quickly create new questions from your new notes and handouts if needed.

b. Pencils or Pens

Regarding the pencil and pen, try to keep at least one spare with you. If all you have is one pen, you could run out of ink. If you have only one pencil, then when the point breaks, you will have to get up and sharpen it. This creates noise that can be disruptive to the class. Keep an ample amount of sharpened pencils in a protective case.

c. Respect

"Good listening pays high dividends."   — Earl Nightingale
"If anyone is to learn in a learning environment, then everyone must feel respected." — teacher from South Africa (name unknown), Springfield College, Springfield, Massachusetts.

We are about to look at a classroom from three perspectives:

a. The Teacher
b. Classmates
c. The Talking Student

a. The Teacher

Some students don't understand the importance of not talking while the teacher is talking. Talking while the teacher is trying to teach is disrespectful to the teacher. The matter of disrespecting a teacher in the classroom is necessary to discuss. Why? In some schools, the teachers and the students sometimes argue about how students hold private conversations and use their smartphones while the teacher is speaking. A teacher cannot concentrate on what she/he is presenting when a student is talking or texting.

b. Classmates

If a student is talking, then the other students in the classroom cannot hear what the teacher is saying. This causes the students to miss out on important information that they should be placing in their notes. We've got to stop doing this. It is disrespectful and unproductive because no one can learn if just one student is talking while the teacher is trying to teach.

c. The Talking Student

Every teacher knows that if a student is talking, they aren't learning, because no one can talk and learn at the same time. Some students say that they were talking in class because they had a question about what the teacher was presenting. If you have a question that you need answering, then ask the teacher, not your fellow students. If the time is not right for asking the teacher, then write the question in your notes and ask your teacher the question when the time is right.

The solution is simple: don't hold conversations with other students while the teacher is talking. Someone, including you, will miss hearing something important that should be in your notes.

2. Place the following information at the top of the first page of your notes:

Subject

Teacher's Name   Month/Day/Year

This is more self-explanatory than #1. As soon as class begins, you should write at the top of the first page of your notes this information. This is done so that when you go to review your notes (which you should do before every class), you will be able to determine the subject, when the notes were taken and who taught the class. Who taught the class is particularly important because sometimes your notes need further clarification. With this system, you can approach your teacher and say,

"I took math notes on May 29, 2015, and I cannot understand what is meant by the term lowest common denominator. Can you clarify this for me?"

The mere fact that you took notes proves to your teacher that you value the information that was presented. She or he will appreciate that attitude and be inclined to give you whatever attention you need to learn the information thoroughly. It may even help your grade. You might even get an "A" for effort.

3. If it's on the board, it's in your notes.

Some excellent teachers have poor penmanship, so they don't really like writing things on the board. To compensate for this, they will rely on

PowerPoint presentations or some other method of helping you to visualize the information. However, no matter what method they use to display something on a board or screen, put it in your notes. No one goes through the effort or expense of putting something on the board or developing a PowerPoint Presentation unless it is vitally important. Make sure you record this information in your notes.

4. If it is repeated or restated

If a teacher repeats something, he or she is trying to show how important it is. Hearing something repeated and then writing it down is important, but no more important than writing down something that is restated. Restating means saying the same thing over and over again but in a different way. You will have to listen carefully for restated words and phrases but they are well worth catching. Look for those repeated or restated statements and write them down. You will probably see them again on a test.

5. Dates and Locations

It has been said many times before but it bears repeating: "Visualization is the greatest learning tool in the world." This pertains to our next recommendation: "What should I write in my notes?" If your teacher gives you a date or location during a presentation, write it down and list the occurrence next to it. This will help you picture what you are learning. An example would be:

December 7, 1941, the start of WWII for the U.S.
Pearl Harbor, where the Second World War began for the U. S.

Also under the subheading "remembering dates", Try to remember some dates by comparing them with other dates. For example, if something happened the year that you were born, it is easier to remember. Whenever you hear a year or a location, picture something unique to that time and place, like the clothing people wore, or an object.

In the above example related to the start of WWII, envision a palm tree and you are likely to remember Hawaii.

Visualizing what you hear helps you to learn, understand and remember information. It can also help make a presentation more entertaining, if you can see the information in your mind's eye. It's like the difference between radio and television.

6. The names of people mentioned and their contributions

Should your teacher mention the name of someone during a class, write that name down and write down the contribution that person made. An example would be:

Franklin Delano Roosevelt, President of the U.S.

7. Unfamiliar Words

In some learning environments it is not acceptable to raise your hand and ask "what does that word mean." As your courses become more advanced, your teacher will expect you to know what a word means. If you don't know what it means they will expect you to take the initiative and look that word up.

If your teacher says a word that you don't know, estimate the meaning of the word by listening to how it is used in a sentence. Then, write that word down in your notes. The exact spelling is not necessary.

As soon as possible after class, look up unknown words using:

i. notes or a memo application.
ii. a website like Dictionary.com.
iii. a dictionary.

That one word can mean the difference between learning the information you want to learn and you not learning the information at all. This can also prevent you from using words that don't exist, like "conversate" (there's no such word).

8. If your teacher says an expression that you don't know the meaning of, write it in your notes.

As soon as you find the time, look up that expression and place the meaning of it in your notes. If the expression is one that does not exist, then check the Internet to see if you can find one that is close to it. An example of this would be "for all intensive purposes." There is no such expression. The correct expression is "for all intents and purposes."

9. If you can see the potential benefit of the information

It doesn't happen often, but sometimes we can sense when information is important enough for us to remember for other than just school. Sometimes, information has great potential in a professional and even personal way. One example that I can think of is the statement made by the teacher from South Africa that I mentioned earlier: "If people are to learn in a school environment, then everyone must feel respected." I can remember those words more than 20 later because I saw how valuable the information could be academically, personally and professionally way back in 1992. This realization led me to write it in my notes and review it for future use. Always remember that someday you will be paid for what you know, not just how many tests you have passed.

10. The need for prerequisite information

Prerequisite (Students must know the meaning of this word.)

Sometimes a student can feel like everything the teacher is saying is important enough for us to put in our notes. If this happens to you, then you lack the prerequisite information necessary to be taking that course in the first place. Notes should be for new information, not for information you already know. If everything your teacher says sounds new, you must do either of the following:

a. Take a course that covers the prerequisite information.
b. Get a tutor.

Let's put the recommendations in your workbook to use. Take notes for the next five minutes. At the end of the following presentation, let's see if you can answer some of my questions by using your notes.

Note to instructors: While giving this presentation, write some of the information on the board.

Why I Remember Roberto Clemente

When I was a teenager growing up in Hartford, I had lots of respect for athletes. One of the people who I came to respect the most was a baseball player by the name of Roberto Clemente. He was born in Puerto Rico in 1934. Even as a very young man, he identified with the people who worked hard. He appreciated "the people who struggle." Initially, the Brooklyn Dodgers signed Clemente in 1954 when he was practically right out of high school. Sadly, the Dodgers never played him. At one time, Clemente was told that he was their secret weapon and that he would get a chance to play when he was needed the most. He didn't like that answer, so the next year, in 1955, he went to the Pittsburg Pirates.

Although some of Clemente's teammates, the media, and the fans of the teams he played for did sometimes not appreciate him, he remained proud of his heritage. Everywhere he went, when people would call him "Bob" or "Bobby", he would correct them by saying "Roberto". What I liked most about him was if he didn't think he could play well, he wouldn't play. He was like an artist. An artist isn't going to paint something he think looks bad and sign his name to it. He had a "passion for excellence". He once said, "If the ball is in the park and the game is on the line, I will catch the ball."

In 1960, Clemente's team won the World Series. During that decade, he led the National League four times when it came to batting averages. In 1971, he played in the World Series again. Just before the series began, he was quoted as saying, "nobody does anything better than me in baseball," and his team won the World Series again. That year, he was voted the Most Valuable Player. On September 30, 1972, he became the first Hispanic to get 3,000 hits in the major leagues. At one point he said, "I now have peace of mind."

Soon after the World Series and his 3,000th hit, Clemente and his wife Vera visited the people of Managua, Nicaragua so that he could teach the children how to play baseball. He and his wife fell in love with the people of Managua, but they had to leave to go back home to San Juan, Puerto Rico. Three weeks later, there was a terrible earthquake in Managua, and the people were left without food or medical supplies. Clemente chartered two cargo planes to transport supplies to the affected people. Unfortunately, corrupt people in Nicaragua took control of the supplies before they reached the people in need. Clemente heard of this and on December 31, 1972, he chartered another plane, loaded it with supplies and got on the plane. He was quoted as saying, "If I go with the plane, the supplies will get to the people." The plane was so loaded with supplies, that as soon as it got over the ocean it went down in the water. Clemente and everyone else on the plane were killed. His body was never found.

As time passed by, I came to realize why I appreciated Roberto Clemente so much. It wasn't his athleticism; it was his humanitarianism.

His most famous quote was, "If you see someone in need and you do nothing to help, you're wasting your time on this earth."

That's why I remember Roberto Clemente.

My questions to the class:

1. What essential Tools of Learning for your profession did you have?
2. Did you place the subject, presenter and date at the top of the first page?
3. What important information did was written on the board?
4. What information was repeated or restated?
5. What dates and locations did you mention?
6. What other name or names were mentioned other than the main character?
7. Name any unfamiliar words that were mentioned?
8. What unfamiliar expressions were used during the presentation?
9. What one thing was mentioned that you think will be beneficial in the future?   How so?
10. What prerequisite information might have helped you to understand this presentation more?

Activity 3
How to Remember Information

Review the Roberto Clemente questions before beginning this activity.

In the Tools of Learning, the section on "Remembering" consists of four separate tools. The most effective of these four is called "Use SQ5R". SQ5R is a composite. It includes: a system of visualizing information taught to me by a fellow recruit named Eddie Lopez, the SQ3R system created by Francis Pleasant Robinson and presented by the International Fire Service and Training Association, and this writer's contributions, which are:

a. Recent and relevance
b. Audibleizing the information (my made-up use of what some people call a made up word)
c. Precise pronunciation as a psychomotor function
d. Repetition instead of reciting

In this activity, we will examine and practice the basic method used to enhance our ability to memorize large amounts of information. After all, what's the point of learning and understanding it if you forget it?

1. Identify the information you want to remember

Although this might seem easy to do, it is sometimes very difficult to accomplish. The steps generally consist of:

a. hearing or seeing something that you think is important enough for you to put in your notes.
b. reading something you think is important enough for you to highlight.

From these two sources, you will be able to identify the information that you want to understand. If it is very important, you may elect to remember it for extended periods of time. An example of this could be our multiplication tables. As students, being able to remember this information precisely is imperative. Being close is not good enough.

2. A person's got to know their limitations

In the fire department, there is a term known as "critical velocity". What it means is that no matter how much additional pressure you place on a fire hose, you are not going to get more water out of the end of it. You may even burst the hose. Therefore, the point here is to pace yourself. If you attempt to memorize too much information within a short amount of time, you are going to get frustrated and give up. It may even prevent you from believing in your ability to remember information.

3. Create an environment without distractions

While we are memorizing new information, it is beneficial to imagine what that information looks like and sounds like, if possible. You can't do that with distractions. Trying to memorize information with the T.V. or radio on is like holding a conversation while someone else is making a lot of noise. You can't concentrate on what the person you are listening to is saying. This means no television, no radio, no computers and definitely no smartphones. Smartphones have become an assassin of time. They have become necessary in the sense that someone might try to contact you during an emergency. However, when you are studying, ask the person contacting you if you can get back to them when you are done.

4. Make sure that you understand what you want to remember

Don't make the mistake of reciting information over and over again, just so you can say that you have it memorized. Understanding the information before you attempt to memorize it saves time, and it enhances your ability to remember the information long term.

5. Determine the relevance of the information

The word relevance means "connected with the matter at hand." In other words, ask yourself the question *how am I going to use this information?* Information must be relevant for us to enjoy the process of memorizing it. Determine how you can use information before you go about the process of placing this information in your long-term memory or neocortex.

One example that illustrates the importance of relevance is defining words. Ask yourself *why is it important for me to know what this word means,* and *will I be able to use this information in my academic, personal or professional life?* If you can answer "yes" to these questions, then the information is truly relevant. The Tools of Learning recommends the "S times 5" system of building a powerful vocabulary. This system is found in Tool #4 entitled "Keep a Dictionary on Hand".

6. Decrease anxiety

The number one reason why a person cannot learn, understand or remember something is because of anxiety. Anxiety is a feeling of worry, nervousness, or unease, usually about something that is about to happen. Something like a test. The one word that stands out more than all the others in this definition is the word "worry". Some people think that worrying is necessary if you are thinking about solving a problem. Well, that "ain't necessarily so." (Ira Gershwin)

Some of you might be thinking *what does he know about worrying?* Well, I have a long-standing history of worrying that dates back to when I was in the second grade. My teacher wrote on my report card, "Charles is a worry wart." When I got older, I developed test anxiety. I can study information for years and when that test gets in front of me, I draw a blank due to worry and nervousness. To get me through this experience during promotional exams, I used to trick myself into thinking that the test was not that important. I would say to myself, *If I don't pass it this time, I'll be just fine and I will pass it the next time.* Then I would calm down. However, I continued worrying throughout my career as fire chief.

Then one day I read the words of Willis Carrier, inventor of Carrier air conditioners. Mr. Carrier said that there were three ways to prevent worrying. They are:

a. Think of the worst thing that can happen to you
b. Learn to accept the worst
c. Work at improving on the situation

The worst thing that <u>you may think</u> can happen to you is that you don't pass the test. That's what happened to me the first time that I took my GED, when I failed to get good grades in college (twice), and when I took the oral interview for my Captain's exam. The world did not end, and thanks to the Tools of Learning, I eventually succeeded in them all.

Also, if you were in a body of water and your arms and legs were moving, it does not mean that you are swimming. You could be drowning because swimming requires a coordinated effort using your arms and legs, if you are to go from one place to another. Well, so it is with the thinking process. The point that I am trying to make is that your mind could be moving constantly. However, if you are not getting closer to your destination (which is solving the problem), then you could be just worrying. In both cases, you will use a lot of energy and never get closer to where you want to be. When you accept the worst, your worrying stops and your nerves calm down. Once your nerves calm down, you can work at improving the situation.

The work that we must do to improve the situation may not be the same for everyone, but I ask that you too consider using the methods that I have used throughout my academic and professional career:

a. Don't let what you don't know get in the way of what you do know. This can happen if you have not been able to master all of the information that might be on a test. Sometimes a test will consist of 100 questions and just 10 of those questions are on the concept that you have not mastered. If you get anxious about those 10 questions, you may not be able to answer the other 90 correctly. Focus on what you know and you could still pass that test with 90 percent of the answers right.

b. Think of reasons to believe that this test is not the all-important one. If you start thinking that everything is riding on this test, and if you pass it your life will be great, and if you don't your life will be over, then you will start to feel anxious about the test. Instead, think about what you will do if you don't pass, like taking it again or being content with what you have. Just think of options that will help keep you from worrying or being overly anxious.

c. Find a way to take as many tests that are similar to the one you have to take for graduation or promotion as possible. Take the tests in the same location, with the same time constraint, if you can. If you are unable to take a test in the same location and you want to practice on your own anyway, be certain to time yourself as you take your practice test. Working under a time constraint creates anxiety, but that is how tests are given, and you can only get used to that source of anxiety through practice, practice, practice while being timed.

d. Don't tell everyone that you are taking the test. If you tell everyone, you will be thinking about their disappointment (or possibly, laughter) if you don't pass the test. In the words of my cousin, Finitia Armstrong, "Some people will pray for you and others will prey on you." You don't need these things on your mind when you are trying to focus on remembering information and thinking about the negative reactions of other people leads to anxiety.

d. My grandfather, Candido Pina, once said, "Relax. Knowing that when a person has done their best, they can do no more." This one is self-explanatory. If you have studied properly for a test, then you have the right to relax.

Where the Rubber Meets the Road

7. "Be not afraid of moving slowly; be afraid only of standing still."

— Chinese proverb.

Memorize vs. Remember

Memorize: to commit to memory; to learn by heart
Remember: to recall to the mind by an act or an effort of memory; to think of again

Memorizing and remembering are not the same thing. One is putting information in our minds and the other is taking information out. Expect the process of memorizing information to take some time and be content with improving what you remember, even if the improvement is very slight. A two percent improvement in information memorized per week equals 100 percent in less than a year. Have you ever met someone who received good grades in a course but a year later couldn't remember what he or she learned? That's because that person didn't take the time to memorize the information properly or he or she didn't take the time to review what he or she knew. If you don't take enough time to memorize the information thoroughly, you won't be able to remember it when you need it under pressure.

8. The mother of all retention

Repeating:
Let's take a block of information that we want to memorize so that we can remember it later, like our multiplication tables. Most people who have a difficult time with division, adding and subtracting fractions, and algebra have difficulties with these types of mathematics because they have not mastered the multiplication tables.

To get through multiplication problems, they often use a filled-in chart of the multiplication tables. Unfortunately, that chart is not allowed when they are taking a test. Other people who don't know their multiplication tables will add to get their answer. To figure out how much is 8 times 8, they will start at 8 times one equals 8. Next, they will continue with 8 times 2 equals 16, etcetera, until they get to 8 times 8 equals 64. That is not multiplying; that's adding, and it takes a long time to arrive at the right answer. Because most tests are timed, they run out of time before they can finish the test.

Math's Foundation

The foundation of math includes addition, subtraction, multiplication and division. If you do not know your multiplication tables, you will not be able to check a division answer. That means that two walls of your foundation will either be weak or missing entirely.

If this is the case, you will have a difficult time solving the following types of problems. You may not be able to solve them at all.

We Need to Know
Our Multiplication Tables

Ms. Marcia Rodriguez

Ms. Rodriguez is a math teacher at the Hartford Adult Education Center in Hartford, Connecticut. She began teaching math in Teacher Corps during the years 1971 to 1973. She has taught math in the Hartford Public School system ever since. With 44 years of experience in her field, I asked her to construct a list of all the types of math problems in a GED program that require knowledge of multiplication. The following is what she provided.

1. Multiplying whole numbers
2. Dividing whole numbers
3. Solving word problems
4. Solving multi-step problems
5. Fractions and multiples
6. Order of operations
7. Changing mixed numbers to fractions
8. Changing improper fractions to mixed numbers
9. Finding equivalent fractions
10. Reducing fractions
11. Raising fractions to higher terms
12. Finding equivalent fractions with given denominators
13. Adding, subtracting, multiplying and dividing fractions and mixed numbers
14. Multiplying decimals
15. Dividing decimals
16. Changing fractions to decimals
17. Changing decimals to fractions
18. Changing a fraction to a percent
19. Changing a percent to a fraction
20. Changing a percent to a mixed number
21. Compare and order fractions and decimals including on a number line
22. Finding unit rates
23. Using proportions to solve problems including similar figures
24. Scale drawings and scale factor
25. Solving percent problems
26. Finding rate of change
27. Solving interest problems
28. Converting measurements

29. Finding perimeter of two-dimensional figures including circumference of a circle
30. Changing radius to diameter
31. Finding area of two-dimensional figures including circles
32. Finding surface area and volume of three-dimensional figures
33. Finding perimeter, area or volume of combined or irregular figures
34. Finding congruent angles
35. Finding complementary and supplementary angles
36. Corresponding sides of similar triangles
37. Determining the measure of an angle
38. Determining the measure of an angle in a quadrilateral
39. Finding the measure of central tendency
40. Finding a weighted average
41. Tables and graphs
42. Determining independent probability
43. Determining dependent probability
44. Combinations and permutations *
45. Multiplying integers
46. Dividing integers
47. Evaluating algebraic expressions
48. Multiplying variables
49. Simplifying expressions
50. Commutative and associative properties
51. Properties of 1 and 0
52. Distributive property
53. Inverse operations involving multiplication
54. Inverse operations involving division
55. Using distance formulas
56. Using cost formulas
57. Power and roots including zero and negative exponents
58. Multiplying powers with the same base
59. Raising a power to a power
60. Dividing powers with the same base
61. Multiplying factors
62. Solving and graphing linear equations
63. Solving and graphing linear inequalities
64. Finding slope using a graph, table of values or formula
65. Use equations to graph real-world situations
66. Using slope intercept form to graph equations
67. Writing an equation in point-slope form
68. Solving systems of equations by graphing, substitution and elimination
69. Scientific notation

Let's test our ability to know our multiplication tables with the following charts. The goal is to finish both in five minutes or less. However, you may do just one if you'd like.

x	1	2	3	4	5	6	7	8	9	10
1										
2										
3										
4										
5										
6										
7										
8										
9										
10										

For those of you who don't find the above chart challenging, or you find yourself adding instead of multiplying, please use the following chart.

X	6	5	3	8	7	9	2	4	10	1
5										
1										
6										
2										
9										
8										
3										
4										
10										
7										

Note: While the students are working on these tables, write the definition of the term "critical thinking" on the board (see #10 below).

a. After filling out each column and row, identify those that you had problems with by circling them. If you find it difficult to do any of them from a specified point onward, make a note of it (for example, I don't know them from 4x3 on).

b. Write in a notebook or on a folded piece of paper the one(s) you find challenging (example 9x7=63).

c. Look at that problem and read it to yourself.
d. Raise your head, close your eyes, visualize the problem and say it to yourself. This step is easy to pretend, so you must be disciplined, and do it exactly as written.

e. Look at it again to check yourself for accuracy.

f. Raise your head again and say it out loud. Saying it out loud not only helps you pronounce important words and phrases, it also helps you to "audibleize" the information.   I made up the word and the definition for the word "audibleize" to illustrate a point. Essentially, "visualize" means to form a mental picture of information. Well, my made up definition for the word "audibleize " means to form a mental sound of information. If you can see and hear information in your mind, you are better able to remember it. That's especially true of those who learn best by listening, and that's why songs are easy to remember.

g. Look at it again while saying it out loud again to check for accuracy

It may take time, but eventually, you will be able to recite them all. Make sure you have an adequate system of review. For me, Tuesday is Times Day and even though it may take less then five minutes, I practice my times table on that day.

This process can be used for math or definitions. See Tool #17 of your Tools of Learning presentation for more on this.

9. Organize the information that you want to remember

"Repetition is the mother of retention."   — Old expression

To help insure retention of the information, you must organize it and review it from time to time. Even if it is too much information for you to review daily, you can develop a system of rotation so that eventually all of it will be reviewed periodically. After a while, it won't be necessary to review it anymore, you will know it like the Pledge of Allegiance, and you can erase it or remove it from your list of things to review.

10. Retention vs. Critical Thinking

It is the belief of the Tools of Learning that critical thinking and the Tools of Learning are two sides of the same coin.

Of the many definitions for the term "critical thinking" the following one will help prove the point best.

"The mental process of actively and skillfully conceptualizing, applying, analyzing, synthesizing, and evaluating information to reach an answer or conclusion." — Dictionary.com

This definition is shared with the reader to illustrate two things:

1. As you will see in the books you must study, you are going to have to prove that you have critical thinking skills. If you have not learned, understood or remembered what critical thinking means, how are you going to prove that you have it? As stated in Tool #4, don't let words and phrases pass you by without you knowing the meaning of them.

2. Also, I want to show you how to remember long complicated definitions like this one.

To learn this definition you must use some of the basics of the Tools of Learning like "eliminate distractions" and "use a dictionary". Once you have turned off the television and picked up a dictionary (or used a web site like Dictionary.com), you are ready to understand it. To understand this definition so that it can be remembered, you must understand each word in the definition.

Notice how the words "conceptualizing, applying, analyzing, synthesizing and evaluating" revolve around the word "information". Without the ability to remember that information, critical thinking is simply not possible.

One word that we don't use often is "conceptualize" which comes from the word "concept", and it means:

Concept: Something formed in the mind.

It does not matter if we are building a house or making a meal, it all starts with thinking about exactly what it is that we want to do. A concept car is just someone's idea of what a car will look like in the future. On the Internet is a drawing of a 2057 concept car that turns into a suit of clothes when you arrive at your destination. This car does not exist, but the idea of it does. That's a concept.

The next thing that we should be concerned with is "applying" the information. That means using what we have retained and using that information to do what we want.

The next thing we must do is "analyze" the information. This means if something goes wrong with our plans, like the walls are not level on the house we are building or the main course of the meal we are making tastes bad, we will be able to think of the information that we have learned, understood, and remembered and fix the problem.

The next word is called "synthesizing" which means to combine the parts and make a whole. That includes taking the information we have learned, understood and remembered about building different parts of a house or making different parts of a meal and combining them to build an entire house or making an entire meal.

The next word is "evaluating" and that just means to test what we have done. It's like checking the walls to see if they are straight or tasting a portion of the meal to see if it tastes good. If the walls are not straight and you know how to straighten them or the meal does not taste good and you know what seasoning to add to make it taste good, then you have the ability to "evaluate" information, which is part of critical thinking.

The important thing that I would like for us all to remember is that "critical thinking requires the ability to learn, understand and remember information." Some people will tell you that remembering information is not as important as it used to be. Don't believe them. If you know a lot about a subject, you can engage in critical thinking much more easily than if you know little or nothing about the subject at all. If you can't remember information about the subject, then you are lost.

Let's use the steps found in the "Repeat" portion (sections a-g) of the SQ5R system to remember definitions. You must say the words in each definition exactly as they should be pronounced. You must practice this perfectly. Perfect practice will:

a. Enhance your ability to remember the information
b. Improve your ability to pronounce words the way they should be said

Keep in mind that, this system can be used for any definition. If it is necessary to remember pages of information, then an additional step (h) must be added to the "repeat" portion of SQ5R. That step includes the following.

1. Use steps a to g of "repeat" to help you remember a large section of the page you want to remember. You may have the ability to remember a paragraph of it.
2. Use steps a to g rehearse the next sentence of that page.
3. Once you have mastered that sentence, attempt to recite the section you have already retained, and then add to it the new section that you have just learned.
4. Continue using this process until all of the pages you want to remember are retained.

"Once you can recite, the old with the new,
Then all that is left is for you to review."

Don't be surprised if it takes a week to master a definition or months to master pages. Remember that the goal is just two percent per week or more. If you move at this pace, you will have improved yourself 100 percent in less than a year.

Appendix B

The Evaluation Tool

The Tools of Learning is useless unless you put it to good use.

It may happen someday that a student will say, "I've tried the Tools of Learning and it doesn't work." Well, it won't if he or she doesn't use it.

To determine if a student is using the Tools of Learning correctly, ask the student to answer following questions. (Note: Students may also ask these questions of themselves.)

1. What time of the day do you study?
2. Where do you keep your study schedule?
3. Do you study with distractions around you like a television, radio, video games, cell phone, etc.?
4. What do you use to look up words you don't know?
5. When do you look those words up?
6. What do you do when your teacher uses a word you don't know the meaning of?
7. When was the last time you asked your teacher a question in the classroom?
8. What kind of homework did you do when you were on vacation?
9. Do you rewrite your notes?
10. If you get homework today, when do you expect to get it done?

At this point, the teacher, tutor or student must select important sections of the chapter the student is having trouble with. The student must then talk about the section in his/her own words. Based on the student's responses, the teacher can determine how to proceed.

For example, if the challenges are math related, try the following steps:

1. Start as far back as addition, subtraction, multiplication and division. Then, determine if the student can perform these basic operations before proceeding to more complex problems. The student must know the multiplication tables, asked in random fashion (see Activity 3 of the Student Workbook).

2. Determine if the student knows the "order of operations" and "inverse operations."

3. Determine if the student can liken abstract problems to something concrete, or something that can be detected with any of the five senses.

4. Ask the student to show his/her personal study guide (PSG) used to help him/her remember information.

5. Determine if the student uses acronyms or acrostics to remember information and if the student knows how to create acronyms or acrostics.

6. Determine if the student knows what SQ5R means or what it is used for.

7. Determine if the student has ever used SQ5R.

8. Ask the student what they are aspiring to do with their education.

9. Determine if the student has another strategy for learning, understanding and remembering information other than the Tools of Learning.

Appendix C

Which One is More Work?

A.K.A. The Top 10 reasons to Use the Tools of Learning

Some people have told me that the Tools of Learning looks and sounds like a lot of work. Let's make a brief comparison. By failing to attain an education when I first went to Greater Hartford Community College, it cost me:

a. the work I needed to get into the New Careers program.
b. the work I needed to sign up for classes.
c. the work I needed to get a student loan to pay for courses.
d. the work it took to get to classes each day.
e. the work I did as an employee in the program.
f. the work of resigning from the program when my grades were bad.
g. the work of explaining to everyone what happened to my status in the program.
h. the loss of my apartment.
i. the work of moving in with my in-laws.
j. the work of finding another job.
k. the work of finding another apartment.
l. the work of moving into the new apartment.
m. the work of paying back a student loan that didn't even benefit me.
n. the work of applying to another college, Manchester Community College.
o. the work of driving out to Manchester Community College for classes.
If I had had the Tools of Learning I would have been able to avoid f. through o.

"Overall, success is less work — by far."   — C.A. Teale, Sr.

Appendix D

The Premises

"Premise: a proposition upon which an argument is based or from which a conclusion is drawn." — The Free Dictionary

There are 134 premises of the Tools of Learning. All of them support one main conclusion, we should never teach anyone anything without first teaching them how to learn, understand and remember the information.

After each presentation, the teacher of this program must look at the following and determine how many were addressed or omitted. If the premise is consistently missed, re-study that information.

Each Tool has a key premise followed by an asterisk*

Learn

Tool #1: Use a Study Schedule

- 1. A strategy for learning, understanding and remembering information has been created.

- 2. The Hotchkiss School taught lifelong lessons through the GO Program.

- 3. A study schedule keeps you from doing anything but studying, when you should be studying. *

- 4. Study schedules should be prominently placed.

- 5. Media has dramatically diminished the time we have for studying.

- 6. Smartphones are an adversary of learning that we can use to our advantage.

Tool #2: Enhance Enthusiasm

- 7. A = (H+S) D
- 8. The Tools of Learning is a strategy for learning, understanding and remembering information.

- 9. "H" stands for mental, emotional and physical health.

- 10. The most common form of emotional disorder is depression.

- 11. Depression can keep you from studying.

- 12. The "Triple A's" of enthusiasm combat depression.

- 13. We must "Aspire" to do great things because good is not good enough.

- 14. We must create and adhere to a list of "Accomplishments".

- 15. We must "Attain" educational and professional goals like getting a diploma or a degree.

- 16. A two percent per week increase in information retained is 104 percent per year.

- 17. We must keep goals in mind that fuel enthusiasm. Aspire. *

Tool #3: Avoid Distractions

- 18. The television can prevent us from focusing even with the volume down.

- 19. Our minds can process thousands of words per minute.

- 20. We can study hundreds of words per minute.

- 21. When the TV is on, we subconsciously watch it.

- 22. When the radio is on, we subconsciously listen to it.

- 23. Success is all about focus. *

- 24. We cannot focus on two things at one time.

- 25. To learn anything, we must "turn off the television and pick up the books." — Richard Epps

Tool #4: Keep a dictionary on hand

- 26. There are over 500,000 words in the English language.

- 27. We must know the correct spelling of words (for exams).

- 28. We must know the meaning of words (for exams and personal conversations).

- 29. Malapropisms can be damaging both academically and professionally.

- 30. The 5-S's of building a powerful vocabulary: sense, search, synonym, sentence and story.

- 31. One word can alter our understanding of major portions of a subject. *

Tool #5: Know their contributions

- 32. Contributions of individuals are as important as the meaning of words.

- 33. Unknown contributors must be researched. *

- 34. Three sources of information are needed to determine a person's contribution.

Tool #6: Get a tutor

- 35. The ancient purposes of a tutor are many.

- 36. Some libraries and Boys and Girls Clubs provide tutors at no cost.

- 37. Most colleges provide tutors free of charge.

- 38. Expecting trouble? Get a tutor before the course begins. *

- 39. If you wait until you start failing exams, it may be too late to get a tutor.

Understand

Tool #7: Examine your own ability

- 40. There are at least five levels of technical knowledge.

- 41. We are not tape recorders learning just to recite information. *

- 42. We must know how to say what something means in our own words.

Tool #8: Ask questions

- 43. Rudyard Kipling learned from "six honest serving-men."

- 44. Asking questions prevents classroom hypnosis.

- 45. There are two types of students who don't ask questions. *

- 46. If you don't understand it, someone else in the classroom might not understand it either.

- 47. The negative thoughts we have when we don't understand something said by the teacher can lead to <u>anxiety and a lack of focus</u> on the material being presented.

- 48. Asking questions shows that you "value" the information presented to you.

- 49. Obtaining individual attention from your teacher after class is beneficial.

Tool #9: Be the Teacher

- 50. Archimedes discovered the power of the lever.

- 51. Visualization is to learning what the lever is to tools.

- 52. To help insure understanding, you should visualize a classroom with you teaching the information you want to learn. *

- 53. "The best way to learn is to teach."
                                — Old expression

Tool #10: Give yourself homework

- 54. Some nations send their students to school more than 11 months out of the year.

- 55. No one knows what you don't know better than you do.

- 56. When you have some spare time, you should review difficult to remember information. *

- 57. Summer vacation is the ideal time to implement a system of review.

- 58. A system of review must include the subject of math.

Tool #11: Rewrite your notes

- 59. "We will forget 90 percent of what a speaker says if we don't take notes."　　— Earl Nightingale

- 60. Notes must be legible (my Drill School note taking experience).

- There are at least five benefits of rewriting your notes as soon after class as possible:
    - o 61. If your handwriting is bad, you can remember what was said during class.

    - o 62. You can develop a legible record of what was said by the teacher.

    - o 63. You can recall some of the things that were said that you didn't originally write in your notes at all.

    - o 64. You are physically active while learning. This means you are using the psychomotor domain.

    - o 65. You will experience the teacher's presentation a second time through "visualization" at mind speed.

Tool #12: Complete quickly

- 66. You should do difficult homework assignments ASAP after you rewrite you notes. *

- 67. You must review completed assignments until they are scheduled to be handed in.

Tool #13: Get a Math Foundation

- 68. Absence from class due to health challenges and moving frequently decreases our ability to learn, understand and remember.

- 60. The times (or multiplication) tables are part of the ABCs of math.

- 70. If you do not know your times tables, your math problems will multiply.*

- 71. Students who move frequently miss out on math essentials.

- 72. Infrequent math courses in college create an erosion of our math foundation.

- 73. Memorizing the steps needed to solve a problem is not as effective as knowing the rules governing how to solve the problem (drill school math formulas and memorization vs. PEMDAS).
- 74. We must master the language of math. Know the meaning of math's words and phrases.

- 75. We must memorize and never forget our times tables and the order of operations (A/C Kehoe and the order of operations).

- 76. Reading and math require foundational knowledge (how I teach reading and how a similar system can be used to learn math).

- To learn math, we must consider utilizing either or all of the following:

  - o 77. We must relate the new to what you already know (like money).

  - o 78. We should liken the abstract to the concrete.

  - o 79. We need a solid foundation or prerequisite knowledge.

  - o 80. We must remember the general rules.

  - o 81. Sometimes it is beneficial and/or necessary to list the specific steps needed to solve a problem.

  - o 82. Free websites provide an abundance of information on any subject.

- 83. To review math means to do math (psychomotor learning domain).*

- 84. Reading or watching someone else perform problems is not an adequate system of review.

- 85. Following the math performed by an author or teacher proves only that you understand how the problem was done, not that you remember how to do it.

- 86. If all of the above fails, a tutor may be necessary.

Remember

Tool #14: Write questions

- 87. The neocortex is that part of our brain where we store our long term knowledge.

- 88. The best way to exercise your brain is to ask yourself questions.

- 89. To test yourself regarding the information you should know, create your personal study guide. *
- 90. You must practice answering these questions until you can answer them readily.

Tool #15: Use mnemonics

- 91. A mnemonic is any learning technique that can be used to aid memory.

- 92. One way to remember the number of days in a month is to use the knuckles of your hand as a mnemonic.

- 93. Acronym. A form of mnemonic that is a word made from the first letter of a group of words. H.O.M.E.S.

- 94. An acrostic is a group of words from the first letter of other words. Example: My very educated mother just served us nachos = the eight planets of our solar system.

- 95. Learning mnemonics is good; creating them is excellent. *

- 96. We must learn to anticipate the questions we will be tested on.

- 97. We must be aware of repeat letters like the letter "M" in premise 94.

Tool #16: Use short periods of inactivity wisely

- 98. Firefighters must know the location of streets in their city or town.

- 99. A small pad can be used to assist in this or a comparable purpose.

- 100. A smartphone can be used for this purpose too.

- 101. The more you look at difficult to understand and remember info, the easier it will be to learn, understand and remember. *

Tool #17: Use SQ5R

- 102. Reading is too passive to be considered studying.

- 103. To understand a challenging assignment, two or more readings may be required.

- 104. You should highlight important sections as you read, using: a. Hash marks / b. Underlining (___) c. Brackets [ ] d. Very Important Page (V.I.P.) e. Asterisks (see Tool #18: Organizing)

- 105. We must pay particular attention to captions and figures. They reemphasize and help you to visualize the written words of the author.

- 106. Reciting is the mother of all learning. Fun is the father of all learning. Repeating is the mother of retention.

- 107. The "taxonomy" of a subject is the foundational knowledge of that field.

- 108. To be considered a true professional, you must memorize the taxonomy of your field. *

- 109. SQ5R uses as many of your five senses as possible to enhance retention.

- 110. "We become what we think about."   — Napoleon Hill

- 111. We must vary our means of review: tapes, pads etc.

Conclusion

Tool #18: Organize

- 112. When finishing a diploma or degree program we must save our books, notes and handouts.

- 113. The larger the amount of the information that must be read, the lower the rate of retention.

- 114. Information that has been learned must be organized and reviewed according to subject and date to insure long-term retention.*

- 115. Highlighting with a marker is not necessary; a pencil will do.

- 116. The following is a specific system of highlighting information:

    a. Hash marks (/) b. Underlining (___) c. Brackets [ ]
    d. Very Important Page (V.I.P.)   e. Asterisks (*)

- 117. The asterisk system compels us to review information out of order if necessary; the way tests are given.

- 118. Tool #16 may be necessary if the problem persists (the pad, notes or memo application).

Tool #19: Problem Solving

- 119. "Knowledge is like faith. Without works, it's dead."
  — C.A.Teale, Sr.

- 120. Passing of tests is enhanced by ToL but is not the ultimate goal.

- 121. Solving problems is the ultimate goal of the ToL.

- 122. The ToL is the prerequisite to critical thinking.

- 123. You can't go to an attorney with excellent critical thinking skills for a heart operation.

- 124. Solutions to problems are like medication for an illness: there may be side effects. *

- 125. Solutions to problems must be managed.

- 126. The ToL manages its solution via tutoring, and email feedback.

Tool #20: Learn, understand and remember the positive history of your city, state and our nation

- 127. Focusing on the negative things about our history can diminish our appreciation for it.

- 128. Our nation's history is not being taught in some of our public schools.

- 129. It is frequently being taught in our college classrooms.

- 130. We may be offended by what we hear from our teachers.

- 131. To control our attitude takes F.A.B. *

- 132. Many people spent their lives, risked their lives and sometimes gave their lives so that we could have the opportunity to succeed (the Bill Edmonds experience).

- 133. We can show gratitude to those who made sacrifices by pursuing excellence.

- 134. Anything less is stealing from your nation, your loved ones and your future.

Please send all questions to TealeInk@gmail.com.